Downloading
the Poetic Self

Downloading the Poetic Self:

An Anatomy of Poetic Character

By

Frederic Will

**Cambridge
Scholars**
Publishing

Downloading the Poetic Self: An Anatomy of Poetic Character
Series: Inside Selfhood And History

By Frederic Will

This book first published 2018

Cambridge Scholars Publishing

Lady Stephenson Library, Newcastle upon Tyne, NE6 2PA, UK

British Library Cataloguing in Publication Data
A catalogue record for this book is available from the British Library

ISBN (10): 1-5275-0555-3
ISBN (13): 978-1-5275-0555-1

For Big Bear

I live life as though it were, in itself, a standing into a future condition, in which orders I can't imagine will recapacitate me, assigning me to the rights of place.

TABLE OF CONTENTS

Introduction 1

Part One: Poems of Intervention

Chapter One.. 21
I as Intervention in Poetry: *Guatemala*

Chapter Two 29
The Long Poem in the Age of Twitter and *The Being Here Site of the Poetic*

Chapter Three... 49
The Epics of America

Chapter Four... 55
That Postmodern Mention

Chapter Five 57
Some Prose Poems, 1975–82

Chapter Six... 65
We Jes' Chawin'

Chapter Seven... 97
Dranster, Dranster, Who's Got the Dranster?

Part Two: Modifying Intervention

Chapter Eight.. 123
Translation: Practice in the Third Language

Chapter Nine... 133
Me, That's All

Chapter Ten 205
Kids' Morbid

Part Three: Serene Years

Chapter Eleven 217
Serenity

Part Four: Arguments with Charon

Chapter Twelve 277
Arguments with Charon

Part Five: Gosh, after all That?

Chapter Thirteen... 313
Flying to Byzantium

Postlude

Chapter Fourteen 329
End and Beginning

Textualities

Poem Texts and Translations.. 331

Index.. 333

INTRODUCTION

In this book we begin with the poetic work of one contemporary writer, Frederic Will, and take it as the lab material for an experiment. The experiment is to determine whether a poet deploys and expresses a *character* in his poetry, and if so whether the author's character flows from him-/herself into his/her work. (There might be a poetic creator who had "character," but from whom that character did not flow into his work. Homer is often cited as such a character-free but omniscient poetic maker. For many eighteenth-century British critics, Homer and nature were "the same"; "character, like nature," said the poet Kathleen Raine, "is always in the year one.") We could have asked this same character-question about any of the millions of writers who have tweaked language and voice during their time, and for whom the poetry of that voice was to them a stirring component of enriching life with meaning. (The notion of the "poet writer" is still laden with "romanesque connotations" and is under heavy transformation in a world of writers' workshops, little-guy street-writers, smartphone novelists, gay, lesbian, and transgender writers, hermit epic makers, you name it, as well as the higher diversified reading consumption markets. It is rare to find a person for whom poetry and complex sentiment link who does not acknowledge a "past in poetry." So the broad issue of character in poetry intersects with a virtually global psychiatry of individual expression.)

Look at a seemingly stern example! Is the character of John Milton, the man *himself*, to be found inside *Paradise Lost*? (Go scrambling through those knotty lines and fast-tied intricacies of syntax, even through the first ten epic lines you have memorized, in an effort to feel the workmanship from the inside: do you feel the throb of personality in there as perhaps you find it in Hart Crane's *The Bridge* or Shelley's *Alastor*?) This pragmatic question, which could be posed to Joe Schmoe in your writer's group as well as to T. S. Eliot or Cleanth Brooks, is as down-to-earth as they get. It's like asking whether you penetrate—or can't—the manner of the Assistant Secretary of State, as he discusses global arms treaties in Tehran. Pretty hard to penetrate the guy, no? Milton, as we all know, *was* a real person. We even "know a lot" about his life. We could biopsy him at any of the points onto which our attention hooks: onto the youngster writing his teenage Latin elegies at Cambridge (1625–29), onto the brilliant and preciously mature poet of *L'Allegro* and *Il Penseroso* (1645), those fancy English texts we strangled on in high school—the guy was 37 by that time—or onto the blind creator of *Paradise Lost* (1667), on a level with the giant largeness of the human condition, or even onto the guy who *did all that*, but in real honest fact did none of it *at this date or at that date* crap, but was working more or less *all the time* in his head, so that now and then something would happen to make a section of it get published out of the long scrolled work-world of his life. We could biopsy at many a point of entry! Would we find something like Milton's "character" appearing in the "published works" of those different periods, and if so would that "character" be a hopelessly vague amalgam of tones—something milky in your hands—something we could never *quite get our hands on*; would Milton's "character thing" vacillate from one period to another; or would it bear the hard stamp of a set of linguistic habits, such as those Leo Spitzer tracked to their style homes in *Linguistics and Literary History*, and which for Spitzer seemed to justify thinking of literary character in the old Greek sense of *stamp, inscribed signum*?

We could ask the same sequence of questions of any author. Has Shakespeare's character permeated *The Tempest*? *King Lear*? Is his character the same in each work, in every part of each work? What does "character" have to mean, to render the idea of it relevant to an assertion of any of these propositions? What kind of "character" would we be talking about here, anyhow? Does "character" in the old-fashioned *moral sense* belong to such a discussion—as when we talk of "this young man's sterling character"? Or are we talking about "character" as the Greek word *character* implies it, a unique tonal engraving scratched onto a metallic surface, the *stamp* mentioned above?

The word *character*, while not easy to pin to the wall when it comes to great poetry at any period, is not easy to dismiss as irrelevant to this or that body of work. In fact, the notion of *character* may in this discussion push us to rethink our entire vocabulary of criticism. (Certainly the broad-sweep genres of criticism—New Criticism, Structuralism, Postmodernism—sit uncomfortably with the notion of literary character, except perhaps in the vein of Foulcauldian querying of whether the author is, whether the author is at all *present with his personality* in the work.) Or in "dealing with Shakespeare" would we need to redefine "character" altogether, with the help of another kind of explanatory language, like that of neuroscience, in order for the notion of character to lay claim to flowing from author to text? Would character have to be some habitual style of inflecting one's reactions in language, almost a tic of response? My broad sense is that in the instances of Milton and Shakespeare we will get most mileage by taking "character" to mean *trademark, tweak,* or *tone*; whichever most clearly signals a cachet that seals or at least partially identifies the work or series of works in question. My sense is also this; that if we adopt this broad sense of character, in our quick look at Milton or Shakespeare, we will find it both in word-choice and in phrase-construction, and in whatever we find in an author's work that we want to call *style.* Writings reflect authorial style as much as a person's speech reflects his style. My character, in what I write, is likely to be about the same as my style.

We will work with details, and close analysis, of a good many Frederic Will poems which will seem to belong inside a long development of the story of this person's poetic character. In tracking this development we will be paying attention to the dates of publication of the works in question, the times in Will's and our communal life in which this or that was happening. (Ultimately we will be looking for a way to study how Will's character-download helps to place him *in* his time.)

The unromantic, hard-edged poems inspected with a hard eye at the beginning (particularly Chapters 1–7) of this book—all drawn from the middle period of Will's work, from say the late 1960s to 1995—are meant to bring out a reigning language strategy in Will's poetry of that time, a strategy of dislocating the mutually reinforcing relation of poet with reader, and of imposing flavor or style that is at the same time a cloaking of the writer's individual presence. In that of course Will was to some extent simply acting out the stance of a "modern poet." Since Baudelaire, the theme of "Western poetry has been marked by a fretful complexity, an interposition, between poet and reader, of cat-and-mouse identity games, the poet arch, the poet half-concealed, the reader led this way or that, as a *dolmetscher* of mini revelations. It may be said that Will was, in all his poetic since his earliest books, *Mosaic, A Wedge of Words, Planets*— 1959, 1963, 1968—carefully breaking from the romantic mode, the mode of the open heart, and cryptofying himself. In all that, agreed, Will is standing inside the history of the language as it intersected with periods of human awareness—nascent global conflict, growth in technical skills for penetrating minds (psychologies, technologies, windows onto sociology), and from-within evolution of skills sets—like those of the Pléiade in Renaissance France—which promoted verbal dexterities and counter-plays of cross-cultural implications.

There is, though, more than just a resistance to character-sharing in those middle period—the guy was forty to sixty-five—poems. There is a discomfort, even an anger, in these midlife poems that sits astraddle Will's personal life in the midlife years, and that perhaps—we will almost go there, quietly—reflects arguments with itself that his own time was indulging then—the quarrels of American exceptionalism vs. the need for compromise during the Cold War; the fight club mentality which infected this under-stable period of latish capitalism, the cast-it-to-the-winds audacity of the intellectual discovering that what we think *matters* in America—the period of *Armies of the Night* (1968), Civil Rights, and the March on Washington—can move social and cultural mountains. (We will, from inside this historical wind-tossed midlife Will, remark an invisible politics of the retrograde, a progressive conservatism, a politics which can take its bearing on finial issues like prosody, the nerve system of the verbal creator, but which also plays out in a diffuse historicism that ranges from agricultural pastoralism to social communalism; thematics that floated in and out of Will's lines, and that contributed to this guy's intemperant moods about the friendliness of poetry.) Where can such a politics more subtly intrude than in the desire to take a stance for a library of the subtle ulatramontane forgotten: for the work of de Bonald and Lamenais, in the French Restoration, for Maurice Barrès' *Les Déracinés*, for Evelyn Waugh's post as a foe of ecumenism in the Catholic tradition, even for Robert Bork as a doughty champion of hard thought in the face of nimble secular adjustmentism? We will fly tentative thoughts, throughout this discussion, about the relation between art work and culture work; the relation of the individual with a pen to the overgrid of socio-political in which he lives, and which he may teeth on for the sharpening of his own *tweakus linguisticus*. Many a spice, in other words, went into the taste buds of the by 1984 twice-divorced Mr. Will.

From a look at this banquet of interventionist mid-career poem-things, in which Will trademarks himself as never so clearly, we slide back into the history of Will the young poet, *el poeta*, whose sprudelling of poems, and would-be *lavishing* of character through poetry, already makes itself felt from a wide long bed in Honolulu, in 1936. There the eight-year-old chap lay, post-concussion, for sunny weeks of gazing down onto Waikiki Bay in what now seems prehistory, and was in fact concurrent with a true history, the Nazi takeover in Poland, the maturing of FDR as an international president, the dekulkization of the Soviet Union—plenty of history to place young Will's idyll in one version of the real world. There he lay, embedded innocently in that island paradise setting he had little awareness of, stretched out as the victim of a rashly cutting hoe, the weapon of choice for a hostile neighbor kid—all one remembers of the kid is Nicky, the name—on a hot afternoon at the bottom of the grandparental garden near the hibiscus plants. And from that pain-free consciousness, bathed in sun, poured epics of the sea, of the weed that clogs it, and of the great cloudy naval fleets visible out there on the bright blue sheen, poetry flowed from every point into that pre-lapsarian mindscape, and back out through the eyes of a wondering eight-year-old. This was a poetry of innocent world give-back, and lived by pleading for the mercy of the world. Something of that guilelessness was a large as the ocean, itself but a single teardrop.

It would be six years later, as a mid-teenager, that the same youngster would put together an eighteen-page pamphlet of poems, *Fragments*, for his (at least so Freddy thought) startled father. The I of the maker spilled like egg yolk across the screen of the gift. We have here a default position against which to measure the "see-me-now" softness of the early romantic poetry (in *Mosaic*, 1959, and *A Wedge of Words*, 1963), the stridency of the middle-years interventionist language of Will's poetry, or the "epic" elongations of spirit in the later long poems, *The World of John Holmes* (2014–15) or *Anonymous Assault* (2017). The character-download of *Fragments* is gothic and pantheistic; a teenager's no-holds-barred, take-me-to-the-world testimony, natural enough at sixteen, to the sense that nature carries one's own feelings in its heart, that sadness and *Weltschmerz* are twinned with power, and that talking about death is the only way to talk about life. The amalgam of heart feelings, in this open-souled romanticism, blends to a vulnerability Will's midlife poems eschew. (Note, in *Fragments*, the preoccupation with the name of death, as well as with end-stopped colors, the preoccupation with blue; the omnipresence of the windswept, the dry hills, the dawns and dusks; shards of the all-formative two-year experience that had made young Will at nine and ten a part of the central Arizona mesa desert, a soulscape of buttes, bleached cow skulls, and red cactus.) He has his feelings, like any sixteen-year-old, and longs to be shared by other users of the language he too is. The preface to *Fragments* could not be more eloquent, in its obeisance to open-souledness.

Preface to *Fragments* (1944)

The intention of this collection is to demonstrate the validity of my philosophy of Irrationalism, which I consider to be of especial significance in the field of poetry. This embodies the concept that man's truest, most natural, and hence most basic reaction to any stimulus is thoroughly irrational and passionate, particularly when measured by the standards of the scientifically frigid twentieth century. The supposed progress to logic and the exercise of reason appears to draw man away from the spontaneous and uninvolved state which he now manifests only in his primary reactions to immediately external circumstances. I believe that poetry is one of the few areas that can still maintain the right to record spontaneously the impacts on the human mind of the materialistic, causal, and external world which has been created by the Industrial Revolution.

The objection to this art, on the grounds that it is exclusive, and unnecessarily personal, may possibly be well-founded. However, I think the fault lies rather with the poet than with his medium. These creations may be considered overly personal only insofar as they fail to coincide with the impressions and reactions gathered during the life of the reader. It is the job of the impressionistic poet to depict images of such sort that they so correspond with certain fragments of the reader's existence as to both vivify the imagination and loosen the steel fetters which are progressively being fastened around our modern scientific limbs. It is with the desire of so doing and the conviction of failure that I present the following selection of "fragments."

***

Nine selected "fragments" will launch us on this teenage work:

First Sin

Torpid snake in the slinky underbrush
Slide
Glide
Fall from your peak—snake.
Shine forth serpent
Lighting
Blighting
Drawing blood and dying—snake.
Move young quickly—not old,
Snake. Dusk is soon, not late—torpid serpent.
The reeds rain white roses.
Deep joy through steamy pores
For you serpent
For you
Only.

Tumor

What I can now say is small pieces of gingham
Cut from a large bolt; is blue thread drawn
Across a rise of water. The fields are wild but
There is birth still.
A tan fawn beside the old post
And there is birth still.
Trembling are the long-gutted fields after
Holding iron long.
Must movement go on forever?
Have we lost too much?

Trends recollected

In the samovar tinkled the airs of white men
Drinking their tea. These were the long hours,
Passive in the reception of wet clammy imprints.
Open thine eyes, Marushka.
A pot of sound, shared equally by
A man and a door, lay
Quiet on the floor.

In the kitchen fell a spark blowing
White into white hearts blowing
Blue dreams in blue faces.
This is your bed song, child.
Many are the bright sparks—their flashes.
These are the long blue languid hours
Foreign beyond despair, pouring
Light through dark walls
And the fresh chanting
Fails.

In Victory

In victory we cross the peas and
The white inches.
Here is movement slow—time running like

A young hare. The units are small here.
Here the empty blue fields
Spotted with a small torrent of little
(very little) rivers.
Animate nothingness and the white stone.
These only do we love—the blue sounds
Drifting.
But drifting is a sound too sure.
A long sensuous expression of day on
White cloth and
Long. Endless.

Death and transfiguration

Shall we break the barrier?
Will you tell the oak that dawn tomorrow
Is once but not at present? And the frightened
Brook? Can you tell three thousand years that
Smoke is not blue nor the mountain clean?
Try, train your ears and hear
Blue water on blue stones and
Fresh wind on fresh graves.

Sighing, dying, reflecting some light and
Dying—expiring on the maple leaves, on the
Petticoats of a crisp autumn dying.
Bearing two sons (both dead now in large tombs)
Had torn her bready features and pallid.
Anyway a farm and pig are work and work's no
Fun and kids (now dead) and whistling.
Oh yes and money.
"Sooner can a camel go through the eye of a needle
Than a rich man enter into the Kingdom of God."

When the flowers were laid it was still
Young but the sameness was that of a past
Merging (in cobwebs) with an equally
Well-discovered future (in chains).
An apple may fall too—but slowly,
Not Icarus nor Phaethon—but slowly,

"And the might of the Gentile, unsmote by the sword,
Hath melted like ice in the glance of the Lord."

Lament

Last night, throwing sixteen years of pleasure
Into the waste-basket
I died.
The new moon holds on, and the clouds.
Why do we let go, must we let go,
Dropping pleasure into the inferno
Like hot tongs?
Though the figure be inexact, the emotion
Is as certain as winter rain on tombs
And slate-gray life.
Waste-basket full of dreams, and a cold floor
On the cold floor pulpy with dreams,
Last night sixteen years of life falling
Into the waste-basket dropped
Onto the floor
And died.

Nobility

Will you not have an apple, Princess?
The blossoms of the tree are pink and
Your heart will sail out to an apple,
Princess.
Whip the wild waves, Princess. Beat their knobby heads,
Princess.
Drive a stake in this quiet cove and moor
Your thoughts to the red oak—Princess.
The night blows softer.
Green shadows fall across your valley, my virgin,
Cutting as a bread knife thin slices of your
Form.
Flee to the blue coast—smell the white weed and
Chain thyself to red oak—tender young oak.
There is the voice casuistry and the step

Impartial.
Love a green frog, Princess.

Trial and Error

Blue saints scurry into the night and the
Pungency of fresh trees, and
Blue green organisms.
This part is called deserted—deserted.
Last man departed long since.
Yet into the limestone hills permeates a
Sweet, hand-picked ichor
Small wonder men died singing a
Young song on
Ancient hills.
Green hills—
Too old.

Plaint

Will you not pray for me, little man?
Will you not give the musty earth a fig for
My salvation, furry one.
Green roots fall quickly into the small caverns
And I am sure it would be slight bother.
Hand the white fowl a young heart and the
Blue snake a black rod, little man.
The night song is peculiar not to an
Individual but to a race of little things
Playing in the arroyos of a timeless
Twilight.
These are those forgotten
And for them flows not the
Wine and the
Long breath.

*(Never published. Copy of Fragments in author's archive in the
Humanities Research Center, University of Texas, Austin)*

***

Can we say that the poetic self cries unashamedly for attention here? Are we in the pose-stance of *Werther*, of early Keats or Shelley, or of a fragment of Novalis, whose wounds and joys beg for an uninhibited airing? Literary historical thinking makes this way of putting it seem attractive. We seem to find here a pigeonhole into which to slip young Will, the maker of *Fragments* and an Hawaiian oral epic, an invert lad for whom the sound of the sensuality of the world seems to be entrapping enough formality to become a poem. Of course, there is another way of looking at this pre-pubescent style of youth poetry: one can warm up the Oscar Wilde in us—language is the means by which we hide our thoughts from one another—and around it the heavier baggage of language critique, which has in our time trained its guns on battlements as lofty as theology. Many today will report that language is a weaponry stronger than any IBM when it comes to the demolition of the walls of accepted thought. This is the side of us which says that our language is no direct portraiture of the person making it, is in poetry hardly the bearer of an ounce of character, that it can be a distorting mirror of whatever it reflects, and that the imprecisions of the verbal are fatal limitations on the cognitive usefulness of language. This will be an unromantic, if you like Wittgensteinian, language, which so far from reflecting character establishes it. This bias of thought will gleefully undermine the efforts of Romantic language to express, will confine them to "emoting," and will leave few shreds of dignity to the sixteen-year-old hoping to share a heartful, with dad and the world.

Far in the future of Will's kid-stuff Romanticism, and even of the midlife period (1970s and 80s, plus a bit) from which we will be sampling generously in Parts One and Two of this book, will lie a semi-final discussion of the prose poems, of the "later poems of serenity," then even of the *mini-epic* itself, which make up Will's last set of testimonies, indeed the oblation in terms of which Will becomes increasingly fond of describing what he was trying to "leave behind him." (That classic bequeathing metaphor, Shakespeare at its head, crawls into the bedsheets with death. We will there be beyond the zone of poetry as alignment, or even of poetry as testimony, and into the zone of poetry as a way of standing into things with full throat. We will be daring ourselves to think of poetry as a way in which we are already the victory over our own defeat.) Will's earliest poems will spring from the period, we say, when Will was already framing the definition of the "living situation" we picture-frame in the banner-heading of this book. (*I live life as though it were, in itself, a standing into a future condition, in which orders I can't imagine will recapacitate me, assigning me to the rights of place).* Under that banner many volumes of poetry, and of prose that nothing essential divides from poetry, stand together with the decalogy, *Selfhood and History*, which Will is currently constructing for Cambridge Scholars Publishing, and which unapologetically factors poetry, fiction, philosophemata, and the poetry of prose into the tumbler of world perspectives which keeps making up what Will embraces as his "opus." (Take that work term from Will, take that grandiosity, and you may see him topple like Achilles with an arrow just piercing the fiber of his crusty heel. Of course, he is made up of promises to himself, and can see the artificial world crumbling around him as unconcernedly as Prospero sees the painted world of art in vanishing mode.)

In the formative of the *period of intervention*, so named here for pure convenience—to point to the aggressive and unseductive of Will's mid-life poems—we will carry the query of *character* into the stage where character is first being formed. In *Fragments* we have looked at character-material incomplete in itself, passionately verbal, at times pseudo-epic in tone, in which the creator, though not yet in thought of that self-masking anger that goes with intervention, will simply deploy a self-figure across loosely joined thematics, and bask in the sense of a give and take with fellow word users. (*I'm here, you're there, shake!* This will be the period of clubs, support groups, of the first thrill of the Oscar Williams anthology, which opens out to you the possibilities of loosened tongues, adroit and unexpected perceptions. It will be the social period, to be exact, in which one discovers the desire to be with others, as a driver for his language.) It will be out of this thrilling early trove that we pull *An Emphasis for Easter*, a plug of evening reading in the author's living room, on a well-remembered shmooze session with fellow graduate students Geoffrey Hartman and Harold Bloom—guys who went on, with a bravura vaster than Will's, to makes themselves part of a wide literary consciousness—and others, deep helpers in the author's own attitude formation. Shall we say that the character stamp, on this epyllion (1950), is only just more distinct than that on the poems in *Fragments* (1944)? Language is taking its own head, and streaming.

An Emphasis for Easter (1950)

Stine—mother
Trole—father

Gwin—daughter
Nelle—old servant
Liane—son
Brane—married to Gwin

ST. Back to a center of love, from your cold circumference
Of manors; back to the womb whose shelter three times split
You left to wither in a winter land.
This flesh has shriveled as your father's acres,
Worn with war, sapless and trenched…

TR. Your emphasis I disavow. The land is twisted,
Repair required, a summer's trust, and walls
Enough to calm our urgency. Myself
Can never doubt, my son and girl, your strength
Reminds your mother that each pod
Must play the wind.

GW. And you, the sceptic bear.
A world of Swedish nights I've improvised the sun,
I've urged the spirit of a Spanish feast, yet won
But little sympathy for every southern
Sentiment. Of thirty months a drought
Has cracked and peeled…

NE. I know, the southern luster
From thy southern rind. I place the turn
Of image which thy puberty was wont to
Fashion up for every shape of flesh,
In eyes, the sun or God, for breasts, red pears,
For hair, the lily-tree which agonizes
In a wind-embrace. The trace of heaven, found in
Things, beguiled thee from a truest joy
In fleshlessness. The one fire that is Christ,
Too heavily befigured here, invites
A naked soul. A bowl of parts, alas,
Thy father bids enkindle thee—for thee…

GW. Ambiguous thanks, old crone…

LI. (to Gwin) Evade no less eternal judgment thinking

To outwit a god too well aware.
His vision tears the trumpery no less
From Gwin than Nelle, and governs by his own
Consent. He meant to save us through Aquinas.

BR. And therefore did he nurse and hatch
The leather eggs of Aristotle in the groins
Of sexless southerners. Arose that quaint salvation
With its vicious brood of wars and obstinacies.
Arose enlightenment, the black barbarians,
And that disharmony which mutilates the family's being,
Between the love of man for woman puts
Abstractions, cries at lust, besieges flesh
With spectral, bony carcasses.

ST. That you
Dissociate Christ's love from man's enough
Reveals your blackness; which to dissipate
My daughter's born gentility suffices.
Her from me raped, you shattered the punctilio
Of her hereditary right, dishonoring her birth...

TR. The worth of which exceeds that of old Nelle
Less than act exceeds conception, be she not
Thereby more rich for receptivity,
Uninstitutional, and open to each tense
And mood that nature's grammar plays across
Its vital fields. Her heart that yields to southern
Longing can shape out its fibred, less
Elusive order in the North, take
The wind into her...

NE.   over-blown impetuosity.
I disagree, and opt for home and church,
The which alone I've known joy-bearing.

GW. I feel I'm at the center, frankly, of your judgements
On the old and new. My view, not philosophical,
Distinguishes two issues, one of heaven,
One not quite. My Swedish knight, this Brane,
Whom you doubtless find inelegant,

Is bent to find his spirit's locus
In a sympathy with man's infections. Hocus pocus
Though he dubs that Latin which the northern
Ear finds uncongenial, still the spirit's
Spirit he observes, deplores injustice, serves in act
Our whole community. He preaches love in deed
And in the fields. He'll wield, in short,
A most undoubted force for equity in Sweden.

BR. Sweeting, you have just put my case
Before those in-laws whom I care not greatly to appease.
So little, truth to tell, do I incline
To placate older forms, that I'll be bold
To clarify the intrigue which demands
My presence here…

LI. I fear the family piety dictates
A less irreverent leisure. The impulse which
Our northern friend extends to this exchange
May well derange and tickle our tradition,
But falls regrettably inapropos.
Below Christ, I honor Stine and Trole,
To them I urge the guidance of our talk be turned.

BR. A dainty turn he's learned, this fawn.

GW. Pray, Brane, still more respect our home punctilio.

TR. Not angry as the stormwind that has found
Its mountain crags invaded, its domain assayed,
But clearly, as well-oiled thinker meets
The other, answers every challenge, joys in
Clarity. Yet this too with a difference,
That I am past defeat, past blood
Within myself. I am a skull in contemplation.
What time I skinned the Saracen, employed
A restless bronze with restless ballet, stayed
Far first in rank, that time I had the peasant for my mate,
Our hates were but a single love. But to complete
My own incertitude, I turned home to this nest
Of the belongers, of the meanings, this file

Of life-solutions in the drawers of which
Each problem's classified. I lied, and squirmed,
And threatened to abjure my birth-rite. Then,
One night, the body's birth-right laid its claim,
The Thane of Crawl assumed for wife this spark,
This burning letter, and his life, his Stine.
A new life-order, personal and rich,
Could supersede the former forms.

ST. Not unembittered I have seen the children go
Below the horizon of my daily day, they've
Faded. Leaving me a possibility,
A hope that springs would bring one down
On melting ice,
The other lure back to our twilights and our cherries,
Lure back for a talk, an afternoon. The bloom
Is off this joy. Return a
heart-worn woman
And a learned priest.

NE. We ceased regret when two springs passed.

BR. And when another spring is gone, you'll long
For battered Spain; the pain of my discourse
Must now reveal that I have come in force,
Over the ice, furred and fatted with
A million Scandinavians. The tone of our
Adventure is a serious one. Northern
Progress in the social arts we shall
Encourage in this Spanish land.
Red will be the sand with just so many
As command financially. Christ lives this day and learns
To rule in Spain. To you, old Trole, I extend
The hand of ally, bear the offer of a
Sinecure…and to the rest, saving Liane,
Whom we shall later question, offer time for swift escape
To Tangier, where your summer house awaits.
There need you fear no violence from a too
Intense majority.

GW. My husband and my home I cannot equally

Respect, or so the world will have it.
Yet poles apart are aspects, not real difference;
The treasure of my vigor is absorption.
Below the surface of intentions, lies the movement of
Experience, which I,
Seeing the ends in the beginning, love in
Motion, will call an Easter Emphasis.

MI 1965 (I,1) (Publisher acronyms can be tracked down in the *Textualities* section, at the end of this book).

With that move through the backdrop of Will's poetic work as character formation—exuberant, synthetic, baroque, even pantheistic, as in *Fragments*—we will have a loop around Will's early trials. This early work (1944–1950) is not really work but an accentuation of lifestyle, an effort to leave that style in a name. *Naming*, we will have occasion to see in these examples, has been Will's password to the "standing into" which is trueness to the presence of the human situation, and which on an occasion, while he was dodging through the minefields of the biological situation, he nominated as an action descriptor for the maturing, aging, and ultimately surviving process. We repeat: *I live life as though it were, in itself, a standing-into a future condition, in which orders I can't imagine will recapacitate me, assigning me to the rights of place.* With a return to the barer anatomy of the making process, as he ages within, Will will return also to the original thoughts awakening gave him, into the essential process of giving things a name, and thus giving ourselves a place in what-is. (Will's earliest essays—cf. bibliography in *The Modernist Impulse and a Contemporary Opus: Replaced by Writing*, 2017—were precisely about the naming act, and the changes naming establishes in the world it interprets.) It will be no surprise to find that the poetry of Will's later stage oblation, babbles up out of the childish acquisitions of his initial steps onto the stage of being-with-other-people-in-language.

And within that degree of closure, in our overall flight through and out the other side of Will's juvenilia, we will have been able to imagine that the mid-life interventionist poems, with which we will begin Part One, are conscious moves to dissimulate the self, to prioritize language itself—think of the Tupus poems (ahead; the meat of *The Being Here Site of the Poetic*, 2011), in which a language invents itself. By contrast, the poems of childhood and of youth were a laying bare, a gesture to the innocence of language. (That is, to the innocence and transparency we ascribe to language, supposing that the fantasies, drives, and dreads of the late teens, say, are closer than are the "reservations" of the mid-life sophisticate, to who and what we "really are.") The "later poems," prose poems, and mini-epics tend to the wry and colloquial, and in direction order new edicts to character-in-language, such as *let them see* you and *close no doors*. Edicts, however, are edicts, and never to be mistaken for the charming outbursts of just being here, while not even saying that you are here.

PART ONE:

POEMS OF INTERVENTION

CHAPTER ONE

I AS INTERVENTION IN POETRY: *GUATEMALA*

Stéphane Mallarmé, master of invention in language, depreciator of the naïve, wrote that: *L'oeuvre poétique implique la disparition élucutoire du poète, qui cède l'initiative aux mots, par le heurt de leur inégalité mobilisés* ("Crise de vers", *Divagations*; 1897). The poetic work implies the *élucutoire* (elocutionary) disappearance of the poet, his disappearance behind the very language he makes himself poet in—the poet who yields initiative to the poem's words, by allowing that asymmetrical knocking together, by allowing the words' deployment of their difference from one another. The poet disappears in this process. All that is left is the poet's words, bruising against one another. The keyword for us may be *heurt*, a knocking against, a hitting. Not only does the poet yield the initiative—the creative power "behind" the poem—to the words of the poem, but he yields to them the power that accrues from their inequality, *inégalité*, the joust of power relations among these words. (Lack of interior proportion and balance is the price paid by the words for their free-market adventure among their fellows.) Having yielded so much to the words, then, what happens to the poet himself? Where did Milton *go*, on the far side of the work in *L'Allegro*? (Character may have been taken from him, and given over to the words of his poem, but what kind of ontological placeholder then *takes the place of his poetic character?* He has one, he's got a *character* we know for sure, for we all do; but where is it? Has he yielded himself out of existence? Is major creation a self-obliteration, for all the semblances to the opposite, the senses that big creator and big ego go together? Is there any *moi*, "personal identity," left as guidance for the poet's poem? Is the poet's character not simply left somewhere in the poem, either as a residue or as a pervasive flow?

I am asking myself that question, as I unshelve an old pamphlet, in which I had long ago (1973), twenty-three years after "An Emphasis for Easter," crowded what I thought were hot metaphors that rose from the condensed experience of creation and sacrifice, and which I now think heralded in the midlife interventional period of my own poetry, the period where ole Mallarmé caught me with my pants down, pulling back from the intra-shocks of my own words. Did my "poetic" *character* survive into these midlife poems?

The hot-metaphor pamphlet in question was *Guatemala* (Bellevue Press, Binghamton), a pennyworth of fyre I thought at the time. The life-text to it was a trip to what at the time I took to be that searing polity—or so I characterized it, tripping off of banner headlines and the jargons that constitute a personal geopolitics as tame in fact as pussycat soup—where corruption and the jungle (sounds good, don't it? Very Graham Greene, who was doubtless subtler than yours truly at makeover jobs on the daily news, like in *The Quiet American*) vied in real-life hotness. I am there again today in my version of this poem as I surround the action re-do with the feel of it, and look for what I was; the time (I constructed) was between the lines. There again? I am watching (well I was there being, no?) a row of image-bare stelae, sixteenth-century victims of Spanish priests' ardor to remove the relics of an earlier priesthood as it was, aligned adoringly before the great temple of Tikal. (A little historical packaging here, harmless, and spot on conceptually, the meat of teacher digressions.) I was being the designated and expected attitude pose of the event. Language took the place of the stage set, abruptly.

Guatemala II 1973

Suddenly the stela takes a turn for the worse.
Who cut the priesthood back
Shaved innocent features from their diamond of sense?

Suddenly the power goes like wind from the stela.
We dash our lips to history's throat.
We breathe like tornados
Through the rock's hollow skin.

Suddenly the stela takes a turn for the better.
Forgotten features puff like cysts on the tattered rock.
The priest breaks his eyes
Open from the carnal rock.
He has seven fingers of blood in his vision.

Suddenly the stela takes a turn for the worse.
It devours the earnest face of a child.
It opens from the silence yet is only the silence.

It swells and blossoms before our eyes.
Then it dries like a heart,
It dries like a heart and blows away.

GU II 1973

As if to underline Mallarmé's point, about the way of the disappearance of the poet, the poet's *moi* makes virtually no appearance in this poem. (Virtually? Someone guides the "suddenly" for sure, but has it a personal nature? It's our nagging question, sooner or later sure to turn up a pincushion of insight.) Or rather no *named* appearance; no pronoun backs up the poet's *moi*. There is no "I" here, no "character of the poet" monitoring your read, but of course there is an implied "I" who is asking the questions the poem is made of, and who *is* thus there. "Who cut the priesthood back?" comes at you from some questioner, but that questioner is leached of distinctive characteristics, emerges from a traitless language *intervention. The intervention is simply an intrusion. You didn't ask about the stela's health, or ask to follow the course of that health. It was laid on you.* The intervention in question, however, does take place as part of a relationship. The intervention's question is directed at someone; "who cut the priesthood back" is legible only if the reader acknowledges the presence of a *hearer* of the question. Asking means hearing, yourself hearing yourself, no? The hearer is not named, and may best be thought of as the reader. (Reading, then, is a kind of hearing? But there is no reason why the reader couldn't also be the writer.) So though there is no "I" at the outset of this poem, there is a questioning which seems to belong to a questioner and a hearer who are constructing one another. Does this quasi-"I" questioner count as a surrogate for the poet's "character?" Our answer involves trying to describe how this questioner gets onto the scene.

Perhaps the question that starts this poem should be considered an "intervention," a legal accusation, an intervening into the origin and course of the poem. (What line of discourse among folks is not interventional? There's a flow. There's an invitation for fulfillment and sometimes for reduction. One person moves the croquet ball a few meters to the west. There is "conversation.") The intervention can take the form of a question, *who did this or that,* but by the second paragraph the initial peremptory question, loaded as it is with tightly compressed laments, bursts its grammatical bounds by bursting out in response to itself...with a third-person statement that "suddenly the power goes like wind from the stela." The statement is not *exactly* a response to the intervention question of the first three lines, but is rather the introduction of an emergency, onto the interrogation of the first three lines. The cry of alarm, as though to locate the peril in the immediate presence of the intervention, opens out onto a "we," for the peril of "power loss" is so great that collective resuscitative action is required. The intervention now resembles a Big Bang from which emerges a personal speaking voice, like the voice of the Abrahamic God from the desert. Is the "we" of "we dash our lips to history's throat" the "person" questioned by the interrogations that open the poem? Is the "we" the consciousness reading the poem and saying it over to him/herself? Is the "we" a person? If so, is it a person so embedded in history that mouth-to-mouth resuscitation is possible for it, as it lives its history; in other words, is this "we" the size of history? This "we" fits its history exactly. And this "we" is that from which power "has gone like wind from the stela." The alarm is personal, though collective, and itself seems little more than an intrusion, humanity intervening on behalf of its historical control, the stelae which in archaic Mayan Guatemala are the inscriptions of history, inscriptions which, as we know, the conquistadores leveled like stalks of grain, as they vented their Christian time frame against the cancellable Mayan underdogs. A retributory violence—"suddenly the stela takes a turn for the better"—follows the effort of the "we" to resuscitate the historical thread. This "we," no personable collective but the action-face of the initial intervention, treats us to a bloody commentary on priestly vision, the price the priests' eyes must pay, to retrieve the meanings of the rock they are carved from.

At the same time, the intervention offers us a passing hope for historical continuity—this is the conceptual melt-down of the interventional voice—which will again be demystified and stripped at the end of the poem. For in the voice of the intervention the stela once more falls fatally ill, and blows away in the wind. The stela grows silent and dry, and supports no more knowing faces. Has an "I" made itself discernible through the filter of intervention, "we," and the "our" of the "our eyes" at the end? We listen inwardly to what has just transpired. We put the artifact back on the shelf. We have lunch and take a walk. We "do our thing." Then we return to our study, pull down the page, and look again at the word *artifact*. What is it saying? It is saying there is this upstraight stony record of historical meaning, that this record is a lifeline to the meaning of the past, and that (in some world) this record is scattered and lost. It, this poem thing, is somehow both what a person is saying to another person, actually me to me in this case, and what this person's grammar is refusing to acknowledge as anything but intervention with the odd sucker-attached app of personal verbiage.

Meanwhile the *words*, as Mallarmé says: *L'oeuvre poétique implique la disparition élucutoire du poète, qui cède l'initiative aux mots, par le heurt de leur inégalité mobiilsés* ("Crise de vers", *Divagations*, 1897). Okay. The poet gets out of the way, after intervening, after playing with a "we," after under-muffling a kind of I-thou relation to a reader, who is kinda the poet himself. Okay. Nothing then like a transparent statement with a job to do, *hey bob bring me that sack of potatoes over in the corner.* And yet when this poet gets out of the way it's like after having landed a rabbit punch and you Fred Astaire it nimbly just off to the side and there's no reaching you with a return punch, but you're sort of there. You've landed your load, and its doing its work, chewing up blood vessels, scribbling contusions, and making a Halloween mask out of an emeritus professor. Character download? Shall we say this is a hop skip and a jump download? Now you see me, now you don't? Super different from the fruity personal download we read in *Fragments*, or intuited in "An Emphasis for Easter."

All that junk that follows the destructive blow against the stelae is like the life the words are leading, after the poet leaves them, stepping out of the way of the impact of his/her statement. Mallarmé calls the interaction of those words, left on their own, an *heurt*, a blow, or a whole scene of blows as the words slam against each other like go-carts at a country fair. And that's not all he says about those words. He says they are mobilized by their "asymmetrical knocking together against each other." Because they are of different sizes and shapes, their interchanged blows send them spinning, like ricocheting billiard balls, over the surface of the poem. These spinning words, themselves, "get the initiative."

The farther we pursue this imagery, the more uncertain it seems that we are going to find a "poet" or "character" serving as the voice at the center of poetry in general, and certainly of the *Guatemala* poem before us. Robot or computer-generated poetry, we might be starting to think, would lack nothing characteristic of the intervention poem before us. It might, in fact, further tweak that element of alienation which is so often a factor in getting a poem to make us pay attention to it. What, though, if that frivolous divagation—zombie poetry—is a key to a new formulation of the poetic character available to the intervention itself? The very hardness of the poem before us, as though eating its own face as it courts ours, is a tease of person. Poems that refuse to make friends with us, that are intelligible but only to the suckering-in point, do the work archaic Greek imputed to the creator of *character*, the one who burins a sharply incised figure or imprint into a coin or other piece of metal. That creator of *character*, say of the individual sculpting his own character for himself, burins a sharply incised figure or emblem, the profile of a unique individual into the coin of being, and does so in the way the zombie poet might be thought to invoke a personality onto what Mallarmé sees as the mobilized counters of the words the poet uses.

The words of the *stela* poem, above, open their intra-textual knocking about through the portal of the paragraph. The interfaces among the paragraphs are where you can see this. Look at the four lines beginning with "suddenly," each of which introduces a shock to the thought which preceded it. Three of those lines open with "suddenly" then segue immediately into an account of the kind of turn the stela takes. What preceded that turn is in each case as brusque, and without antecedent, as any intervention. Aren't we reading over a chasm in which such eruptions as an originating creation, the ultimate in abruptness, seem promised? Those turns are alternately worse, better, and worse, in a darkening plait, into which the alarm of stanza two is woven, that the sense of crisis may be maximized. One might say, then, that the word-group stanzas beat menacingly against one another.

How do the nuclei of those stanzas, the unit-words, treat one another? What do they do with the "initiative" the poet, according to Mallarmé, accords them? ("Initiative" may be a useful word to describe the kind of hanging around his poem the poet has.) The words of the poem disaggregate as they are compiled. They allow no "I" to assemble them. Hard, disaggregated nouns batter one another, silence dries and blows away, stone puffs out like cysts, we breathe into the rock's hollow skin, innocent features congregate around a diamond of sense. None of these stony language components comes to us as a humanized offering, dressed for the suave of person to person. There is no *moi* to take its children by the hand, and lead them back into the fold of voice.

Zombie poetry? If zombie implies not quite melded into an emotional oneness, not quite coming to you as the work of another *person*, it may be correct to call this thing before you *zombie poetry*. While there are elements of *Einbildungskraft*, of *ineins-bildung*, before us, and we can, as we did above, see those elements coalescing into somewhat sterterous conceptual strands—the historical as marker, the death and resurrection of innocence, the vulnerability of the temporal—we can hardly feel we are in the presence of a speaking voice with whom we are already present as a partner in dialogue. Is this the same as saying that we are re-inciting poetry which was *not* in the first place character-stamped?

And if this is a way of saying that, about the kind of poetry we are reading here, should we say we are reading poetry that has slipped past the Romantic tradition? Are we reading in the vein of George Oppen poetry, and not in that of e. e. cummings? The present author has always sported a crush on the poetry of George Oppen. In fact, the author has a bunch of crushes on hard-edged—Robert Grenier, Christopher Middleton, Gary Snyder—poets who have slipped the noose of the Romantic, who have in their ways gone on reading Pindar, Horace, and Pope, even while recognizing that "The Prelude" was a game-changer not to be underestimated. What was the draw to those crushes? It was that fascination with the geometrical, the Mayan hardness—what else than "Mayan" is the stela poem?—the angularity and sheer history of the artifact. And from where can have come this gnashing taste for the angry of hardedge? Seasons, stillness, insecurity. The sense of wanting to be the last man standing, one who proffers a hard oblation at the end, and makes it an act of love. That's where it comes from, that draw and that team.

CHAPTER TWO

THE LONG POEM IN THE AGE OF TWITTER AND *THE BEING HERE SITE OF THE POETIC* (2011)

Guatemala is our portal into what we call interventionist poetry, designed as it is to tell but under conditions that mask the teller, and to do what the poem can to conceal or redirect the voice of the poet. It will be seen, in what follows in Part II, which digs back into the work of Will's first three volumes of poetry, *Mosaic* (1959), *A Wedge of Words* 1963), and *Planets* (1968), that the distortions, closings-off of self, and angers which generate so much post-Baudelairian poetry, are not part of the repertoire Will brought on stage with him. From *Fragments* on, until Will's life started hitting the fan in the mid-1960s, his poetry is in the Romantic tradition, battening where it can off the gamesmanship-metaphysic of Marianne Moore or the sucked in *rausch* of a Hart Crane. By the time of *Guatemala* the cloaking of the narrator is fully fashioned, and the carving against childhood is on the contingency curve which will have full voice by the time of the following from *The Long Poem in the Age of Twitter and The Being Here Site of the Poetic* (2011).

2.1

…it's a hollow
　　you rode it? well
　let's jes…it's a hollow,
　　　it has a side,
here, there's a distich, n'
　in the centre a…
　　　it's a hollow,
　　　　it melts…
flies away in yr
　　hand…tren
　　　the old doggo,
　the fire captain…

                    makes a stop at the
little tren's room,
        slithers...
                there's a dog-o,
                there's a cheese—
        o slip me one...
        he dons
        tren, it's hollow,
                fills it...
    it spills...
                but it's hollow...
                        he takes a ride...
                there's a...furtive...
        tren derives from...
                he's there smiling
                surely, ready to pinch
        it's a local wear
                sure, a fire sergeant...
                clop clop...
    isn't it rocky?
            isn't there local motion,
                n' stir...
                    he hollows
            it's tren, zippo zippo,
        bursts, tren, sense-data...
                    minima...
            amoralia? rather hollow...
            rather a jettison
            n'a tree...he winces,
        tren, it's a hollow,
                        there's zuma...
                from it drops
                drips, drips...it's a hollow...
                    you make a fyst
                of leaves, shplunk...
                    n' drive...
                it's a tren,
                it's hollow, it catches...
BHSP 279–281

Any narrator there?

2. 2

It isn't or...
Well...said
Let's say it was
Not, not is safer
Dry as in...
Tack, tack, hard
tickety...
It is not, o
tell, me it is
not ill...he cries...
ten-
dons snap he cries...
dragging....
his gown clod
pure dirt
has it not, it
is, not, he
streams...there will be uh
briss? brisket?
clutching...a word?
it isn'
t or might...you gaul
you Fulani, or
did u try,
tribe, defending case
law hand...
he said, meestah...
his gown clod
pure...dirt
devil ain't seen...
he stirs, there's a
mogha, mogha...
he fingers its
a or is
not at all, no
knot..ah mean
clotted, his gown,
he draws
is there a packet?

he frisks…
is it tack,
tack, jack, metal?...
or frozen,
his gown, u
dread? not snap?
is there a pretense
"red"…
hard not is safer?
he deems,
and in that
slight motion, dork…
well there's a trend…
it extends…
follow the Lieder,
they blew…
ugh a snack
a dervish in a sac
pack cracked
gown pure
duhrt it isn't or
well, maybe it
ees…he flogs…
there's a smell…
a jerbil flaying,
dukn, dukn,
mogha, mogha…in a
free duhrt colored
gown snaps
draggin sure's
enveloped, simply enticed…
he rises a…
it's a
frail Bodenschap…
ahm kneelin…
he's a seed he
dips dips tacks…
dips dip

BHSP 281–284

Or are there innumerable characters, a mosaic of them, downloading one another criss-cross? Establishing hearers as they go?

2.4

The flower you
   Held
      To my temple…
    It was a fever,
  Like Dirce…
       Like the road…
     I took no sheer
    From wind but
      Tacked
    Diagonally back
    I rowed
  Say, air
      Currently from my shoulder…
      I took a barn…
   Battles in farmland,
    They singe,
       Whence…
     Oh you did?
      You rode,
    Ultramontane into
     Tren…?
   I guess a fyre,
    Windy, yes, no?
  Stippled the lobe
     U held…well flowers
    Gergamite, flodge…
      U will hold up
   We all know
    Is costly,
  Taints…it was a feint
   Ur
   …dress was it?
     Insyde out…
   And a frank
     Torment wimpling…
   As at Scheria…

Voluble, then last an ear
Tong a long a lobe...
The flower,
U held?
I hold two
It was
"trying," the air
wonko bonko
Shstakovitch
Bryttle
No hear
Riding on this
Lobgesang
Fyre...they dredge
Pinko from his nostril
She shrinks
Then assaults...
The ear
Wig slithers...u
O u do the
Funniest...he
Rappels, the moment
Hollows
By his foot...
He drags
With him a tale
U
Oh you! Lobe
Maddening sprite
Trick hymn out...
Did you gear him?
He went
Easily into that couch
Where all...
Almost all, well...
Where hearing begins
At the lobe
U held
To my temple
My priest's...
O feverish

I will not drain
Bickerstaff...
The smile...ur lip
File, file it
Under
Temple, faint,
Rowbyrowbyrow
Til
You feigned
I took ur...
Lady, of Spain,
Winkle, winkle, little
The "starry heavens..."
Above, a setter,
You tricked me.
I'll sue,
Ah'll sue ya
Sure, samanthee,
Surenahll...
He faints...
Roses from noses
Blossom, flow sprays.
U floor me he says
Temple
Of my being
Touched, a lobe...
A flower...
Did Archilochos
N' Neobule
Not rinse one two three
The flowers
Of
Paros?
He winks,
A dish
Drying in his hand,
Makes the difference...
She says
Touching, "fyre?"
He tackles,
He feints...

> Turns yr gesture…
>   His features he prays
>   Lighttemple templelight
>   A lite touch
>   She recedes…
> She gives hymn
>   Voice, Calvin
>   No Klein thanks rough,
> Fingers kiss.
>   He stills,
>   He pulls back
>   Was that not a
>   Feint, a brink?,
>   His temple
>   Blown shortly
>   Her
>   No did I say…
>   Flow?

BHSP 289–295

Is there not a parade of interventions here, each thought-line taken up fresh by the semblance of a response which, serving a new interrogator, becomes the #1 instance of trigger?

***

Will has at this point for some time been concerned with poetry written by no one. He can see many collateral reasons for such a concern. There is always Homer, who is the great inspiration, for his nearly total authorial selflessness, his magisterial control over poetic effects, and his fascination both with suffering and with its remedies. Homer always seems very present as no one except the other side of himself. Then there is—because it caught Will's grad-student attention, poor thing—that compelling vortex movement, late nineteenth century, in which early Yeats or T. E. Hulme or Wyndham Lewis shed an instructive spell of symbolic coldness, onto the art enterprise, and then a little later, across the channel, Mallarmé himself made the cold seem the only suitable preservative for characterful poetic emotion. Like Prospero Will turned these bookish excursions into long trips into an other from which he never returned the same. There is also that funny trip to Postmodernism, which to Will—maybe to all of us for a while in the 1970s and after?—became a flashword for personal use, embedded in a nearly borderless sense of our time, and of what in it was most beginning to have to be formulated. Among the paths down which Will took that flashword, *Postmodernism,* were the quagmires of language theory, and especially the notionary zone that language creates the self, rather than being created, for a purpose no less, *by* the self. The turns and twists, of this latter concept, take Will on regular dates with cultural anthropology, and with the arguable notion that culture takes its own linguistic mandates wherever it goes, and "at the deepest level." Far inside the arguments choked back, here, lies a steady interest in whether any one writes the poem, or whether language writes it—and if so what that could mean. The shades of Foucault's "What is an Author?" again hover around this internal dialogue, which directs broad fire against the idea of the integrated self. But Will won't go that far, for he thinks around the need for a concept of character inside literary authorship, even though, as you see, he is in training for a multi-faceted midlife attack on that bulwark.

In *The Being Here Site of the Poetic* (2011), Will outlines his perception of the authorless poem in front line combat with intelligibility. He is, to make his point, throwing words in a pile, the way Pollock threw paint at a canvas, and yet he is immediately aware, upon inspection of his pile, that he is reading the world through it; that there is somebody using that pile, even if it is himself deciding what to do with that pile. Many of the Tupus poems, which form a kind of self-obliterating narrative for *Being Here*, show off both the humor and the subversion intended in the present language challenge.

Tupus is ready to state.
He grtspn carefully, faces the cameras,
Marks the point on the wall
To which he will bgr.

Thousands 8tpaz.
The pope is there prnntn10d.
The only thing that prevents a riot is pr>sz.
Tupus knows where he is going,

Takes his itrp and climbs carefully out of the town.
Saviors are seldom welcome,
In the yt2^ they came from.

BH 119

Tupus might as well be the everybody or nobody who writes the Tupus poem, or is written by it. He can be grand, "ready to state," *ahem ahem*, and he can be ready to offer a routine power point presentation. He is professional, like the great cartoon of responsible legibility each of is from the inside these days. But basic language equipment is nonetheless reluctant to define him. He doesn't forget English, English forgets him. When he "*grtsp*," English has dangled him in formative mode, and *bgr*, to which he is to bring his skills, is trying him on. (We *could* think of the inner drama, in this poem coming to be, as born into existence by the "individual" hoping to find through language invention new spaces to occupy. But this Tupus is not an individual, rather a type, and hasn't inside him the velocities needed to generate a new language. He is just enough language to be being made.) Is there a right answer to the question of what *8tpaz* is trying to signify? Of course an automatic insert is there in each of us, to fill the meaning void, yet the "applaud" may actually be intended as the space for "wipe their asses" or, for that matter, more betwitchingly, might be there for precisely *8tpaz*. This latter possibility is thrilling. *8tpaz* could be the name for itself. Thousands of words could be of this sort. The wild cards sprinkled throughout the remainder of the Tupus poem enjoy the same mobile status. They could be what they suggest, something totally different from what they suggest, or precisely what they are, which would make us think laterally.

What kind of had-to-be-as-it-is language do the words in the above Tupus poem enjoy? Do some words enjoy more blessings from the king than others? Or are they all piles of sound begging our valence? If they seem to us such "piles of sound" is it that they lack certain historical credentials—say certain Latinate or Germanic roots—or is it that we lack the inventiveness or energy to hear them as what they are? We can't answer this question by book, but can place it with other questions concerning the levels of insistence language has for us when it comes at us in a poem. Questions like: isn't there a poem for every kind of cognitive or emotional pressure? Hasn't the poem language for a deepest forebear, into whom the *poietes* taps?

***

Or four little Tupus bits:

*What kind of African king would I make, wonders Tupus,
Glargin sleepily, torgge in shuttered places, I would wonder
Am I stolggew, rungiog, corwal?*

There are training wheels for everything.

BH 75

***

I am not Tupus, Ergijjn.
I am not the son of the powers, grahgg.
Or the one who washes out the buckets.

I am, shrosggh, friendly, I am shurggw.

BH 79

***

Tupus takes the trail straight up the hillside
Pertinently. He is always where he should be,
In the shroggs, left there, nshuernint, a signal,
Lipersure, frosd, a tendency.

BH 80

***

Glabrous and smoky, walks euro cool into his garden
And begins rearranging the phlox.
Let's put gitr9 here this summer, for it goes with the ptrmv.

To make the garden supple
he goes down to the garden shop,
orders a truckload of hsdf and forks it onto the humus
with results the neighbors will applaud
when they return from praising his 7yncs.

It is thus that each of us, doing a task that is appointed,
meshes with the purposes of the other,
constructing thereby the house of a society
in which old-fashioned 7ws complement the racier virtues of 7rb.

BH 99

Will intervenes, as character-creator in the Tupus poems? Let's say it again, what it means. He mock creates a character for himself, but what that character is made of is the absurdity of Tupus being made of anything except language. Well, language plus impulses, plus a Chaplinesque inclination to start out on projects, ta dum ta dum ta dum, and then to trip or fall down in the mud or fart in church. Is the author, this Will guy, pulling our legs, or mocking himself? He is muddying the waters of whatever character he might want to ascribe to *himself*.

The Long Poem in the Age of Twitter (2011) began as an effort to let some poetry write itself, another version of allowing poetry simply to be language. The author recognizes, in this form of the desire to drain character from language, the potent whiff he imbibed, during his earlier making years, from circumambient sounds that felt as though they derived from a single concern with language as maker of *itself*. (Had he a hidden Ariel charming him on the breeze, but never self-disclosing?) He had word friends in many ports, thanks to what for a while became his professional tweak, working in and around workshops for writing, especially as director or co-director with translation workshops. In other words he was close to *that* philosophically interesting feeler toward placing self in the world through its doing language. He was immersed in the living issues the existence of one's language introduced into one's sense of simple being-here. It was a little like being a rap artist collecting the detritus of the streets into a malleable foster child of pure representation.

***

Come now, your discourse falters? The upward flight
Time promised you, whither is it tending? Let me clear
My throat and with it my mind. As long as my back doesn't hurt
I can think about the witness the stars provide.

I know darned well that my mission is a go, yet where, yet
Who is able to tell me? Is it not Mother Philosophy,
With her train of Acolytes, who bubbles here beside me?
Who glosses Meyerson or Quine? Is it not the faith I had?

Or is it not the simplest philosophy in the world?
The ward of my telephone, the comfort of an occasional jello,
A pat on the back? Sometimes I think I can settle for the very

Least things in the world. They are so savory.

They are best, let me assure you, when accompanied by least,
When given as a child gives a gift, with a little embarrassment.
I could swear that what I heard this morning, when dressing,

Was the ultra-simple turning of the spheres, which I've heard before,
And along with that, barely visible on the horizon,
A line of the robed figures that dance each morning for the ashram.
There is such salt in the undissolved peace of these moments.

What I mean by philosophy, then, was really just openness.
Friends dropping in are inevitably the best explanation,
For they just happen, and suddenly you find apples,
And a pint of rum, and go out onto the back porch,

And are very loquacious under the moon. One of you, like Pepe,
May actually think he is a philosopher and may open a topic.
Perhaps it's that freedom's the enemy of originality for it's only
In chains that we know how to be free. That was always Pepe's point.

Always he spoke for discipline, and always for tightening the net over
possible meanings. I fully comprehend him. I know that when you write,
Which fewer do now, learning to stop the line is part of the wonder.
It's important to control breath. It's important to do this and not that.

Ordinary speech is far too much like driving down the highway
And filling yourself chiefly with peripheral vision.
Nothing has a line or fervor when you drive.
On the other hand living too rigidly, caring too much about cleaning

Up the kitchen before going to bed, or expunging meaningless traces
Will get you down. It will make you compulsive.

LPAT 211–214

***

It's a silent afternoon, all Sunday.
Sunday covers my shirt and my forearms,
Sunday grows tall at my expense
There where festivals stagger home.

I have in truth no future to recapture, only a future
To bring home slowly to sit beside me.
I have absolute governance over my shirtsleeves
And over the trial balloons I send up.

As for the respectable I might try fooling them with my tie
Collection which is doggedly risking, or I might
Walk onstage during the Emmys in my underpants.

Instead, however, I'm likely to remain precisely here,
To browse more sedulously in hopes of remuneration.
Ya see my pride is swallowed like soda pop.
I will go down before you

If you promise me a dollar.
Full-service registration, however, will cost a lot more.
Technicians will have to be called in, busybodies of science,
And where they intrude it is ugly.

Stop watches and time clocks turn softly and vomit.
Nice little children, in nice little schools,
Up their pinafores and giggle like Benny Hill.
Decorum pours like treacle into the streets.

If you have a wiggle waggle, with which to keep me silent,
I guarantee to tame you.
Sunday's only Sunday.
The sun's only the sun.

LPAT 215–217

***

Chapter 2, "Might be Sattiday" is where, in *The Long Poem in the Age of Twitter*, the narrative action opens from the inside of its author, not from imagination but from the streets of the daily which is the author where he eats, drinks, and shits. We are, in our fashion, approaching the point Eliot and Stevens—*The Waste Land* (1922) and *Sunday Morning* (1917)—brought us to, to the point where conflict divides grace from fall, as the sun hits a warm porch or history drifting away from its archaic truths. How far we seem from the formulations those two gents happened on, but how useable and contemporary seem the ways their texts speak to us today.

Might be Sattiday (2011)

He's known of course throughout
the county, not of course
As an architect of but as an
Whaddidya say? Epistemologist?

Sure an that's it, a collector of
Percipia...admire yer percipia mam?
Cut em a little shorter, like
This, he says, snipping her...

Young man I want cher to know...
Then when they've finished dressin.
Sad, a bit, he proposes...
Audis are reliable...she winces

Something about his gums.
Are there cheeses? Is there a,
Well, Sattiday smell in the room?
He rounds on her, don't go for that talk,

Amsterdam direct, and in a trice
Mornin's there, it's Sattiday
An sure an it's Stevens,
Wallace, drawin distinctions,

This rinsed weave, that...
Ain't Sunday though, an' the
Apparition wavers.
Litachur's alluhs on target

Fabric here, fabric there
Nothin ain't not in parenthesis...

LPAT 22–24

A corny love affair, a pass at the great metaphysical questions of mankind, and a slide off into the bestial ambiguity of literature herself. We range widely, and on the wings of jes plain talk, sliding in and out wherever we go, asking no questions, accepting no excuses. This sliding in and out is but another version of yielding of self to language, which we illustrated above, in the *Guatemala* stela poem—where intervention deprived the author of his very breath—and in the "Tupus is ready to state" poem, where all Tupus could say, to make of himself a personality, is replaced by fake speech which anticipates him. Language takes over, intervenes, in all these *bruchstuecke* of thought. It is not that there is no narrative to follow, but that the narrative shlurps itself up, bars the inroads of the integral ego, which would form, distribute, and harvest the message. The fierce tiger, language, crouches inside us; when we open our gates the beast slavers gracious angers across our page.

***

Wandering at its own pace, but through us, the river of choice samples our values, our crumbiest hopes, our goings beyond, and becomes those potentials on the far side of an aw shucks discourse which is both calamity filled and erudite. In *The Being Here Site of the Poetic,* the author ruminates on the view of language that has to have underlain his poetry to make its existence possible.

***

Governorship, justice, and power snowflake the following exempla, in which the lability of each proposed topic surrogates for the characterless character of the "writer," leaving the language ultimately on its own, free of him. (This is anger? Creator withdrawal? A new kind of sulking? Or the chance for a little indecent exposure, without catching the eye of the cops? Call it what you like, provided you include the care taken by the caretaker of this language, to be absent from it even while making it.)

2.11
You see
We don't need it
   There's an aria
   Goes "che gelida…"
   The "m
Anina" goes
Just before.

Or is it
Just…deserts sweeten
Any system
Justice…, iustitia
After the "gelida"…
Cold first, ladies,
Gentlemen, a bit warmer,
Governor, ship…
It's only just,
Ya see,
The way he …
Guvnuh Winthrop,
Suh, I'd…
The swan strokes
Hand after cold…
Hand me a peesa
That…
She steps back,
Suh, she says,
Ah didn't fer uh
Moment…
Laks ah'd uv
Thunk it
Mam, he says,
Drily,
Guvnuhship goes
Hand-in-hand
With cold.
Cold little…he
Fries, it's a fry!
She smirks, guvnuh,
Muh hand's…
Small n'frigid
He rejoins,
Stroking it…
Guvnuhship's
Privilege, mebbe,
The oak
Drama, folks
Gathered by hillside…
The plain stirs..

What savage crew!
 Yes guvnuhship it's
 Raht fer the mass
 Is missa,
Iustitia, it's
Ave atque
Wally! Petrus! Firmenson!
                Angels and…
Ministers of state
   Gather, pressed,
 Each to each…
        He bends, his
 Hand fumbles
          Over…
 The leaves dry
Tentatively on dishes
 A merger…
                              He spends
        Wristsful, handsful
        Gelida,
   She spends the
 Last Iustitia in Adelaide
        Honey,
     Here, innocence
        Feathers lonely
As doorknobs
          Opening
   Iustitia…them? Where?
 U said town?
     He bustles…
  For Iustitia he'd…
 But when he gets
There she's gone…
     Robbin'
 S Eyeland huntsman…
          The furze…
 He settles, Iustitia's
Done shakin his

   Hand cold…
 Che Gelida

Govnuh, u said?
　His perruque
Stiffens, drily
　Squirming to the…
Rinses
　　"cold hands cold heart"
oh rose of
　　Iustitia…

　The great becalmer…
　Missa est.
　　Dimitte? Pink-
Slipped? He dodges.
　　No Bull
　He whispers…

Bent to the…
　　Hand that rocks the
　　Cold sore wound
　　　Of its patron…
　Che gelida
　　　　　　Chiquita
　　Benina he coughs
　Papal this mass
　No bull
　　Issued…issued from the
　　　　　　　　Warm

　　Into cold dark hell
　　　The thick
　　Set finger of the
　Hand's wrung
Proposition…she coughs
　　Iustitia…

BHSP 313–318

CHAPTER THREE

THE EPICS OF AMERICA (1978)

The foregoing sultry carnage of bad-ass attitudes contrives to enter languagelessness by being the voice-out of a marasmic time traveler, a fly-by-night philosopher of history, to whom as much is allowed as was permitted to the narrator of the downfall of the Mayan stelae. (The swashbuckle, of the three widely time-separated poem-sequences—*Guatemala, Being Here, Twitter*, 73/78/2011–12—only highlights their purposeful singleness of intent; to discern the strains of pure language prioritization in Will's opus. What dominant chords of character-download find themselves central in *The Epics of America*? Is it a guy or the worn voice of history who offers us this wryness?)

Epics of America XXXIV Milktoast

Toast melts in the American mouth.
Soldiers go to the front carrying bowls
Swimming with milktoast. Cannons lob toast
Fierily into the enemy lines. I lay toast
by my bedside, nibble it in the morning.
Toast fills the attic, bulges from trunks,
Suitcases, old paper bags. I feed
Guests on toast, heap their plates.
Now I am reading a book about toast,
How it influenced America, how it taught
Our Founding Fathers principles of law,
Justice, constitutional rigor. I put slices
Of firm brown bread in the toaster
And watch them heat. They pop and grin.
I dip them in butter, nibble them,
Take in their friendship. I think of the people,
Past and to come, who will not know toast.
And I toast one piece for them.

I butter it generously,
And leave it cooling on the edge of the table.

EOA 35

So, back to the question of downloading character into the poetic text. A *persona* addresses us here, though one glad to pretend to be a person talking chummily to a universal mate. It is as though there is some foxy secret being shared, between two figures who do not know each other, but are willing to tap together into a world secret. This then is a new turn on the manufacture of a surrogate creator for the poem, and a new way of ascribing "personality" to the created text. The "I" speaking here is no person we will have known, and no viewpoint we would be able to identify.

The *Epics of America* built broadly on this acidulous-global voice, which arrogates to itself the right to undermine at any point in its culture. It is not a cynical voice, for it is without worldview, but a voice made of language, and backed up by no currency more stable than language-making-language. There is no linguistic Fort Knox behind the language of *Milktoast*, and yet one wonders, and has to foreground right here and now, whether the perspective behind voicing this voice is what we would call *postmodern*. That question lurks behind the whole operation of the first "interventional" part of this book, which is devoted to ways old-fashioned human personality is deflected from the texts in which it invests itself. The personality of the poet is nothing but ways to avoid and channel a wholehearted statement of what and who it is. The poem is a co-conspirator in that effort to deflect, but to deflect while teasing, as though the reader wanted to be duped into conversation with a casual friend but was not comfortable going there.

Epics of America XII: Starlight in the American Stable

Red stables filled with whole horses.
A leather window taped to prairie.
He picks up a rock, holds it
Coldly against the moon.
Takes a knife, peels off the shell,
Cuts back into naked
Central rock.
Starlight, dead in the rock.

Closes the rock. Closes the red stable.
Filled with whole horses.
Takes a knife, peels
Horses back. He pours light
Softly under the peel,
Watches the manes glow.
Then he closes the horses.
He closes the red stables.
Everything is surface.

EOA 12

Poet guy saying to reader guy: look, there are some fundamental layering issues, insides and outsides and embeddednesses, which we could enjoy discussing if we decided to get to know each other better by saying, between us, what it is to exist coldly, foldedly, under a light that exists only to separate the stars. This poem may be the best way to assure our never having that conversation, thanks to having made an effort to have it.

The angers subtending interventionist work are palpable in the *Epics of America*. After all this work is satire etched in disciplined acid, hoping to sneak past the wards with a bit of humor. "The Foreigner" (*Epics II*), and "Horses" (*Epics IV*), give passage to the anger.

Epics of America II: The Foreigner

A foreigner enters the café.
Lying on the wall,
Foreigners, in our eggs,
Mighty in thin toast. I cull
Foreigners from my salad dressing,
Dry them on paper napkins; I eat
Crunchy foreigners.
Foreigners come to our party,
Bubble to the surface. I drink,
Blithely, to the foreigner in my shoe.
I pull him out, plunge him in wine,
Fry him. Foreigner for dinner!
Pepper. Some salad dressing. We sit,
Still, *en famille*, and eat the little…
Easy we have walls, foreigner walls,

Lying in walls. A foreigner
Drops from the plaster, cuts
Vaults into the wall.
I pat his head. I warm
Left over salad dressing to feed him.
I brush him, then I lift him
Gently from the floor, open the window,
And blow. He dissolves in the atmosphere.

EOA 2

   Was the foreigner real, or just a figment of my imagination? He blows
away so easily, "bubbles up," "drops from the plaster." He is as shallow as
the great Republic in which he is consigned to "foreignness."

Epics of America IV: Horses

Horses block the way. Here, over here.
Nothing budges. Manes and tails wave.
He goes around them. Damnable horses.
Here horsey, come. He slaps the horse,
Passing its withers. Auction this baby.
Horses scatter. Here dapple, here roan.
Horses vanish. He sells a horse,
Buys horses to sell; bets on horses.
He wins, seven horses. He pens them,
Runs looking for halters. They break
Easily, reach the highway. He catches
All but one. It flees. He cries
Here horsey, he says to it, lie at my feet.
Horsey kneels before him. A game?
He pats horsey. Nothing to fear.
Angels take horsey covered with feathers.
He pats horsey! Withers! Horsey
Sinks to the ground. A big smile grows.
Horsey laughs at himself. I took that
Seriously? His flank hurts though.
He looks at it closely. It really hurts.
Then he lies down softly. He stretches
One leg at a time. He dozes.

Horsey, am I really horsey?
He puts his head down. Here
Horsey he says to himself.
Here horsey, here horsey horsey.
And then he dies.

EOA 4

What kind of a voice reports this to you? The voice alternates between dry narrative description and shock value—killing its object quietly. Is it a trustworthy voice, that of a friend? Or is it a voice playing with you? I have to think it is the latter. Up ahead, in "The Word for Love in Danish is Hard," you will listen to an ambiguous voice of the sort we are discussing. The speaker is in love but, more than that, loves you because you are listening to him say he is in love. The speaker of "Horses" not only wants to hurt a horse, but he wants to ward you off, by doing so.

Finally, look at the Will who has gone beyond into a place where he incorporates and then remakes the world, a version of the ultra-aestheticism Will has frequently made his default position.

Epics of America XXIX: Zen

He makes an incision.
"Here," he whispers to the orchard,
"enter through my finger."
The trees file in through him.
After them comes the hillside.
After the landscape has been emptied
He tapes his finger.
He closes the incision.

Next day he looks for the orchard,
Perching on the hill.
The orchard has gone.
In its place he sees his finger
Opening around a wound.
It has replaced the trees,
Replaced the landscape.

He makes an incision.

He parts the flesh around the thumb.
He reaches in and tugs.
One by one he pulls out pieces of the landscape
Nature has made.
He sets it up.
It is green and whole.

EOA 30

The aesthetic issues to which Will has consistently returned, both in imaginative and conceptual work, coagulate in this short poem. We can make the world ours, he seems to say, by opening to it, taking it in; then, after that organic transformative passage—is this the definition of imagination?—we can restore the world, "green and whole," rejuvenated. It is the Willian tweak, at this point, to insist that there is a biological to this passage, a true digestion.

CHAPTER FOUR

THAT POSTMODERN MENTION (2000–2017)

Yes, we did let the PM word out of the sound bag, and should say another word or two about it, before driving a couple more character-averse poems into the pen. Then we will soon have a swollen six-pack of *indirection* or *character-deflection* poems tucked away, in which language intervenes sharply between poet and hearer, and we will be better able to talk out where we are going in this thing we have already said we are making into a book. (This thing, you see, that had "book" written all over it, from puerperal issue to bibliographic maturity, despite the insistence, of many of the author's Job-literate buddies, that the *book* is dead, and that only old Joes like yours truly romance about Seine walks in which you passed Jean Paul Sartre shuffling deeply along inside his annotated version of Meyerson.) But having so much as burbled the postmodern thing, we should at least complete *this* degree of throat clearing. *Postmodern* in some sense we may all be now—and that's the reason for this little explanatory interlude—but ready to demystify the Gutenberg revolution we are not, not ready to live outside the magical draw of those leather-bound volumes of Rabelais and Montaigne which lined the living room shelves of some of our childhood homes. Likely though it is that the force of that Gutenberg revolution has already been sapped from within—as I stand here and declare my allegiance—six hundred years of relative success—in the market, in the memory, in the educational projects of our variously staged cultures—there nonetheless can be no doubt that the well-bound book has established value habits we can't readily shake, thrilling as it might seem to substitute emoticons for turns of phrase. We are still within that *old deutscher werkstatt* ambience. Many of the old gods have fled, the most recent to flutter its wings being the print book; though grounded she still be. As we speak, one sees no more *Olympische Fruehling* on the horizon, yet here we sit on the back porch, spine in hand and page-turning fingers in action.

What we are mulling to create, there on the porch, is poems that are still poem things, and novels Gustave Flaubert would have recognized as such, and that are lined up on the page, and bound at the spines to the great warm cunabula which have comforted talkie babies for six hundred years, against the cold of the babulous and the loose. We also admire what courage we have for the traditions of intelligent human achievement, and want memorials left in place, lest we forget what we have been and still need to do. We admire the courage to recognize in contemporary terms the vigor of Herakleitos' observations on the transience of the moment, and we try hard to realize that what we have just said about the present became past before it was formulated. This latter temporal portal insistently reminds us that whatever, in the postmodern condition, reminds us that the sign is forever caught up in a fleeting network of signs is a banner of verity which no amount of historical grumbling should authorize our taking down. What we want out of postmodernism is a fresh sense of the never-permanent quality of the artifact, the constantly self-reformulating relation we adopt to that artifact, and the never complete indicators we leave of the meaning of our creations. Needless to say, it remains of continuing importance to us, to remember all these points about literature as constant inter-critique of other texts, the message Harold Bloom— remember "An Emphasis for Easter"—embedded in *The Anxiety of Influence,* the thrillingly global message of Postmodernism, and above all the fatality with which we are talking and writing through others' mouths, and indeed, while enacting ourselves as varying shadings of our own character—from "see me here!" to "listen to my long tale!" to "out of my way, buster!"—while being at the same time others' characters.

The best answer to our stance toward postmodernism is probably bringing these poem things into the face of the empty world postmodernism promises us, refusing as it does all efforts to trust naming things to hold them in place. It is the present writer's hope that poeming his way through the pearly gates, maximizing thus the modernist impulse, will be the proof of the pudding of the noetic, and that, in consequence, the thrust of postmodernism, which includes accepting the other in the making of itself, will find itself affirmed and even highlighted on the face of the nervous energumen as he stands before the maker he is (at last).

CHAPTER FIVE

SOME PROSE POEMS, 1975–82

A voice making itself a thought instead of a person was another way the recusant Will—from middish life on—managed to dissatisfy those customers for whom the desire to relate to a human voice was the trigger for a character-read.

Lunch, Paint, Modern Ways (1980)

He asked for his lunch. They brought it on a paper plate. But it was painted onto the plate. There was one picture of broccoli, another of mashed potatoes, a third of a veal cutlet. At first he tried to cut them. He tried to pry them off the cardboard. But they were thoroughly embedded in it. Then he picked up the cardboard. He gnawed at the edges of it. Soon he got to the picture of the broccoli. He ate it with pleasure. Then he ate the meat and potatoes. By this time he was nearly full. Still he motioned to the waitress. Have you pie, he asked her? She returned to the kitchen, then brought apple pie. It was beautifully depicted, juicy and crusty. His mouth watered. But something was missing. He took out his ballpoint. He drew in a small piece of cheddar. Then he started in eating. The combination was outstanding. And when he was done he was really done. There was no fuss with silver. There was no fuss with china. There was no fuss with washing himself, or making a stop at the men's room.

TYOB 14

Who is talking to us here? Is it a friend of the "he" who is scoring this modernist meal? Is it a satirist of contemporary culture? Is it a deep-carving philosopher, out to raise ancient questions about the relations between things and our representations of them? Whatever, it is clearly not the voice of a person eager to *express* himself, to characterize himself for our behalf. We are once again far from the poetry in which the human talks to the human, exchanging a new world. We are far from the excitement of the maker of *Fragments* or of "An Emphasis for Easter." We are far from the gesture by which one person reaches to another in language with himself as the offering.

So what's happening here, in this talk-to-talk poetry? Once again, freshly, why does the author create a proxy who refuses to do any of the good natured missionary jobs customarily expected of poetry, in its role as "friend of mankind through the twists and turns of life"? Is our author a subversive who leads a quiet revolution with a wry grimace on his face? Who is pleased when children fall down and skin their knees? Would he be one of those?

The fact is that Will's entire opus in language is contrarian, not subversive. Your friendly author does not blow up the community's new rec center, in an effort to say no to the reigning inequality in property taxes, or to fight for homeless shelters. Will counter-grains as an act of thought, an act of roughing up the fur on the thick coat of intelligibility, so that we will feel the electrical pressure of obstinance on our thinking. Hasn't this been the trigger for the kinds of language Will has been throwing up against expectation? It's intellectual anger!

And is there a perimeter bounding the slashing moves of this language machete, and sparing them the charge that they cut too widely, in too many directions, and seem to harvest from a field so shapeless that we don't know how to process it? As we have seen above, in a salami of possible voicings, Will is interested in an inner negative boundary on character. Rather than full-throat it, that I-stuff inside, he is for choking it back queryingly from the start. Isn't that what philosophy is about? (In that motif Will continues the classical—Horatian, Catullan—discipline from within, his version of holding the field of reference to shape.

Epics of America XXXIX: "His pale color"

i

Bellying green prairie moans
Under his comfortless touch.
Knowledge climbs his leg like a stain.

He grows darker.

ii

Moon you rode him to death.

I saw him fall, dragged by rays.
Saw him rise,
Press the car,
Limp into Dubuque.

iii

I saw his body
Shirt up stiffly
From the black valley around McGregor.

He walked a few
Miles in an expensive derby

Then lay down.

iv

He darkens,
Returns to the lorry
Picks up power and whistles,
Crossing into Kansas.

He is losing color.
In Kansas his body
Assumes the color of his lorry.

He is lost from sight.

Hours later, before they have found him,
He fastens his body to the body of the lorry.

And walks for hours,
Simple and wounded.

EOA 40

Landscape, *mechane* in landscape, and sterterous uncompleted passages across the land, burrow into the skin tones of this darker/paler/color loser, this excrescence on the wounding land. There is no story about him, to which we could attach the interests of our emotions, unless it is the simplest story of labor, motion, and color, a gouache language paints out of itself. As in *Lunch, Paint, Modern Ways* we are faced with edicts of *how it is*, not with invitations to share a point of view toward them. No way to shake hands with *this* guy. Or with these?

Bus

In California a man is eating an old bus. He has given himself two years. Naturally he begins with the tires. The lonely hours will be with the body, though, nibbling on the tired, travelled sides of the Greyhound. The sun will go down in the evening. He will be bent over a piece of metal. As he chews it slowly the metal will remember the continent and will offer the continent to his body. All the fatigue of night, on this enormous landmass, will enter him. He will chew slowly. He, too, will be remembering.

TYOB 13

The pathos of the patient anti-hero, plastered as a piece of memory against the landscape. How my character downloads into this scenario deprived of emoluments, transformed into itself as the communion of the tired created world. How, thinks the author, does the God of Teilhard, with his mass in nature, power up out of this cranky mini-epic! And how long has Will struggled, as he did in his French text, *Miroirs d'éternité*, to let Paul le Diadème outward into a "mass of the minerals," in which the whole earth formulated its adulations!

***

It will escape no attention, that the immediately following prose poem, here, will continue to wrestle with the fertile topic of "nature's mass."

A Little Brandy (1972)

A little brandy in the snow shovels the walks

It eats into the ground
It lets last autumn's old marron blades
cheek into forgotten chlorophyll
it chips the edges of the sidewalks
it makes old men slip
antically and their wives' calves gossip
with each other
and dogs turn green pissing
and speak afrikaans to each other
and professors of philosophy leave the phone
off the hook for hours and dream
and girls take their hair off
in cheesetrays and leave it around the room
and old pieces of cloth turn red

A little brandy in the snow

BIS 85

***

    We tend to be pushed, in these prose or prose like poems, to the point
where the absurdity we discover becomes part of a plausible critique of
our shared world, as well as into a contemporary Western version of the
African praise-song.

***

Five Poems (1978)

Tom Washes the Minerals

    Tom washes the minerals first before putting them on the table. That
way they gleam among the leaves. Tom's wife sets the peas down gently in
the midst of quartz. His son surrounds the potatoes with bauxite.
Mealtimes are reminders, says Tom, of a beautiful marriage between the
organic and the mineral. He patiently longs to consume the mineral. He
wishes his knife could cut into marble, slicing it. He'd butter it carefully,
salt it, add a little paprika, swallow it. From then on he'd eat nothing
organic. He'd nibble on the sides of mountains. In him too the glistening
patina of minerals would grow hard and glossy. Yet when he looks around

the table he sees a row of grimaces, the same old pull toward the organic.
He sees doe-like confidence, and the rotting passion of leafy spinach.

Tom and the Rebellion of the Carrots

   Aloof, Tom planted the garden. Peas, spring up there, he ordered;
tiny green arcs cracked the soil. Potatoes and parsley responded likewise.
Only the carrots refused to answer, sulking in their seed shells. Tom
thereupon called a shaman to aid him. The carrot seeds were charmed.
Spells were laid on the ambient humus. Rain was commanded to fall on
the carrot patch. Several days later a filament of carrot knifed up through
the topsoil. Nature, it reported, is in the midst of revolution. Carrots, you
see, are but the vanguard of trouble. Tom listened closely, wondered at the
countering. Nature, he'd have thought, would be the last resistance. The
next year, however, he had a problem with spinach. And in subsequent
years he found the whole garden stubborn. He turned more and more
inward. He issued fewer orders. He stayed by himself, especially in the
springtime.

(Note the anthropology of refractory nature. The shaman anthropologist
who intervenes to mollify the topsoil. A Miltonic tug of war between
growth and elemental fury!)

Tom's Military Career

   A lone bugle cuts the air, sinks, and leaves the battleground silent.
Tom peers from his tent. The enemy is barely visible. He creeps out and
breakfasts, anxiously. Then he takes his gear, marches out onto the field of
battle. Now he sees the enemy advancing, dust, howitzers, an armored
division. He walks straight toward them, charges at them finally,
galloping, firing. He disables a tank. He turns a flank. Then he is wounded
in the finger. His whole hand comes off.

The German Fellow

   The German fellow comes when I least suspect him. He appears
hanging around. He walks down my chimney, settles on a footstool, talks
about the weather. I hear his rumors about the world on the skyline. I see

what he shows me—papers with headlines. I go to the cupboard. I pour out a whiskey, offer it to the fellow, and light up my meerschaum. We spend hours in conversation. Later he beckons to his spirit, rises, climbs up again through the dusty chimney. I watch him disappearing. I send regards to the capital. Then I go back to my existence. I tie down the shutters. I stoke up the fireplace. I bolt the door, and put a tree trunk across the driveway.

(This time a tree is sent to do the blocking. A world cut back to refractory anality, a world enchanted to growth by demons and "German fellows." Who can endure home invasion by such a combat of forces?)

In the Hollow Provided

In the hollow provided he beaches his canoe, fastens it to a willow, then walks into the village. He finds there a classmate from his old alma mater, goes out drinking, comes back late. He lies down quietly in the hollow provided. He sleeps an hour. Then he rises and wanders. He returns to his vessel. He unties it. He launches it at dawn in the hollow provided.

Paris Review Five poems, 114–116 #73, Spring/Summer (1978)

***

The prose poem, as part of the ongoing dialogue with being, which we settle for calling "philosophy," extends itself in "Bus" and "Space," and unexpectedly, we might say, launchpads out into the nubs of conceptual coherence which make geneses of thought.

***

The Begonia Rises Waxy (1980)

Waxy and thick the begonia rises. It urges us to paint it. So we go up to it with brushes. We paint it red, white, and blue. We admire it and praise it. Then we wish we had it natural. Why had it asked to be painted? We start to strip the paint off. We pull it away in patches. But this makes the plant look blotchy. Its fibers water. The leaves are in shreds. Once again the plant suggests we should paint it. But this time we resist it. We hold a paint can near it, then withdraw it teasingly. We say, paint made you shabby. But again the plant invites us. This time we grow angry. We cover it with turpentine. We light it in a bonfire. We throw it in the landfill. But the plant still assails us. It peers from the dustheap. It begs us for beauty. We take paint and smear it. We take plastic and wrap it. We take a gun and shoot it. Waxy and thick the begonia rises.

TYOB 21

Our love hate relation with the plant once again opens a window into the forces raging for formula-status, right there in the garden.

***

Space (1980)

Man is "the future of man." He is always ahead of himself. You walk down the street. You are planning a thousand things. Whether you name them or think them they pull you apart. At night you dream. You are "what you are not," and are "not what you are." Everything opens always. You go back into yourself each time, you feel certain your body will hold you. And each time it lets you go. There is nothing but room. There is nothing but somewhere to go.

BS 39

What is the dry mystery of these texts? They offer, and produce, a quiet unfolding of the sense of being here. Dry wonderment shadows each of these portraits of mere existence, the brevity of phrasing, and the stressed repetitiveness—summarizing, as in "every thing opens always"—all conspire to immerse the reader in a mindfulness that includes the very eyes with which he is reading.

CHAPTER SIX

WE JES' CHAWIN'

Will has a history of poems direct, free of the wry, passion-slanted, and he will put those on the table "in due time." (We have already tasted "Fragments" and "An Emphasis for Easter." Both these earliest poems and the poems of our two final sections—"serene" poems and poems that talk with Charon—make substantive concessions to the idea of character download in the poetic action.) Before he arrives at these concessions, though, I know he wants to tell you something even he sees, and thinks, strange, in what he is telling you about his poems. He knows he can express feeling right at you, that his love poems could bring a Guernsey cow to her knees, that his poems of head-on fear and anxiety could calcify your frontal lobes. He feels pretty confident that he *can* download his character into his poetry. He can indeed soup it up, that character. He will sooner or later be about helping you to see how in such direct poems as he writes he can try to download his whole bloody self, without margins, onto the platter before you. And yet he is opening himself to you, *in this first interventionist part of his book-thing*, as someone happy to be offering you pieces of language drawn from a disciplinary tradition, the poetic, which is presumed to be a guardian of personal distance, self, and right, of freedom to download yourself onto the page as you like or not. He knows that you are thinking these initial little chapters, in Part One, seem a bizarre introduction to *la joie de la poésie* or the getting-to-know-you stuff that makes for poetic friendship. He knows that you think he's thinking, *I pretend here to be Mr. Nice and yet I'm cutting small angular muscle-tearing incisions into the webwork of silence, painful portals into my point.* But you could just be wrong there.

The difficult and the meaningful twin in poetry, in ways that only exposure to the simplistic in expression can clarify. You have to win a poem back from something, emptiness maybe. You have to deserve a poem. You have to deserve a *rendez vous* with a working soul or earsmith. Let him or her hurt you with care. Or die of boredom? Is that exactly the alternative?

Epics of America XXXIII: Shaman Days

A brook bustles in and out.
Guppies swindle algae of the latest egg.
Night brings travelers like him,
Old sinners to dark streams.

People like him settle for an hour
Around a wrecked car,
Edges of moss.

Crawdads watch them,
Mail thickening like mud
Over old pink shears.

Minnows tell stories
Thoughtful travelers repeat.
For a minute there is no more than one in the world.
For an hour nothing is subtracted
From the sweet brown endless
Silence that holds him.

EOA 34

   Have we here the quiet stasis of a nature poem, plucked somewhere out of the bucolic tradition—Theocritus, Horace, Wordsworth? Does the narratorial promise good faith attitudes, and a representation of the world left to us by humane traditions?
   The narrator introduces us to a "him," "an old sinner to dark streams," to be sure, but perhaps to a "thoughtful traveler" as well. Generic this traveler is—twice we hear of people, or "travelers," like him—and at the same time unique, no more than one in the world, held by the "sweet brown endless silence." Has the narrator established a trusting relation with us, so that we can feel confident that the "him" being introduced to us is at least what he seems to be, and in all probability downloads the actual character of the writer? The "him" seems to be one among many, gathered as he is in the stillness around a wrecked car, and if he is simply a construction in the landscape he is at the same time the construction by the narrator of himself. He is the "simple and wounded" character of the poem above, from *Epics of America XXXIX*: both guys, though perhaps "simple and wounded" belong to the landscape their narrator has created out of

them.

In the following the *he* has become the *I*, which *he* is not greatly different from, and has stationed himself at a feeling point not far from one of those excursions into the raw feeling material of philosophy. (Philosophy? The bias in "issues" which turns them back onto themselves, so that, say, decisions about moral alternatives become concerns about decisions themselves.)

***

Patio Metaphysics (1980)

Now, in the patio, there is a fierce wind, no wind. There is a half-crazed swallow—no bird—leaping, battering the air, crying.

There is a lady—no lady—crossing in dressing gowns, attempting to free the swallow—no swallow—and there is a man of evil intentions chasing the legs of the lady.

All this imagined scene—no scene—plays against a dirty patio of the Hotel Real de Minas.

There is a scruffy chalked surface, patches of bindweed, almost claustrophobic airlessness.

Now, in this patio, I imagine something bitter and fanciful, like Browning's "Soliloquy in a Spanish Cloister."

Imagination makes the patio into something it is not—but might be— something it is, but cannot be.

Imagination makes the moment startle, but not last.

In the end the patio, chalk and bindweed, is more imaginative as simple actuality. Last night a cat sat before me here, crapped in the soil, and for minutes pawed at the earth, covered, sniffed, covered, until the action was hidden.

Now, this morning, I remember the cat, its little pile of secrets, and imagine that the lady, the lady of imagination, is in fact simply crossing to the hidden pile of disaster. She is prying it back with her fingers. But from the pile bursts a swallow! From the swallow bursts a man!

There I go, though, building away from the instant!

American Poetry Review #48 (1980, Nov–Dec).

***

Metaphysics? Well, eruhhh....There is for sure an instruction. In *to on*. Did imagination purvey, above, the soil in which real carrots grow? Or did imagination simply loosen the soil, that the inner voice might warble without too much grunching and grunting? Philosophy as subject matter of poetry is out of the zone of interventionist work? But still with the snap of a wild wolf in it? Philosophy is a source of gongoristic foreplay for the present author, willing at all times to convert serious thought into play, as though to imply—a version of the superscript of this entire book—that one can indeed slip through the pearly gates with a Henny Youngman one-liner. The sass of the affected persona, who works this territory, is as true to life as Will in blackface, and plays real hard with the reader's interests in believing a person is talking to him.

Poetry and Philosophy (2008–9)*

i

Don't matter where I start
It's philosophy.
That is, it's always about being here,
Where…

He hands off the gown
He knows the beat of basic women.
Take off what's inside of you
Madam it'll still be the beating heart.

In the forest of anonymity
He tiptoes out onto the verandah

*An earlier version of this poem appears on pp. 215–23. Differences between the two version are marked in bold.

And peruses the deep passages of the sea.
They sing to him like twists and turns in Vivaldi.

It's as though there were some conductor…
Durned sea playing to the bleachers…
Now he takes an old-fashioned settee
And winds a watch…

Elegance in the face of a barbarian has its charms.
But back to you madam, and your beating heart;
For that's what makes the gown rise and fall
That you might step…

ii

It's an Edwaard Muybridge
Kind of effect.
That's why I say it's philosophy.
You see it's always about being there

Even when you are there with it.
I don't see escaping.
I can walk a long way
Without sidestepping my flesh.

What I do see is taking terribly seriously
Pieces of fallen equipment.
A whiplash fell off a tree.
Some dogwood broke apart in a vase.

When he walks down the road his body falls apart!
Now madam, you know that's not exactly true,
You know the wind can create an illusion
Of *désagrégation*, as the French say, at any time,

Most of all when your tie's straight and your shoes shined.
That's more of the philosophy, you see.
You double back on yourself
Counting the times you've been contradicted,

Contraindicated, contravened, and just plain checked.

You know you've got the stuff to make a real good soldier
And even a good philosopher.
Yet when it comes right down to it, to IT,

There's always been a doubt.
I ain't the doubtin' type, Mam, rest assured of that,
But I do some philosophy, specially Bishop Berkeley,
And I do like the way a breast parts from the side of a gown.

Anyhoo…you might say I've jes' started now,
Been introducin' muhself, shore is hot in this bar,
Been gittin' ready to ask you round to visit the Department
Where me and muh colleagues piss the time of day.

No, seriously, after checking out the inside of that gown
The thing I want most in the world is to engage you
In a little witty conversation about the endgame
You and me's stuck with. Yah know, PHILOSOPHY.

iii

Edmund Gettier, may his name rest in peace,
Forged the VERIFICATION THEORY for thinking to some purpose.
Maintaining a true belief, and being able to justify it,
He said, was productive thought.

What if you maintain the false, and yet it leads you to the true?
He covered that too, imputing to the false, *like there's gotta be a heaven*,
The discovery factor. **Finding** that your belief was wrong's
Like finding that inside this room, just next to the bar,

There was a lemon-colored Philipino woman jes' beggin' for it,
Then discoverin' it was an illusion. That mistake could bear fruit.
You could jerk off over it! Seriously, though,
It's no small matter to know small matter, particles and animalcules

And whatever else Van Leeuvenhoek decided to call the minutiae
That hit his lens. Main thing's gittin' there first
With the names, then with the concepts to fit. Concept's the
Operative thought movement, here, **meanin'** take it in yer hands

Bud, it's a *concipere, concapio, con Capulet* if you prefer, and thus,
Accordin' to literary history, a bit of a bit of a wolf…
"Aye, you have been a mousehunt in your time,"
Mr. Gettier, hanging up the false in front of the true,

That your real character as fallen, as half a leg,
Son of a gun, howling wolf academic, might be hidden.
Hidin' behind a proposition ain't logic at its best,
When the clean truth is as open as air.

iv

I guess we all have our secrets. "Private vices, public virtues,"
And maybe that's the way to go, blimey, in the dark weeds of
Compromise. I'd rather it weren't so.
I'd rather we could go, each of us, openly to our Maker.

Our Maker would embrace us and hold us.
Stead of that, of course, guy's all the time sulking and skulking,
Envying this man's whatchacallit, and that woman's whatchacallit,
And missing out on the fun.

Measure each breath to its line, and there, maybe,
The breath of individual life will ease you, will drop you like a quarter
Into some slot where you become more. Worth grows.
Holding your place and showing your teeth is a lot of fun

And furthermore, in the end, makes an impression.
That's about all I want, **man's makin' an impression,**
Which is why I brought that up about getting out of this bar,
About movin' over to that there motel next door where

Although a Philipino chick's already pullin it down there's at least
Room for a little philosophy. See I wasn't kiddin' about that philosophy.
Now why the hell else, tell me, would I be carryin' Meyerson's *Identity*
And Reality in the back seat? You do? You **really** wanna see it?

v

It would have to be Sunday Morning, wouldn't it, when we decided
No more politics, it don't really matter, my daughter was right

That the earth and our simple humanity on it are what count.
At the same time I was reading this *The Story of B* which my daughter,

The same one, loaned me. It was getting under my skin,
Crudely written though it was, it displayed the same rough energy
I got from *The Celestine Prophecy*, and thirty years ago from
A Yaqui Way of Knowledge. It would have to be Sunday Morning

When the sun was cutting out small strips of light from the hostas
By my computer. For Stevens the "complacencies of the peignoir" have to
have
Melodies triple beautied, to outshine a god. My Sunday Morning,

Philosophy having to have it, was some joint between the Enlightenment
And the aura of sacrifice. I knew I had to produce a killing
In order to live, yet that Diderot was there too, a kind of American
Hero, true to what works and Dewey.

vi

When the dog came bounding in I cringed because I knew
Matter brings with it the whole *stofflich* presence of things
Whereas what I want is freedom from the polis and a text,
Scribbled sacred words. The dog though was to lead me

Downward downward to the water, where a trim
Aquamarine sylph slipt out from the bushes.
I stroked her wormy calcitrance and then followed her
Into someplace subaquatic like Grendel's

Mom's cave. To my surprise it was philosophy again there,
A calculus of public virtues private vices, and I gave
From the heart to the antinomy. I've been where
Something I wrote got better as I sinned, or worse as I

Straightened up and flew right up into the sun.
Beauty and goodness ride separate tricycles but on occasion
When the sky is calm and the velocity perfectly tuned,
They can converge in tandem. Silver rims on fire with each other.

Beauty and goodness can meet in the same kind face,

In the worshipful intensity of a child predator
Hardened to the breaking point of love.
There is a wild beauty, in wild things, that will crash

All the barriers of sound. And fly to the moon.
Ah the moon and my love's hands these summer nights,
Walking slowly past the power plant and the field house
And not unaware of the distant out-folding cornfields

That at ten-thirty p.m. seem like coasts of black possibility.
It's not like when I was young young, and would march through the night,
And would find out there, in the steepest over-flowered valleys,
Secrets of the despair in things, or when in Ohio, coming back with my
parents from the coast,

I stood against a cowface across a fence. I'd emerged to piss,
Gone off into the darkness of a meadow, then looked up and seen
This mottled Hereford, the simplest possible presence of the *stofflich*,
Like that dog back there.

vii

Every now and then the curtain of pollutants falls back
And we see the stars. Those times swarm over us, dealing fell
Blows. We know our mortality is for a second, then we fade,
Yet like Kant we know, too, that meeting this dire perplexity

Directly, consciously, raises up our spirit to praise.
We praise our infinitude, like children singing on the way to school.
Dread, awe raises our song! Why not let the little body
Plaster itself silently against the rain? Why not let it fall

Gently without protest? It's because we are callers!
Nothing about us is still. The dry fact wrings us even drier
Until we shrivel in slivers. Yet the long languid energies
Of the American Midwest continue to uplift us.

viii

Philosophy, darling, is what it is all about, even in the bed,
Where the *philosophie du boudoir*, of the place where one "sulks,"

Moods up, is rampant. Love and lust unleash Philosophy One,
Can I this, can I that? and contribute to our bliss.

I know that the random swathes of longing have carried me
To places that hurt us all. I have no doubt that the equipment
Gods gave me to make wide spaces in the gene pool
Has at times led me astray into pure pain—to me and others.

Now that I am older I want to heal and let heal but with the intensity
Darn it of a heel, for only a heel can do the occasional harm
That explodes beauty from its chest. I see power rising from the chest
The way an Olympic athlete brings a lifetime of rigorous practice

To a minute and a half of explosive efficiency in the hundred meters.
It's the way a poem line that works replaces decades of drossy gleck.
Those who were truly great with the line, like Oppen and Eliot,
Filed and filed. The clean bone they came down to whistled in the wind.

ix

Oh soldiers remember on your way to battle that the stars
Will for a moment align, maybe in your passage through the moonlight,
And in their crosshairs will be framed, for a moment, the fine thin
Purpose that drove the Neolithic hunger. We are never far from our
sources.

We are still the same tragic lovers of beauty that fell in the Long March
To the Sea that brought Xenophon and his men home. Only now it's
Probably the kitchen sink where we will be standing.
The water will be running down a drain that leads to the city sewage plant
And above the drain we will be administering the last rites
To an organically grown carrot. Never mind. Time and circumstances
change.

No two moments are alike in their passion. Keep cutting, boy.
When you rinse, rinse like a sacred butcher, washing the sweat
Of the labor of the world from your arms, and standing for a minute pure,
Stab wounds all over you.

x

Sunday morning, in any case all agree, is a time to take stock.
Laden with achieved learning, all brain cells activated,
We stumble downstairs to the all too familiar.
And at once it is the unfamiliar. It is the life we left.

We are in the far place of reflection and abstraction.
Neither a child nor a dog is the animal of yesterday.
The house of the neighbors is like a long ship
Dug from the peat at Sutton Hoo, and philosophy,

Attired like a Mediaeval schoolmaster, is standing where
Mr. and Mrs. Dockeson used to cut their lawn.
I have said that philosophy it must be, in the long run,
That makes the spheres interlock. It's Dantesque this world.

I cannot imagine it not spouting from my ears in canticles
Like the Canticle of the Sun. You go out into the lawn.
There is a patch of brown grass. It fell victim to Roundup
And you nurse it daily. You inspect some bruised tendrils.

xi

Would not Saint Francis have taken the whole passing scene,
Rioting wood squirrels, squirmy mushrooms,
And replaced them with the love that moves the heavens and the other
stars?
He might have. But he was flesh. He might have gone

Down on his knees among the spores and praised gray,
Which is after all the color first in potential.
From gray you can make white or black or shades.
From gray you can make a suit that befits a businessman

Or an Ampleforth schoolboy. Gray is beyond all
Question the brightest and strangest color in time.
It is the color of the feather that the King wears in the summer crown
Made of fillets. The feather came from a mockingbird.

The feather is nothing to mock, but came from just over the tail

Of the prettiest mockingbird as she knelt to a worm.
Out in the bay there was one less worm to fish with which meant
Salmon the size of your arm escaped, and so it went, the world

One filament of philosophically interconnected possibilities, the kind of
Fabric of causal nexi, Aquinas said, which in itself proves God's
Manifest presence. I don't know about that presence.
Fastened together events, like causes and effects, might be the work of a
devil

Anxious only to seem. *Post hoc ergo propter hoc*, after all,
Can be exploded by any Ampleforth schoolboy, and once that's
Been accomplished the network proof of God gets shaky.
When I said there's always philosophy, then, I meant that

Sometimes, when it appears that the world is making sense,
We might well suspect a trick.

*Philosophy, the queen of the sciences, can take many turns into its
name. It can simply become its name, and all the things its name suggests,
rather than the issues—epistemology, logic, ethics—which might crown
the description of it. Philosophy might become the designation of a kind of
prosody, or simply of a mindset. In the following "chaos of presence" we
let philosophy down into the named empirical world, and let it wallow
there. We do life, in its name, while the runt, quiescence, sits out a
pregnant morning in May.*

                              ***

For Mike Quill (1968)

This, Quill, is Lynchburg.
   Mt. Jackson follows.
   My father's house.
      'Fore he
   turd-crusted
         and fat with
   liver puddings made
Charlottesville home.
         Man I've come from!
Yet not as though,

Man, up
    From the mills
But up from the silence.
Shenandoah silence
        So that what I know
Half-know, even think,
Is at last furrowed
From loam the earlier conscious.

This, Quill, is Mt. Jackson,
Here Parnell was born.
    Here Yeats,
        Who themselves
                With ash-staffs strode
    Kehossic in spring
    Talking of the revolution.
        Yeats and my father.

You are thinking of Ireland,
    The ships' lanes,
        Green Killarney.
                        Seems to you
    This fire is turf,
    The whiskey blessed,
                Cuchulain the topic.
    Remembering north
    All your buddies
Who cart the sea's genius.

Come have another.
I discern in your eyes.
        Men stand in
    Line there,
Down the endless retina.
        The endless vehicles
    A city clumsy with feet.
There are Yeats and father.
    They are coming toward you
The mayor has hands on
        His eyes.

The docks are aortas,
    The world cut open
        Back flat on the sea.
The seas are the world's piss,
                Shores its rank arms.
There is a whiff of despair.

Now you can remember the apples.
    Your mother baked them too.
Yeats came down on Sundays.
        Dad and Parnell joined.
You touched my birth.

Poetry Vol. 111 #4 (1968), 229–231

***

Still intervening against yourself? Or do you self-hear now, even in the midst of this interventionist period, and find the notions of pure character-download and blocked-artificial fake polarities? Look at the following poemlets: do they let you into the conversation that is their maker?

Six Poems (1965)

1
Subaquatic

I suspect we go down into
Ourselves, mate, as deep as we can swim.
That is the depth.
I descry the perennial figures there.

They emerge to the seeing blobbed.
Fishlip lust, loose at the gills,
Charges of hightail salmon
Pricked. Learned
Philosopher seals
Glaucous of eye.
The Boys.

Through what I am.
Indigenous hosts.
I raise my tube through the weeds—
You see it pass.
Its bubbles convince the wary
That I have survived myself.

2
In Time of Tapping

I left microphones in my own wall,
There was no embassy.
The delegates
From the foreign countries
Had taken the latest planes.
I was completely alone.

In the medulla
And under the fingerskins
In the impressions of the toes,
The scalp, its follicles.
And listened there,
And heard
Rumbling the slight
Imaginable torrent of the blood.

There were descriptions of me
In other minds
But nowhere
Anything like this.

I went to the window,
Organs and all,
And slashed
The recumbent world
With glances.

3
After Keats

Silent upon a peak in Iowa City
(the tallest at that)
the wind on every side.
My family is in the house
Over coffee, over conviction.
I have emerged for air.

In the Valleys of the Mohican
Chiefs wave plumes of delirium
Tread the autumn ground to fire.
Ancient Iowa stamped too.
Someone discovered buffalo
Hooves in his basement wall.
Or is that, for final proving,
Only half-comic truth?

Silent upon a peak.
Of the mind.
Of the mind's eye turned
To the mind's interior of darkness.

There are birds passing now.
A type of proof of things.
I offer two eyes to their flight.

4
In Memoriam

I went out into the immensity
(in burying mood) and looked around.
The middle of inspiration, dull,
In touch by sight with one hill,
An acreage of huts and distant sea.
So this is the Greece I am,
Not swollen but hardly mute,
Though far from the nearest shepherd.

It was the excellent midnoon

Most feared. The priests were asleep
In various revelations.
And advancing from town to town
I could see the pretense of the sky
That was for these men prodigious.
I saw an evocative lamb of god.

Toward evening the shingles of other roofs.
I came to the haggard square where
Plane trees chattered the evening in.
A dozen old man birds were cackling.
The funeral was underway
In the softdomed church's hall.

I had known the bereaved before,
In the center of various losses.
And lost myself in the group.
At the casket's corners angels
Of asphalt sealed the defeating lid.

We took the road through town
At the blackening hour.
Chickens and dogs surveyed.
At the graveyard edge we turned
Through thickets of yew to the pit
And stood there holding our breaths
For the priest to take.

Then watched the descent and shovels.
Then strewed our particular salt

On that ground we were first ourselves.

5
Né en Illinois

Among others it is especially
To be sought, whatever *it* is.
There chance yields at least to concern.
For others are eminents of concern
In their yellow jackets, ties

Knotted or flowing, shoes of suède,
Or manners of love wholly
Expectable yet never met
In Urbana, Illinois.

Among others other childhoods.
They are not held to fault, nor you.
Simply there were other gardens,
Others who coddled or scolded,
Other sounds to tipple to language.
I do obeisance, holding
Back only a snickersworth,
and that most nearly hidden.

The United Nations.
The guy next door.
The long fleet rows of cars
With unknown faces.
The slate Atlantic, Europe-bound,
Among others.

Or the I who is other.

6
For a Childhood

Charles and Ross, I thought of you,
Crossing the park this afternoon.
It was one of those afternoons.
And the park was bare except of things.

We had begun, almost begun, together,
In the long afternoons, Illinois,
Constructing childhoods. The days
Then as now end with this kind of sun.

I will tell you a miracle as a result.
We have not parted. Something essential.
The grackles crow still as shifting
Their forms like evil hags in the elms.

Urbana was manifest. Today too.
There is an equality in the thing
Hidden below the intensity of the thing.
This we cannot unbalance.

Or the impossible virtue of aging.
I see us now *in extremis*
By the tennis court. Sweat
Flowing like unction over our wrists.

And imagine you tonight over books.
Reading or leaning against yourselves.
Containing the opened world
With the certitude of dying men.

Poetry Vol. 107, #2 (November 1965), 85–90.

Is there a strong sense in which we can still want to call this work interventionist? The author's self, which forthed itself as other within the reader, as the reader's inner voice, has here become an indirect and mysterious posting, or mini-snap of itself. The theme generated from within it is the furtive.

***

Three from China (1966)

The Scholar

He controlled the Han.
Each historical quest
Each deft angelic raid.
What he was on grew.
It began to look
Like "covers" and "jackets."
But the Han were deft
Too, making bronze.
And bothered him at the last
With a propensity so
Great he could not
Finish, to torture and invade.

Ssu Ma died, for instance,
Because he told the truth.
The Great Emperor Wu
Made pyres of the wise.
The lions, jade,
Telling, cool, wandered
Like still Lears
Through the imperial halls
And into his long mind
Where it was already evening
Grown still more silent
Than a vision of the Yellow River.

Lo-Fu

The prince Lo-Fu
    Would have
  "anti-poems"
        what Confucius
et. al. looked
down on as "harsh,"
        "made in Japan"

And to that end
        Ordered
    Scribes out to
  The imperial bounds.
Collectors of what jarred.

In assembly they
  Broke tabu like bread
      Rhymed
When they liked, said
    Prosody stank, speech
      Gave
  Them their clue;
    Ran, drank,
Bashed the old
      Emblem of "gentle-
      Man" in like tin

The battered rules!
   The mountains wept!
Dykes
    Leaned from unusual force
      Far
Down the frontier.
    Barbarian
    Cavalries stirred
       It was breath-
Taking.

  In the crags birds
     Flew
  Up like omens.
       The landscape
Wu
  Chen's in cloud
 Maple, wisp
    Dried
  Cracked
      Wounded
      Like a bad line.

Inter-cult Talk

     i

I want only to
  Provide
Edges
    For the language you
    Let
    Loose
      To give
 It "inwards"
    By framing

All this I wanted
This is a classical desire.

You in your stead
      Propose
      "letting it fall"
         the Tao
      through language
         phrases like hair
lambent
   then muscular
      regions

There is no end to these...
      Speaking at
   Each other over
      Mountains of neurons
  One imagines the Chinese figure
The vast succession, "changes"
      Those Lao-tzu
Gathered as
   "elements"
                  They are not
   Without
            "consistency"

The center seems
                  Opening
   Faultless, at no
         Place edge.
   Bloodful.

            ii

A new meaning
      That the thing is.
         Tao which
      Both you
And it are.

The center is "other."
As, really,
      is
      "horse";

one of the *chih*
"fingers," or "pointers"
    of Kung-sun Lung;
What guarantees.
  Silence
Below the tongue's roar

As is all
  Being
  inplace yet
sides breaking from sides
    always to
  itself at angle

    iii

I said, by "framing."
  You know our
      habits
    of speech.
  I suspect,
      Simply,
  Your affluent Tao,
    Your trust toward
      The
    "Quality of the event"
    above all
—listen!—
  your trust
in the humble.
Small things are not
      Great,
  The Buddhists'
I draw water, I carry fuel.
What a miracle, this!

A song crafted in space, a paean to ideation. Is there character here to download?

Poetry Vol. 109, #2 (November 1966), 77–82.

***

Three poems (1972)

Dawn

Is dawn within?
The flying figure is tackled
Reduced to size
Led to a waiting car.
She had shattered glass

From behind, her shoulders grow small.
Her drastic hair
Nags at the lawn.
Her delicate hands are laced with cuts.

She sits beside them
Nothing left in her face.
They take her hands
Place her.

Then she rides away,
The car gains speed on the nubbly moor.
It breaks away.

We must sweep the glass.
We must learn to make
What order there is.

Catechism

Has the car a house?
The car has a house.
Has the mind a house?
The mind has a house.

Draconian laws are passed.
The brain slips into a silver case.
The mind stacks its trying thoughts

In sheets of metal.

Has the car a house?
The mind has a house of silver.
The mind has a house where songs
Carved out of metal lie.

Draconian laws.
The mind carves the laws on silver.

Has the mind a house?
The mind has a house of silver
And stacks it high.
The silver sings
Reaches the silent roof of the world.

Hands

What darkens the hand?
Another, touching it.
What sleeps in the hand?

The sleep in the hand
Fights off the deadlier sleep.
It runs half-awake down the tree.
What darkens the hand?

Music darkens the hand.
For music is only still
Painting. It starves the veins.
What sleeps in the vein?

Blood that another touches
Fights the deadlier sleep.
Another, sleeping beside it,
Music, music that darkens the hand.

Chicago Review (Winter, 1973), 134–5

***

To claim that character fails to pass into the poet's text is like saying that the poetic self is easily locked away, and concealed, that intervention can easily, with a light touch, diffract messages that pass its way. The poems we air in these last pages, from the 1960s and 70s, fall in the zone we have labeled interventionist, yet are also voices of persons in your ear. The long poem "Myosotis", years in gestation, as we said, grows from a delight in fracturing and redirecting language, which leaves only the shifting and feinting of a would-be character behind it.

Six Poems (1982)

Two for You, Eyes of Blue

i

I start up into my own balloon of neighborless flapdoodle.
The wind boils with me, chucks me up like a baseboard up and out,
over the steamy Atlantic,
Mills me 'til I am chaff falling on a luxury liner. I wake,
Millet and dust, on the captain's boiled red table, stumble there,
Pack my way up onto the deck like a bleary white duckling.
Chomping and chewing I stagger like a salt,
Bubble in and out among the laborious lounges, the cocktail
Figmentations, the musical blue stumpstools.
Long about midnight I run into this flute player, dickey-
Bird, fall in love as though I were a rainstorm over Haiti,
Shuffle and shumple into the side of her head,
Black and blue meself on the Pamela Whitehorere of her vag.
Years later
We're chomping on life bread, teasing each other's donut, rolling and
ballooning.
Lying like a dog I start up into the old discrepancy, find
Though that it is long past one,
That the gongorisms are over
That the music she leaves me with is the only music I love with.

ii

I feel I might burst with the uncontained longing to stick

You in my pocket, to mush with you, to take you out in some
Fiery Western living room, natter with you, to spend the night
Fucking and punning.
I feel that only the old Schlitz brewery horses would have a
Chance to separate us now, to tear us from our axles,
And that even torn from our axles, cut from one another as
Lassie was cut from her home in Northern Scotland,
Severed, broken, rendered,
We would find our way back into each other's arms, mewling,
Helpless as babies. From one baby to another I feel
I should tell you that I love you more than ever I loved my mother,
More than the aster loves the living button of sun, more
Than the signpost the tiny milk of semantics, the cheese
The whey, the whey the speckled udder, the udder the creamy
Fallopian or the fallopian the milk-heavy cow eye where the
Teenager's passion floats like a gumdrop.

Lully's Foot

Lully beat time up his leg all the way to
The red tassel on his nuts.
He beat himself blue, green, finally gan-greenous, then
Tucked himself away in the invidious hatred of
The history books.
Time, beat away, opened his face like a vast beaker of
Malted milk, leaving only the atrophied solids.
Watteau, Fragonard, Clèves died the same way, the same
Time, fawned on by courtiers. Lully alone
Beat the measures up into his ear, then took it off, fired it.
Fact is, Lully beat time into his foot, stamped,
Lopsided himself into a bushel basket of potatoes, stamped his baton
Through his foot, yanked it off, threw it at the audience,
Waited 'til there was absolute silence.
Then flew into the darling Mecklenburg rage.
But it was far too late—heaven was full—and to this date
He is rotted, stashed like a glance inside the cover of
My jackboot.

Lully and the Wrecked Ornaments

Lully packs a wallop.
Straight in straight in through the living room window
And slaughters a dog.
Correction, all he really does is to batter his hand
Against the sink, run to his wife for a band aid,
And douse a few cries in the midmorning grocery store.
Lully, you see, is a braggadocio baby.
In the seventeenth century he composed serial sonatas,
Windjammer fugues, long thin arias for clavichord and
Jew's harp. Today he simply dreams of all that.
Smiling, he tells you that he is from Château du
Reaucomfort, that his ancestors fought at Roncesvalles,
That he himself composed madrigals.
Nothing about him supports this grandiloquent image. He is
Small, semitic. His teeth protrude like weevils. He wears
His clothes like a garbage can.
Lully packs a wallop.
That wallop, though, is but the fist of a doorman, futilely
Defending his condominium.
His fingers, tips, fly like egg custard over the Franck
Sonata.

L'histoire d'un soldat

Looney straight up straight up thicken the air
I cried
And to my astonishment the bird clomb.
I fired and slew
And shook to see it fall
Silent as a dishmop,
Wing over wing into the center of the forest.
That looney was part of the shirt of a child
And billowed onto an infant's voice.
I scratched at the carcass
Knowing the infant was in it,
And in time saw the infant too rise cackling.
Rise up too into the imageful sky,
Saw the whole forest vanish.

I left the forest, left the looney,
Then myself, in pieces, spread on a tree trunk;
What remained of the forest was emptied of a rooting
But the forest sky retained a small green charge,
A half child in orbit
A sweating cackler tucked into bold green treetops.
I staggered from that forest—
What was no longer standing
And pulled my shirt tight,
And clung to the sidewalk.
Looney I cried to myself, looney and scalliwag,
Then fled jerkily across the landscape,
Mechanically triumphant.

But the child I had fled
Fled backward inside me
And flopped up onto a building and cackled,
And before I knew it the city had become a forest.
The skyscrapers were covered with loonies.
I at once began firing,
Aiming at random,
But the loonies grew uncontrollable,
Crawled like beetles til every surface was blackened.
The child I had fled
Flapped in a turbine of threats.
I was freed of nothing.

For years I wandered through that city of images,
Battering the air with shots.
There was no place to hide
In the death that became me,
Except the original forest,
And with pain I created it.
Once more I stood beneath the jagged single looney,
Watched it climb upward,
And with astonishment killed it.

And once more I bent
Across the shirt of my childhood
But this time it opened to show a pink ceramic childface,
A newish reproduction,

And I fell on it jaggedly.
I coiled with that infant
Wreathed in the mudline
Until it basted me with weakness,
Sucked in my features.
I disassembled into a fern
And dripped like soggy guttae
Into the raked lanes of a mudbank.

Flower power at last, you said it

In the American countryside there is a low moan of anti-business.
Cows wake giving. Rabbits abandon their offices, lie on their backs in
the sun. Birds fool around.
Tommy abandons his office in the city, hurries back on the 2:17, takes
off his shoes.
He runs his toes into a clay-pit, chanting *anti-business, anti-business.*
Inevitably, though, he is overheard by a daisy.
The daisy, as it just so happens, is upwardly mobile, dreams of an
office in the city, of trading with Tommy.
Accordingly they trade.
The next day the daisy sits at Tommy's desk, handles orders for the
company, goes to lunch with his secretary.
Tommy meanwhile lies sprawling in the hayfield.
In mid-afternoon he falls asleep, dreams he is back at work; he wakens
to find the field full of former executives.
They are lying thick on the ground, like slugs.
The flowers, however, have almost completely vanished.
The 7:15 express was crowded with geraniums tucked into business
suits, carrying petal shaped cases.
The 8:04 disgorged a small army of heart-shaped marigolds.
Businesses everywhere are being directed by flowers.
The low hum of anti-business swells from a thousand tweeds, rises into
the country air and is swallowed, far out over Weehawken, by the
nervous cackle of executive-level mudhens.
A secretary hen crosses her drumsticks,
And takes corporate dictation from a potted zinnia in a bright yellow
four-in-hand.

Winter nocturne

Memory failed the rose.
Twitching red-shaped filaments,
Climbing upward from a stem,
Writhed, tried to represent.
The rose was nothing it was not.

Always these chunks:
Memory in slices from the head.
Roses—did I say the head?
The petal did bleed
When it was torn from my worm-eaten face.
And an aster,

Crown-heavy, sank.
Memory gave it a color
Stimulant as acid,
Yet the aster sank.

Sinking, the aster's face
Opened for a second like a rose,
Outwarded a freakish stamen.
A blossom crawled over it,
Then degenerated,

Eyed causally
By a simple tendentious tear.
Roses were ripped from the ground.
Was there nought to remember?
No pail of soil?

Roses—the blue stimulant.
Fans—in paper thin palms—
Wrecking air over the thick rose.
And an aphid—purple friend
Dining too, in blight,

And an aster,
Crown-heavy, sinking.
Memory gave it a color,

Stimulant as acid,
Yet the aster sank.

American Poetry Review XI (1982), #4, 28–29

CHAPTER SEVEN

DRANSTER, DRANSTER, WHO'S GOT
THE DRANSTER?

Our overarching theme is the download of character in the work of poetry. Clearly, folks—and we both know that—the poem has its existence as a download, a sprawl of expressive signa, cast from the linguistic genetic. Poems are character downloads. By saying that some poems—*Guatemala, The Epics of America, The Being Here Site of the Poetic, The Long Poem in the Age of Twitter*—make *relatively* forceful moves against character transfer, deflect the self *relatively*, we mean just that, *relatively*. The proof of that pudding may be clearer by the time we complete this book, when we have seen that in his "serene" period, as in his two long poems of the second decade of the twenty-first century, Will has returned to the default position of poetry as conversation, and wants to talk with you, as he had wanted to "talk to you" in Hawaii, as he lay outstretched over Waikiki Bay.

***

One would hardly call the Dranster poems "serene," and yet though they scrape against you they should at the same time invite the pure "language-friendly ear" in you, and thus stand somewhere between "serene" and hustle, at a street corner we have been agreeing to call *interventional*, but tending to interpret, as we push ahead, as promisingly amiable.

Some Dranster Poems (2007)*

He refused, or strove? I think he strove.
She was certainly not the first one I saw
To come bursting off the tennis court
With a steel. And she brandished.

* Compare *Some Dranster Poems* with part xxii of *Myosotis*, p. 159

Far as we could get in the bourgeois hymnal
We found little to convert us.
We found a tripod covered with the dust of time.
We saw notes by a Rabbi
Scribbled in a Tuareg encampment.

Do you see how we return, here, to a partially diffracted narrator, one even more elusively part of our time than Tupus the language inventor, or the fierce impersonal introducer of *Guatemala*, yet at the same time wooing your eye with a glance of friendship.

**

The Sentence (1995–2000)*

i

When darkness fell we were appropriately bewildered
And scquitched up our aprons and ran to our mothers.
The soft flame of taxonomy curdled around our hairpins.
That was the day of the transposition,

Truant lights. A soft broth fell on the Israelites.
We ate a tea made of strangers and walked.
Sometimes each sentence ended. It just ended.
There was a time when every sentence ended

And every paragraph started up and then turned around.
There was a time when the very thought of time
Wounded germane fellows. That sentence ended.
That sentence went backward and was left crawling.

ii

We had to pick it up, three strong men.
It was a sentence longer and darker than.
It seemed to. It sounded as though.
Then when the sentence ended it was as though

* Compare *The Sentence* with part v of *Nine Poems of Striving*, p. 110, and part xxii of *Myosotis*, p. 159

Falling. I strained at it, believe me.
I turned it in my strong arms and held it.
I made a woven cradle where the sentence
Could lie at night, but still it went on weeping.

The sentence went on slowly…o was it a side
Of the old mutton? We broke down the sentence.
We rode up and down on the sentence.
We made a thing. But that was a thing, not a sentence.

The sentence, a thing in itself, flashes in and out of meaning.
As language about language, the present quatrains test the willingness of
the language maker to agree that he is both subject and object of his
reflections.

***

His garter got caught in an oak
And strive he must and strove.
Oh there's an edge on his tooth

And it is part egg. He caught it.
You see he caught an egg and drifted.
He stuck it in the edge of the fridge like an egg.
After breakfast he looked at it again

And strove. He grew weary striving.
Hence the mountain he climbed and the shoe.
The shoe came after him, in a bit of a panic.
It strove. He rode it to pieces, believe you me.

***

There is an order in things he strove to say.
There is an order in the motor, parts of flowers
Say to others we're parts of a whole,
And very good dinners taste one another.

Have you a shoe you can offer me for my date?
We're going out tonight he said striving,
We're going to go out shoe dancing.

There's a toll. What costs nothing?

A nisus pounds its way across this ground, intemperately believing that the character download issue is a beast; that poetic character, for all it is scrutinized in this volume, may in fact nestle even where we least expect it. For character is a slippery wench, and can out in a pocket handkerchief. Are we truly aborting personality, in our crush to write the interventional, and to stamp the romantic under heel?

***

Some more dranster poems:

Dog Days (2008)

Pepper darns the sock!
Amazed by what words,
Packed and aimless, can set
Fire to, the shapeless?

Smell it, parted by fiber,
Print of toe? Now pepper it,
sauces help, baste, sauté.
Sandpaper sounds sheared to meaning?

Meaning's this? Putrid phonemes?
The aleatory tuck of a nanosecond's
Fold? There? Just off n'

Zap, chaos? Pepper darns the sock?
Erodes it, chews up the Dacron?
Of just plain pepper is pepper,
Sits in a plastic bottle,

Sock being as ever on Jim's foot?
That way language is just things in place.
Everything means what it means.
The sock ain't fussin', the pepper ain't fussin'.

Darn it though the sock

Peppers muh little pinkie.
I try walking this way, snaillike.
I try brackets, isn't it?, feather light?

N' once again the pencil
Lighting the paper's edge is
Screwed up, unbalanced, the table,
patta patta, wrinkles like a face.

That seam was so rich?
It yielded ore. The darned sock
Opened to let in Christmas festivities.
The bruised jaw, the hacked aileron?

The bag of winds burst!
911's emergency put-together crew
Flies through the night to the language.
There's the darned breach.

One guy blocks it with a finger
No more pepper flights!
The corner of a sock was caught
And shoved back roughly.

Didn't you go to work the next day,
And put "desk" here, "computer" there,
And "men's room"…u bet u did!
Ain't nothing to worry bout no way,

God's in his expletive tight as a drum,
Only keep the I mean the key
For a sanitary rode worker…
And then again the fear, n'

A kid in Des Moines parks his bike
Slightly at an angle, n'
Whaddy'a know, there's a tsunami…
A trend was noted, "rare weather"…

Best then to leave the world "in place"?
Has this ring to be so insistent?

What nap wants adjusting?
Mr. Google, fix things as they are,
Photograph them, n' I swear
Never two part the seasoned,
Joints holy enough, nor to crank
Joints to seem higher than high.

I fear you, Master!
I fear the dragged seine!
I fear for my sole!
Now let me just take this little chewing

Gum wrapper n' gum n' toss it.
Promise not to tell?
I even fear you, tiny spirits of order,
The milk white finger under the canister.

I know there's a peach wrinkle there!
I know there's a drastic tale
Not quite being told;
Is that because it wasn't heard?

*May I suggest we are in the kind of poem Mallarmé made room for, in
which the shock of words against one another provided the internal
combustion energy of the poem? The poem as thing, referencing the
"real" but simply as a trigger to the "events" of the poem, is a new
species of intervention. "Dranster" let it be for a few pages, until we have
aired this mode of intervening between poet and poem.*

                              ***

There Must Be No Limit (2006)

There must be a way to get around the side
When the front door is blocked.
At the side there are other choices.
Other choices though are inside the house.

Inside the house there are locked doors.
At the side there is a key you need to find.
The front door is locked and there it is.

You go around to the side and look.

Inside the front door there are locks.
The way to open those locks is at the side.
You go around to the side and look.
There is a road on that side; you go.

The road though is what you remembered.
It leads to the house, a village away.
You cannot see the village from the house.
It was locked in a corner of the house.

You go back to the side.
There must be no limit, and then.
You take a long breath at the side of the house.
Last winter you were beside the house.

When you came to the house it was locked.
You drew a long road leading to it.
Then when you came around to the side
It was darkness all over again.

That was enough you thought
And locked it. The side was closed.
Afterwards you came to the house again.
But this time from another village.

We will want to be asking whether the tactile-embedded mover of these lines constitutes an implicit narrator-persona-character. Is such lineage as above a character in disguise?

***

Too Much to Watch (2010)

His was a fell garden and he stayed there.
He did that in the morning to keep from watching.
Watching was too bold, it undid.
Face away from what you cannot watch.
Too much to watch,

Temper your road.
Make for it a destination it cannot reach.
If there is a solemnity arm it.
It may fight for you, like winter,
And help you face away from what you cannot watch.

You are aware that this is not the arm,
Nor is that thing over there the leg.
You are aware that where there was a page of writing
There was a hand, by it a sleeve.
You face away from these things, and do not watch.

You go home every night and make a chalk mark.
Decision seems enough, to make a mark.
In the face of others you are as unwilling.
I saw you hand that man the gear.
Face away, please, from what you cannot watch.

If this is your fell garden, tend it.
Pole beans and milkweed thrive here.
When the chicken got loose you gave it a good whipping.
There was a chance that others might come by.
You faced away, I noted, from what was too much to watch.

In the sinkhole under the city you rode a horse.
Its head was tilted and it had an ear, for an installment.
There was not quite enough room for you both
So one of you rode out of the picture.
I saw you face away, from what had been too much to watch.

*The ritual-imprecatory aversion, in this poem, takes the place of
character, intervening onto but at the same time cancelling the personal
voice.*

✳✳✳

*Interventional? Somebody's talking to you—we're not in Tupus
territory, or even (quite) in the broken universe of The Being Here Site of
the Poetic, but we're locked in a room with a guy who keeps promising to
tell you what he wants you to know, and then reneging.*

Aside (2005)

There must be a way to get around the side
When the front door is blocked.
At the side there are other choices.

Inside the house there are locked doors.
At the side there is a key you need to find.
The front door is locked and there it is.
You go around to the side and look.

Inside the front door there are locks.
The way to open those locks is at the side.
You go around to the side and look.
There is a road on that side; you go.

The road though is what you remembered.
It leads to the house, a village away.
You cannot see the village from the house.
It was locked in a corner of the house.

You go back to the side,
There must be no limit, and then.
You take a breath at the side of the house.
Last winter you were beside the house.

When you came to the house it was locked.
You drew a long road leading to it.
Then when you came around to the side
It was darkness again.

Poems of striving and poems of tactile location, of embeddedness and local gusto; the energies of poetry constitute a kind of character. What are they so attractively substantive?

***

Nine Poems of Striving (2008–9)

i
He/she strove

The past tense plus the gender option
Plus the outskirts near Hy-Vee
Where the wreckage of farms ain't strove
Strobe Thurmond Memphis Sanaztrove.

It got away from me!
Took my finger off the the chocktawrockjaw
N she was there, a sheath overwrapt it
Oh we didn't know but it didn't hurt us.

He puts a table on her head and walks away.
I tell you he strove, she strove.
The past tense was not big enough to hold them.
From there they descended into themselves, arsis,

Thesis, the beat we are. I'll tell you, chrome,
You're delicately ripe to trend along a saw.
There's a Chinese flock at the door, Wendy,
Give the good wunklies a taste of…

He sat down beside the Yalu River
But they had destroyed his picnic table. He strove
To reconstruct, how are ye Mam, a breakfast sandwich?
Oh well, I've the past relaxed now,

Strove to eat your bra strap. Fried? No.
Buttered in crumb sauce? No. And so for hours
He strove with recipes. She answered like a doll,
She rode him like a duiker; feathers, n'strove.

ii
There was a dranster

(Five stanzas of "there was a dranster"—the last five—portray a guy, no?
His profile is as fractured—"oleaginous," "frail workday ethic,"
"judicial," "murky," "little temperance"—as glass on a hot sidewalk; the

qualifiers pull at one another. Is there a mission interior to them, thanks to
which we "feel their tissue?" There is a place which is words we are trying
to construct, and this place is the poet's position inside the poem, trying
you out on a variety of "figures.")

He forged ahead, you know that.
A dranster is always a dranster, and tells.
What he tells is from the inside of the mountain.
Inside it is where the mountain talks to itself.

Shrrd, shrrd. The mountain shdrogs.
There is a cake in the mountain at the end.
You are at this end. You are trying.
You have strong teeth and a strong eye.

You are trying, you dranster.
Tell me will there not be a peak
Where the seams come apart?
One long skirt is typically enough to…

Ordinary ranch style, my friends,
Oleaginous. He dopples it, the dranster.
He fiddles with the mountain skirts
Tapping them. He has little sense

My brethren of the values storming in things.
His is a frail workaday ethic
And he has a monopoly of murkiness.
He truly loves to transect…borders…

He is a frank judicial chap.
A dranster, modest enough. He flows.
Oh he's your flow chart alright, sibilant.
Give him but a chance and watch him blossom.

Deep inside him there is a wall.
You may call it the inside of the mountain
Where a dranster perorates.
There is a little temperance in him.

I'd say mountain climb on the outside.

It's faster in the air.
There are sites to tell, and a dog.
Each little thing, each item, each.

iii
He sweltered

He sweltered and dealt a blow.
My was his hand a stick!
He rose with it in a menace
And was contributed briskly, danist.

He was a Zikisk, a Kropotkin fiend,
You name it, no stroller in the streets.
My was his hand a stick, feathery.
At midnight they broke his room

But he was a tennis player, that was
Nothing to him. He soared, I tell you.
He had an ancient signboard, vulgar.
I'll say I distanced myself.

Oh for sure they'll come dubbing.
They have simple sleeves, you know,
Like adders. Fly modern man before...
Geoffrey knows quite well what I mean

And packs an original slowly.
Nothing beat an original, I'll tell you.
Then there is a little forest they bring up,
Mumbling original sir, and backing off.

I hate those guys in their suits,
I do hate their Chinese. They might have arms,
Sure, but who wants the little fellow?
Is a danist ever welcome? Or a chird?

iv
Odd season

Unmistakeable the season.

A road ran through his lilac bush, darnit.
He wheedled. At the window he drove.
There was a very tense air.

For over an hour he sheltered in the reeds.
He was small and whispered.
He gave dense packets of signs to some
And to others he just gave feelers.

What he said was off about a meter,
But the jackwhsiperers knew him by sound
And rode easily past his house in the suburb.
He crowed over a wife and dreamed.

A mean oak was what he paid
For chipping. Ruined a niblet.
It was dark when the company parted.
They had one blue soccer ball.

At the Café des Beaux Arts he choked.
His rhombus was fetching.
Darling did you see the goings and comings
And the fine ones? There was a plate;

On the plate they placed wire.
While they were waiting he strove.
Fyre took advantage of his brow and burst.
He managed an egg-shaped constabulary.

Nine to five he said wearily.
It's all about being sure you don't know.
Physically speaking he had strength enough
But a deer sure is big and eyed him.

(*The ball that never sticks keeps rolling. Attributes assemble him as the hill consumes him from below. He is no Chaplinesque figure being handed on from misfitting to misfitting, but language itself in process of collating.*)

v
Ambition

Of course he grew dark, with the season.
He retrekked to Bloemfontein in shoes,
And turtled in there eggily.
Had a genetic, sure, Table Mountain fyre,

And rose in rank. Did you not test
The long way he wondered, in that shoe?
I thought him strange, perhaps an undoer,
Though after it all he strove, she strove,

We strove. There's no candy he wouldn't take.
Ancient Burgundian potatoes,
Did they taste or lie fallow like life writing?
He grew a sole so the shoe fit,

And walked in it to Bloemfontein.
It's a large jerry can I'll tell, yes,
That will hold the names of the flowers.
You choose one. There you go,

Stick it in, stick it in tight.
You'll be forever itching but take...
Oh well, he strove, his night was long,
He refused. You said refusenik?

He refused, or strove? I think he strove.
His garter got caught in an oak
And strive he must and strove.
Oh there's an edge on his tooth

And it is part egg. He caught it.
You see he caught an egg and drifted.
He stuck it in the edge of the fridge like an egg.
After breakfast he looked at it again

And strove. I grew weary striving.
Hence the mountain I climbed and the shoe.
The shoe came after me, in a bit of a panic.

It strove. I rode it to pieces believe you me.

There is an order in things he strove to say.
There is an order in the motor, parts of flowers
Say to others we're parts of a whole,
And very good dinners taste one another.

Have you a shoe you can offer me for my date?
We're going out tonight he said striving,
We're going to go out shoe dancing.
There's toll. What costs nothing?

(No rhyme or reason to these inserts. They are breaks in attention and gargoyles playfully located at the ends of the architrave. From them we know we are observed, and by them we are offered free parking spaces for mind. To react in. To ask itself what kind of engagement could be expected from a reader of slantwise sound and metaphysic poetry like the present. Is there a blend of thought with the sound of thought that triggers new modes of being-here? New ways of adopting your position in the micro of your room, your body embed, your poise within a day shape?)

vi
Wrapping it up

There's no assurance.
Nothing he strove to do did he do.
There were blocks against every streetlamp
And he fell, and his shoe too, his shoe.

Much as he had tried to achieve, striving,
He strove in vain. Things curled at his feet.
He kicked a duck from his toe, and charged
Too much just to see it. You see he strove,

And when fyre caught on he eluded.
He eluded and he strove, for he feared.
He took on the past tense fearlessly,
Eating his heart out with strive, and strove,

And Itchygumi and Kitchygumi.

His was absolutely a fiery line,
And he followed it straight up. He strove
Manfully to…his cheese softened,

It was a dreadful canton, and in the pepper.
There he strove. Gruessli said the mountain
Women on their way down, he choked.
He buttoned a desire in a tooth, and ran

Fingers over the down. There was a still.
Oh it was a merger, and inside it…
There too cantons, there too bright spots.
He knew how to teethe, to get it right.

The syntax of the language that constructs, or is, him, is intermittent; grammar book phrase—"it was a dreadful canton"—followed by detached prepositional phrase, "in the pepper."

vii
Jubilance

It was well past midnight.
He knew he had acquired a power, and strove.
Whatever it was he strove, and it was smaller
Each time he rode. He felt the domination.

In the shadows of the streets he held.
He went through dark green corridors.
Grave markers ribbed him; he strove
Though until they said yes, darling.

It was a stone like none other and he rode.
Hail to me, diamond, did you not strive?
Did you not bear me. I bore you
And it was a wound, so I strove, strive,

viii
Immobility

There is no way to move from here.

It is said that there is a stark toilet
In a bar. That is not hard to find.
But it is hard to use for it is forgotten.

There are many things forgotten in this time.
There's no end to what I forgot in a closet
When I moved. A paint can, three dogs, hard
Nails, stubble, a cross between a man and a heart.

I didn't care to count them. There were too many.
Didn't you see the solar eclipse?
A dog woke in Berlin to see that eclipse and howled.
There was no other way to address it.

Now I'm not worried. I too howl.
I can enrich the postman with a snivel,
A beryl in his fob, China men come; it is
Seventy-two minutes past the hour.

ix
The magic in poetry

This poetry is magic like all poetry.
Names of things eat the things, eat the hand
With all its rings. It is good to be startled,
Sometimes, when there are dogs.

Dogs take the sting out of surprise,
Howling. There's a bitter for dogs.
Didn't you heal one once, feeding it?
Wasn't there a space within it to emerge?

Oh well, dogs and caterpillars and heads
And toes of state, they charge. They charge a lot.
Like all things created they move in circles
Among our legs. We tender them.

There is no currency in legs but what we put there.
We simply don't know the price of a leg, or drod,
Or Roman or tinsel. Words fly off. Did you see?
Did you see the word fly? It hit the wall.

We scraped if off. All of us scraped it. It came
Off in paper shreds, on the floor.
Oh man, how we had to route it then.

***

*There is, you are right, no end to the wordstock available to a kitten
like yours truly. Did the real good poets of a long time ago, like Pindar,
and Propertius, and Donne, and Baudelaire also spin out without end, just
let the reams of language pour from them, or is it only a poor wop like me,
with a pearly laptop in hand, who is able to mass produce the progeny of
words?*

Somebody Was in the Way (2005)

Somebody was in the way
last night, far and away.
They were tipplers, and started
To go in pairs. They were not old.

They had the strength of the young
And the minds of the young.
They were not old. They were tipplers.
They walked in gray cold circles.

They were tipplers of the idea.
They imbibed long draughts of common material.
They furnished their rooms with roughage.
They were in the way, terribly.

The night was for tipplers.
Though in a way they were young,
And could move. They had a portal.
They went through their portal in suits.

Woven from tippling they went home.
That was last night, far and away
The longest night. They sighed.
Parts of them awaited by children
Who were interested in them.

The children were interested in them.
One two three seven and ten say the children
Separating them, for they were in the way.
They were in the way but they went.

They moved away. Dawn tipplers,
Easy stars in easy constellations.
They had fabricated heads
But they moved away slowly.

Somebody was in the way.
But he was old, sunning himself.
Once he drank too much.
Once he moved from one place to another.

***

I Have Long Been Absent (2004)

I have long been absent from the side.
I love the way they say it, worn.
I love side as part of resting.
It was there when we went further.

Something lonely came around to the morning.
It had stillness in quantity, and left it.
We felt the stillness in a place.
We were doctrinal of fire, chose...

I didn't know you would weep.
I was shocked when you wept.
I felt a lazer of friendliness,
When we gathered at the emblem.

I didn't know it first as side.
I knew it as portal. It was a dome.
Driving from Portland on one side;
On the other the dishes, hard ones.

There was always a corner to brush.
You said it is a time lock.

On the side dole was eruh created.
I went around, it was over, timed.

Sentience left pockets, Gortyn.
There we wheeled. The bus tampered.
You blew a sign, a feather, off to the end.
Did you not see the side? Or care for it?

***

It Wasn't Easy (2009)

There is a table mat beside the table.
It is all there is to hold.
Did it but know, then leave space?
It made no gesture of yielding.

A rarity in a stone lay there.
You and it knew it was careless.
You and I could read a sign on a wheel.
It was that the chandler was dying.

***

I fell so in love with the side.
It didn't charge much.
I bought it on credit or I er…
Well, anyway, there it was suddenly.

It sure looked like the side I loved.
But it had a little crack in it.
I forced my hand in at that crack,
Like a foal, or a gymnast.

It didn't seem to matter where I went
With my protruding.
The crack was a monitoring.
But inside I was not on the side,

I was in the place under the side.
My love for the side grew hot.

I browsed over the crowded places of the side,
Hoping there would be a side to love.

But the fact is the side kept being away,
Kept being of another who was monitoring.
O side, return in front. Be of other,
Yes, like a geometry, a stele,

Be a hand at the outside.
Go drench your self in a side.
It is the place to be given away.
Of course there is a fabric.

The fabric and the side may fight.
There may be a quintain of fire.
Go there to the side.
Be careful, fire. Be chosen or smart.

You may take away what is left.
There is a place where you can leave the side.
Put it in a corner.
Let it stay there, an hour around on the side.

(Don't we forever reinvent what we ourselves have written? It is a blistering African afternoon, five p.m. and the sun angry about something, and I get this sense that all this dranster stuff is an attempt at magic, a shuffling of words and meaning into a cosmic card game, which you might join me in watching from the corner of your armchair. Magic leaves us for others, but if we have won it it remains part of our repertoire for paying attention, as when in prayer of whatever sort we bring our attention to a burn point.)

***

The Snail Said (2007)

An hour or two away from here.
Just over there side, wonder, too.
Chomp, marvel system.
An hour or two away from here.

There is a Chinese buffet.
I was mugged in it.
We asked for less sodium glutamate.
Oh that was hard to say.

The snail said no to the tortoise's stride.
You come here baby cry on...
An hour from here there's a buffet...
They serve..the children's...ach dran...

Verweile doch, my little finger.
It was Chinese *deutsch.*
I saw a calendar with a marigold.
That wasn't hard to pluck.

On May 10 I published a spreadsheet.
It had all these words and thoughts.
I believed in them. My mentor
Frowned egg frown. No China.

He bolted from the side,
He was afire a cause nor did it...
An hour from here there is a
Gentle...he tangles, his frosted...

Sentiments like these gel.
They snarl around the leg.
Penitentes hell, they shuffle...
They pray side its wonder.

They will not be still in China.
They wish to return in ease.
Hand them documents. They frown.
They sit at a restaurant, on the side.

They turn their faces to the side.
Blow away Tom. Trust your woe.
Trust the side that broke loose.
In a little German café Chinese

Mustard gives life to the spaetzle.

An almost infinite catalogue is completed.
Except one side is missing. It falls
Away when the other sides wander.

Come to me the narrative.
The tortoise waddles across the line.
The hare on the side. I followed you.
You dominated my…the roundness, fire.

And so I go on saving the world, as any nonagenarian driven by cosmic longing. I know how small is every step on the way, the steps stridden toward Lincoln Park and Leal school, as the crisp youngsters carved through Illinois frost, those first adjutant steps directed into the flood of perceptions, misperceptions, and losses. And all that I might be the default position I occupied a second ago as I prepared to use once again that worn out metaphor taken from the repertoire of my time. Borrowing from others to name what they, as well as I, have to endure as read offs of time, speakers whose projects have been vetted long before they were formulated and "turned in."

PART TWO:

MODIFYING INTERVENTION

CHAPTER EIGHT

TRANSLATION: PRACTICE IN THE THIRD LANGUAGE (1965–1980)

The braking of imaginative download, the gear grinding that screeches you down to the flatland, the detour that makes you forget the hue of the author you are working in terms of; all this seems to Will to get paradigm recreation in the act of translation, to which we can add our attention as we muse on Will's continuing strategies for deflecting character away from the giving of the poetic act. In that act, as it revolves around the relation of original to translation, occur multiple opportunities for the Ur maker to get his or her voice transplanted, recalibrated, for that matter enhanced (or diminished). (Will's capstone motto—*I live life as though it were, in itself, a standing into a future condition, in which orders I can't imagine recapacitate me, assigning me to the rights of place*—looks to translation itself as a model for the life-transition act; as though life-end were in fact literature-end, both of them glissando, in act five, into the gene pool of verbal emancipation.) Whose character does the translator of poetry download, his/her own, that of Aristophanes, or that of the two of them blended? Is the translator's voice still recognizable as his own after it has been processed in this way? What happens to whose character in this download?

On occasion, it seems to Will, the translator and the author are one, and the translator's character is in no way "reduced" by becoming identical to x or y who initially made the darned thing—if indeed it was not made *for* them, or read out *at* them by others. Were the author and his translator to be viewed as one, that would make the translation character-download into a parlor game, in which we simply attach the translator's name as that of the original author.

Will sensed, in his translation of *Poem for Christ* (by Steinn Steinarr; from the Icelandic, 1968), that both the poem and the translation wrote themselves, Steinarr voice-doubling his own in perfect harmony.

Poem for Christ (from the Icelandic; trans. Frederic Will, 1968)

That was evening
And we sat in the garden
Two poor boys.
And we watched the sun

Go down
Behind the mountains
In the distance.
That is so strange for a man,

When a man is young,
That the sun must disappear
From the sky
Behind the distant mountains.

As if a stranger's hand
Deprived a man
Of playthings.

And we
Who had not noticed evening
In the peace of the sunwhite day
Sat in silence and wondered
At the sight of the black wall
Which we could not have crossed
The night

And we sat in the garden
Two small boys.
And that was when
You told your secret
Your giant secret
No one knew
Before.
It was so beautiful
And so concealed
The finest secret in the world.
And we sat and whispered
one to another

astounding
leavened words
about the sun
which might shine in the sky
greater and brighter
than ever before
about the sun
and men
who were always good to boys.
"And there," you said,
"all men will be so good
as good as flowers.
And there we will need no more
To fear the dark
For there will never be night
When he has come to free the world."

And we sat in the garden
two poor boys
one night
two thousand years ago.

PL 70–71

    Steinarr, Will had to feel, downloaded exactly into a replica of himself, to a T, the very voice/persona of the original appearing in the translation.

    It was Will's move to describe the braking process, in the above downloading passage, as a moving via a third language; a language through which language A can become language B. What is the third language? It is—Will argues in Translation Theory and Practice: Reassembling the Tower, 1993—the language in which (for example) we translate the first two setting-paragraphs of Kostes Palamas' Twelve Words of the Gypsy (1964) into "English":

T'axedialute skotadia
(The indissoluble darknesses)
Ta charadzei mia ligne leukote,
(A slight crack of light pierces them)
Nychtophernontas kai aute;
(itself bearing with it a night)

Kai etane tou nou mou e prote charavge
(it was the first dawn of my mind)

Kai etane ora melichrotate;
(it was the most honeyed moment)
Kai etane chymeno ologyra
(and it was poured on all sides)
Kati pio chaideutika
(and more soothing)
Ki' apo t'aeraki
(than the breeze)
Otan erchetai giomato apo ta balsama
(when it comes filled with pine aroma)

Proina ton oloprasinon pevkonon,
(from the all green pines)
Ki' apo t'aeraki;
(than the breeze)
Kai etan pera kapou se mia ge,
(and it was somewhere in a land)
Se pege laion kai chronon;
(at the source of people and times)
Kai etane sten Thrake...
(and it was in Thrace)

(Note: No effort is made, here, to characterize the pronunciation of the Greek, or the intricate pattern of stress, tones, and harmonies out of which Palamas makes his "argument"; all we indicate is the significance of the words. The poet the reader is will establish, from the raw stuff before him/her, a path through both euphony and rough stuff, and will be better off making his own poem through earning it the old-fashioned way—stupidly, passionately.)

On the *other side* of the mediating third language, baldly, we get this:

Indissoluble shadows
One thin light invades them
Swaddled itself in night;
It was my mind's first
Dawn.

It was a honey-gentle moment
Outpoured on every side
Somehow more caressing
Than breeze
That comes, burdened with early
Balsam-scent from all-green pines—
Than breeze;
It was somewhere far, some country,
Source of men and times;
It was Thrace.

We just get this, the above. Now can we *add*, to these two specimens of the originating insight of Mr. Kostes Palamas, creator of *The Twelve Words*, the words of some third language *in which* the first was converted into Will's version? You talk about third language, now show it to me! The apparent absurdity of this request is precisely what opens us both to the empty ideality and to the effective actuality of the third-language concept. (Never was it Will's intention to do practice in the real-world bread and cheese fill, though he insisted on the reality of the world filled with the names *cheese* or *bread*. His formulation of a theory of translation was, therefore, poetic creation itself.) Empty ideality because the third language is present here only as the necessity of a place filler, as the Holy Spirit inserts itself, on behalf of meaning, between the Father and the Son. It, this third language, is the intelligibility that has to be there for the translational act to take place, and take place it can when such a poem as Steinnar's or Palamas' fits the translation language like a glove. *Language one* cannot simply become *language two*, as in the fashion of a miracle in which the sanctified wafer is enabled to become the body of Christ in the Catholic Mass. *Language one has to make its way to language two.* So what then is useful about the third language concept? Is it just language retrofitted to fulfill the needs of language?

The third language concept provides a thought-home for all the critical tinkering we must oblige ourselves to do, in order to explain, for example, all that has to be done to *axedialuta skotadia* to make it into "indissoluble shadows." (The surface appearance of the third language, here, is the actuality of language history, the formations within both Greek and English that account for the compositional thought-percept elements in, say, *axedialuta*, "not-dissolved", and are constructive for the end-product "indissoluble".) We can talk about what goes into that transfer, and we can talk about what talking about that transfer is, all as part of explicating the third language. What we come to, as we parse closely and more thickly into the web of transactions that made a meaningful minefield of that transit zone, is that instant calibrations reign there. Darknesses ("kinds of dark") are as it were generated right off the back of *skotadia*; while even *axedialuta*, "not having been dispersed or diluted or dissolved," a compound concept, is as it were the pre-ready mother of "indissoluble". It is not as though a step-by-step process moved *axedialuta* to *indissoluble*, embedding the rational calculus—*indissoluble* or *unseparable* or *unseparable out?*—which goes with a compound language like Greek, but rather as though the mindset assigned to fiddling with *axedialuta* was already at its terminus, giving the third language only that instagram-like semblance of reality it requires, in order not to be language independent of language.

What we say here, by way of short cut and drag out analysis, and with a specificity still unsuitable to a larger argument, suggests that the creative acts of the translator are just what fills the space between languages. These creative acts may be brought to a boil in the working practice of a skilled translator, who like any craftsman has incorporated the lessons that work, lines of desire and intention that settle, once more, onto longed for finales. (The perfect Chippendale, the worked shofar, the narrow netsuke that renders my lady's waist even thinner! These are longed-for finales.) Is that creative translator less a creator in letters than John Donne or Clément Marot? Perhaps the translator is less a creator, in the sense that he/she invents within first-degree parameters, in terms of a *given* language challenge, while the "literary creator" makes those parameters for himself, while submitting to them. (Talk of alchemy! *Mais c'est de la vérité!*) To concentrate on the sputa of the poor translator, however, is to consign yourself, once again, to the job of collecting night soil.

What is the job of these first stanzas of translation of Palamas? It is to get the reader's mind to share the *opening of mind of the poet*, then to descend in that freshened mind to the sense of place which becomes Thrace. A time and a place are to emerge, from the magic fingers of the first lines, which are of the same quality as the awakening mind of the author. So fine is what awakens that it connotes the cool odor of pine tree slopes; "somewhere far, some country." It will be the job of the translator, moving across the immediately self-dissolving space of a third language, to give tone and hue to the old version which is now the new version which is what the old version wished to be.

The third language, as we use it here, is that valence or *clinamen* which brakes the original as it settles down into a new form. There will be any number of brakes to apply—a feather here, a boulder there—and apply them the translator will, to lesser or greater acclaim. In so braking, whatever the case, we invite language transformation.

In the process of language transformation—to bring our chit-chat back to the whipping post—we work with the poetic character, our frontline base of concern here. The translator of course is not the "poetic character" in creating mode. The translator is working with "someone else's" fabric, and entering it at diverse angles, in order to give it working space in a new idiom. The translator is thus, even more actively than the poet, at work on making sure that no uniform character becomes a routine product, that the downloading process doubles down on diverting itself, in translating Palamas or discovering Mayan *stelae* in language.

Tweaks, valences, protective and creative deflections: all these feints make up the repertoire of movements by which the poetic character downloads hints, but no more, of itself. One feels that this is the moment to touch on the postmodernist conversation again, before the direct path is cluttered. Again, what is postmodernism? Isn't it the wide-ranging perception that the stable world of names and their referents is no longer reliable? And doesn't that doubting perception, which will take its generative examples from language, have its roots in the ontological malaise of our time, where not only cultural history but vertical individual profiles are subject to twists and turns—cf. the implications of Planck's quantum physics—we are not prepared to interpret in advance? Given a pervasive holistic dissonance on the personal and cultural level, nothing could be more natural than a deep questioning of the language acts by which we give ourselves expression. Among those acts thus burrowing into intimacy, the acts of art and language most incline to guard their tracks. What do they fear? Recourse to the old-fashioned minefields of word and thing, and their deceptive promises of stability? A wholeness of mind, word, and thing, which is as likely to mislead as the mom-and-apple-pie value syndrome?

The present voice—that of yours truly, prancing around here—hears these reduced and primitive arguments, and will add to them the feeling that language use must be guarded like radioactive material. Language pours from us so easily, and covers a surface so rapidly, like paint, that what it should be discerning and parsing, a ferocious world given us, is obscured and replaced by ugly simulacra of itself. The artist, no doubt, will feel this threat in spades, for he or she lives by discovering ways to share the quality of emplacement in the biosphere, and wants to control the vulgar lateral tendencies, of word, charcoal, oil, or musical note to mop up designata and eradicate their borders.

The postmodern challenge will reinforce the backstory of the present book, for whatever we are foregrounding, about the reluctance of the poetic character to self-reveal, wants further explaining by the cultures which have proven willing to shelter such training as poetic communities provide. Nothing about the making of the poem justifies in itself the simple desire to self-express.

***

The King's Flute (1967)

From the Tenth Word, the speaker Basil the Bulgar killer addresses the Virgin Mary:

And from all the names you took from all
Those places, your wonders, your particular graces,
Names raying like your brow's glory,
Balsam like your own countenance,
Deep like the springs of pity and mercy
Which are your two eyes,
I take—they numberless—and return them to you,
Scapulars, offerings, smoking them richly over,
Glazing them nobly with images worth my soul,
Holiness, my faith, All Queen, Who Pities,
Lover in Sweetness, Ubiquitous, Healer, Freer
There, Seer, Fulfiller, Leader,
Who Answers,
                    Noonsun,
                                    Swift in Response,
Romaic, Athenian, Seen,
Tower goldwoven, throne suntarred,
Rainbow your belt. More vast, more sumptuous
You flooded the sky; path you, more great,
Wearing sun for garment, moon
For footstool, around
Your hair a twelvestar wreath.
At your side strike wings,
Strike eaglewings, to pour
From the light of heaven to the night of hell.

KF 196–197

Where is character download in liturgical language of this sort? We have stumbled through the complexity of the translator's language, and its role on the other side of a third language which ferries intelligibility on its far side. What happens to the mediated language of the translator, when the language he translates strives to be frozen in time, to exclude the individual tone, as the liturgy of, say, the Catholic mass strives to speak through *quod semper quod ubique*, what is always and everywhere the same? The translator of such language steps back from his personality into his persona, if that, and counts on fervor to replace identity.

CHAPTER NINE

ME, THAT'S ALL

The first poem our friend Will wrote, consciously cut out of the marrow of daily, and offered out there as if it represented a person in a place, was "This Autumn's Progress," and for its authenticity the author feels he can vouch, by the decisiveness with which he situates the poem inside himself in time and a need. (The thing still feels like it's in there, in him.) Pre-intervention this action was, dating from the author's first year in graduate school, 1951, in fact from just what he describes, a silent autumn afternoon in the Yale Neo-Gothic Library's central courtyard, from where, in fact, he gazed with astonishment at the inscription *He was born with a gift of laughter and a sense that the world is mad*. (Cf. Rafael Sabatini, *Scaramouche*, 1921; Chapter 1, Book One, line one.) Nothing could have been farther from Will's intention, making this poem, than the desire to hide his character; *he existed as the disposition to make an offering of that character*; and, blessed little fool, he could not imagine that you, yes you, might not share his delight in that itsy-bitsy shroud of individual immortality. (He was one with his mood, and ready to sit down and read it off to you.) It was his first year of graduate school, as I said, and he was both lonely and elated, conscious, perhaps, of the weight of time, passionate to share—but to share what?—rounding on that mood that makes the guy still voluble in the evenings, when the cumulate pressure of the day begs to need to be talked about; and always afraid of being left behind. The piece goes this way:

This Autumn's Progress (1951)

This autumn's progress I have measured by
A quiet courtyard. By its hundred shades of green,
Then by scarlet leaves upon the
Solemn boughs which half a year before
Spring evenings bore into a gentle show
Of furry bloom. While now, today, display

Is made of quite another delicacy,
Of silent, endlessly enchanted death.

Further into simplicity's house
Have I never been than here alone
In a land of fair insistence. Here
Where purpose is subsumed in presence, where
With each leaf's tenuous fall I die
Severally. The pattern formulates
And strangely severed members emphasize
A resolution underneath the grass.

This the time for the horned night, the red
Stream, passion of furred beasts. Passion too
Of the quiet. Smell of leaves, fall's indelible
Fabrication. The incredible phrase of time
Walking giantly through my home, into
Death's raw texture.
Saint Tortoise's sober promenade.

MO 39

Is there a default condition of poetry, in which it downloads the maker's
self without living the environment of ontological defensiveness we have
been fumbling to describe? Was Will finding his way through the maze of
that blurred condition? Did he achieve that condition in "launching pad
love poems," like the following, written a decade later, in the "Texas
years," the years when *Arion*, Harry Ransom, Bill Arrowsmith, and poets
like Christopher Middleton and Richard Emil Braun richened up the
tapestries of Will's still small-town-culture psyche? Was he in these
poems too making an effort at self-identity and stability, in a world
evidently slippery beyond holding?

Letter Back (1962)

Troubled constancies destroy so many
Sleeps. I write you now from past a sleep,
From after all my reasons, from away
Beside white paper, where I sit at windows,
Gorged enormously with sun and spring.

I write to you from past a sleep that flooded
Me with choice upon this highbanked bed.
Yes I feel drowned in restful gaiety
And years alone to write beside this sun.
I should expect to tire or hunger or
To mail these letters, but the door is far,
And I have long mislaid the key, and once
I looked and saw an image of myself
That walked in tireless guard below my room.
I could call thinly on a pulse of air
That you should follow here, and I descend
A flight of stones, and hold you in the sun,
But it is far, by hills, and you were tired,
And I am waking, waking.

WOW 11

It is the author's hope that his reader will have pegged this poem at a date far prior to even the earliest of the high-tweak intervention poems with which we began. (*Guatemala* and *The Epics of America* both date from the mid-70s, while "Letter Back"—the poem before us—was included in a volume, *A Wedge of Words*, published in 1962, some ten years after "This Autumn's Progress.") Did "something happen" to or in the author, in the sixties and seventies of his development, that sharpened the need and impulse for a complexification of the act of poetic downloading? Did he tire of trying to be Shelley, did Eliot and Olson get to him, and did he listen to the multiplicity of diffracting voices asking for attention from inside him? These questions lie at the heart of this book, which concerns character-tone, its expression in poems, and the environing triggers to change in that tone.

What happened was that the rich cusp of the romantic mode, which was allowing this unfulfilled factory of desire to start eyeing a field he had excluded himself from, as a modest dreamer from the plains, opened out into a full paradise of longing, the withering (and thrilling) life of the *affair, yes the affair*, in whose unfolding intemperate strategies deployed themselves, strategies devised—and this process is tightly linked to the highly tweaked download of many of Will's poems of the 70s and 80s—to erect Potemkin Villages around a rotting inner life. (The "affair" itself being a masquerade constructed from the *papier-mâché* of pretense.) To explain this "spiritual" transition, from the open *lettre d'amour* ("Letter Back") to the highly tweaked refusenik poems of the guy's intervention

period, in which it is all about "being there while hiding yourself," and
from there, by George, to what Will ended up at, at this present point,
doing with the long poem, the long jagged out-there-in-the-open poem of
self-discovery through life-summation, will be an assignment more than
large enough to direct the energies of the rest of this *libellum*. By the time
we have tracked grumpy old Will, crouching, into the side rooms of
serenity—welcome early twenty-first century—and ultimately into long
talks with the Charon whom he has never since childhood failed to flirt
with—hey, remember the death-fascination in *Fragments*, 1944?—by that
time we will have written our own *petite histoire de la littérature
américaine*.

For the nonce, though, have we thoroughly outed the innocences of
"Letter Back"? There is some poison working even in the invitation
indirectly proffered in this poem. The word-maker considers that he could
call the beloved to his chambers, make place for her (for these poems are
strikingly hetero, but in a Burne-Jones mode, presuming frocks on grassy
swards), at the end of his thin call, and yet, all things considered, he has to
concede to himself that she is far from him, and probably not up to the
journey. In fact, upon a third read, this poem is probably likely to yield its
single fruit: the construction, by the word person, of an inner world
impregnable even to those he might want to invite inside its doors. Not a
tweak precluding a view of the author's character, as in the intervention
poems, but a stylized look at a real person.

The volume from which this poem is taken, *A Wedge of Words*, was
preceded, in 1959, by Will's first formal book of poems, *Mosaic*. Where
but there should we look for an innocence even more pretend-vulnerable
than that of "Letter Back"? "The Wound and the Grace" corners the same
market, on sulky eros, that we read in "Letter Back", and yet it has curdled
less over the soft fire of self-interest.

The Wound and the Grace (1959)

Could it have been otherwise, the wound
And the grace of our meeting? Unique music tuned
In another key, could it have been? Well,
As it is it will play in me stilly, like the tell-
Tale pulse of a ripening child, the secret
A womb cannot still. And though we are to forget
Wars, our rights, even the time for lunch,
This will be different. Bern, the fountain, the hunch-

Back bear dancing for carrots, the tower that gave
A scope of the city at noon; we shall save
These things well. They will not come again.
Like wine of the best year they will quench when
The seasons grow dry. But this tune and grace
Of our meeting, we will not drain it. The trace
Of a wound will stay, too. Leaving made it, of course.
There was an end and no end, there was force
Done to the *conte de fées*. So it was best
Though. No time for mood, complaint, or a test
Of affection. Nothing protested, no voice repeating
It could be otherwise, the grace and the wound of our meeting.

MO 32

Music carries the feast of schmooze here, importing just the needed loss into the idyll, training the idyll itself on its central point—the charms of Romantic romance, *ô temps suspends ton vol* blended into *nessun maggior dolore che nella miseria ricordarsi del tempo felice*. Literarily propped up, this pretty touching account of an inwardly staged vagary, set on a landscape half-drained of reality because created by words, leaves the mark of sadness and desire, without indulging the excluding narcissism, which, in "Letter Back", has already morphed into a dangerous *noli me tangere* mode. ("Interventionist" not quite, yet, but cautiously self-protective.) "Letter Back", fluid and inviting as it is, has not yet "gone mean," in the fashion of those mid-life interventionist tweak poems with which we opened this discussion, poems written by someone not speaking to you, or by no one at all.

The Romantic, then, stands before us. What else does Wordsworth strive for than organic flow, the concept embedded and embodied, so that when we finish reading one of his poems we are *in* an experience and not in an action of learning how to do something, or know something? The collusion of reason with emotion, the working space of Pindar, Horace, and Pope, has in Romanticism been eroded at the edges. Wouldn't you say that "Letter Back" is basically a mood? What would you say of "Three Snow Moods" (1956) written when Will was teaching in the snowy effervescence of his first job, at Dartmouth College in the old male days. We have jumped twelve years "ahead" from *Fragments*, and five from "This Autumn's Progress"; we are ready to "intervene."

Three Snowmoods (1956)

i

I turn to enter, turning from those frozen sunfields,
when I see the rage of flakes
diminished into shaves of gold, and streaming
Each its up or down, until it strikes
Out of that suncaught area.
This depth of air on fire will reel within my mind.
When summer shines a spin of pollen, leapt
Up madly to my careless eye.
No doubting
Much of flux careens unseen by eyes
Where we walk knowingless: a different sun,
A rare career of brilliance takes the eye.
Zeus came in a golden shower, seeding Danae
With violent light, until she burned all known.
But we must wait for sun on snow so long
That analogues of sunrage fail our minds.
And realms of sense in spin lack issue.
One old claim of thought had guessed us all such spin.
The heart and tendon, genitals and
hands,
A gross and ceaseless churn of atoms destined
To the finer airs at last.
Or why do I turn back to stare such rage of flakes?

ii

Every change that winter could astound
Me with might start here, now alone in snow.
Beside a bridge, in air that lack of sound
Weighs down, and there the bank of pines that grow

Without me. Lord the massive snow surrounds.
Until the pressing scene lends weight to match
This grand downdrift of massless flakes. Oh pounds
uncountable of me weight down the patch

Of snowsoil I am standing on. Oh change,

surprise me now with purpose which had lost
Its name, and losses which breed strength for strange
Redemptions. Vacant realms in me are crossed

And leavened by an inner fall of peace,
Which solemn single falls of flake release.

iii

I call up yesterday's alarm of storm
That stirred me, walking peaceward in the dusk,
That charged this narrow corridor through pines,
That blew a windy hour wildly warm
For autumn's ways. Oh how could I agree
To guess at weathers then? A hint of sea,

A scent of some disturbance over waters
Found me where I lay last night, and waged
Excitements with my falltime ease of self.
Unrestful sense of absent arctics stirs
Some inner summer: but how was I to guess
At freeze and flake? I would have more success,

I've heard, to plan by starshapes: then I slept
But now I stand, alarmed by lightfierce shed
Of snow about this corridor of pines.
And sift of flakes through needly pine boughs. Leapt
Up will to summer takes dismay at beauty.
And this newmoon aches the eyes of me.

I'm swiftly taken by a widened sense.
To guess beneath this forest snowgrace, ways
That I had walked through dusk, and snowy season's
Rule inaugurated in immense
Obscurities of silence while I slept.
The lossful pain of yesterdays unkept.

Paris Review (1956, Spring), 104–105

***

Whether to nature or to love, Will is open in the above language things. We are dealing with a freshness to us, discovering. By the time of "Circe", coming up a decade later, 1969, we are more interested in the language with which we let a love story deploy itself, than in the story itself. We are tapping into what we started by calling an interventionist perspective, in which screens are interposed between the person of the teller and the tale. (That's what the *Guatemala* sequence was about, ostensibly transparent to visibilia, rows of stelae, yet undermining from you, as you read, the humane guide desired for company and direction.) "Circe", more than a decade later, prolongs this screening strategy, replacing the narrative I, which is so directly on top of you in the *Three Snowmoods* and the two earlier romantic poems, with an I, and a partner you, who are nowhere except in language, though there they are—"you shuffled out dreamily / close with beasts," "I swallowed it and tried to look lonely"—representing folks. And here's where we're going, right now, to the long poem we will let out of the bag just on the other side of "Circe". Tagged at 2013, the long-growing *Myosotis* (below) came to birth decades earlier in the dialogue of self with self that felt growing inside itself the wonder of the poem thing, and the fascination with poetic autonomy *which* has been struggling to self-articulate since Mallarmé and Valéry, and which a recent reading of Hamburger's *The Truth of Poetry* (1969) has given fresh terms to control. *Myosotis, chers amis*, is about the language that *Myosotis* is about, but of course it is about more than that, for it is also about the kind of reality created by language which is about itself.

Circe (1969)

i

A careless red dog closed
the distance between us
like the Easter in *Faust*
his eyes were feathers.

I let him come,
his scrofulous ears
printed neatly upward,
his bones coral thin,

until he lay and talked.
Said you were across
the valley, sealed, lonely,
capable of hatred now.

Would I follow him there?

ii

Arriving, you
shuffled out dreamily
close with beasts.
Hung like them.

I touched my ring.
It promised, at once,
so that I risked.
That harm seemed gone.

Under rocks, Lorrain's
setting made for your hair.
You opened topics
like ripe fruit.

On all sides
friendly animals
nuzzled me like a chance
to confirm their soft eyes.

In a while we remembered
the one thing that had broken us
from each other like a blade.
I swallowed it and tried to look lonely.

iii

In the late afternoon
you made some tea
out of antelope horns.
I touched my ring.

From there I walked.
A kind of DMZ
it was, then, flogged
with craters, scrub

pines. I didn't know.
What had we left?
What had left us?
It was nearly eight.

In an hour a moon would rise.
It would entangle
itself in the corners of my body,
it would trip and fall.

Could I pick it up?
There were also squirrels.
They were running too.
And there was a man

with a gun the size
of a toothpick. He passed,
shrinking into an owl's
ear. I hurried.

Really the wood between us
was maddening.
My bones rattled
in their caned going.

iv

I went back to you later,
(it seemed more familiar),
and grew sleepy. You brought
nursing cubs to show,

trains of wee colts,
sidelong glances. The night
wandered in and out
of itself. The fire went down.

Did you bring me, seeing,
a fire I could never?
Or stir the ash womb
I had born in you once?

I flattened myself
suddenly on a bank of red
mosses and went to sleep.
The silence was endless.

It must have been then I
dropped. I became my body.
I entered my body like a hand.
It would not come out.

v
In the morning you'd gone.
I woke like a stone,
Dry inside, veined, stiff,
Sniffing its hill. Pieces

Of the known passed.
A flower came up
Quietly beside me
Then broke down in tears.

A bird bothered me
With a call nearly human.
Snails crossed me
With their vast caravans

In search. I opened
Slightly each time.
But wanted to close
Over the impressions.

When you came
Back I could only half
Feel the earth's nerve
Warble. And could answer

Only this, wanded.
My tongue frozen
Into dry crystal sounds,
Thin phonemes, mica.

Poetry (1969, Autumn), 6–10

***

The prefatory note to "Circe" will have been an iteration of this whole book's gradual climb of stages and autobiography of forms. We pack our punches in small units, guys, and repeat them, repeat the hell out of them, so that in the long run the increments of a global argument can disengage themselves from the present text. So you already know, of course, that this *Myosotis* thing, which is facing you straight in the eye, is some kind of move ahead from reference, to a new place where the poem has started to become not about something but something. And even in our coyness we have probably let fall the concern, at this point, that on the far side even of this self-referential condition we will be stepping off into a wild ocean— we speak of *Serenity*.

***

Myosotis: Ninety Canzonettas (2013; gestating for 20 years, in many forms)

i

Yes mouse ear plant
Forget me not etcetera
Blatant underperformer
In the Regency of glass houses

We wander in the shadow
Of your hard petroleum forest
Longing like brickbats
Green tufts on our shoulders…

That was Bill Murray I believe
In Iris Murdoch's garden

Oh how we pissed away the coordinates
On the far corner

ii

He collates his memories.
There is a flow chart in his heel
And he takes to the wind.
Oh mercurial sagesse!

A pint and a half of him before
Matins will drain you.
The sands will grow mawkish
Taming his prayers with scent.

He will go tap tap like a bucket
Outside your bready window.
I dare say a fire would twist him.
I don't doubt the denizens

But they too are likely.
You see it is harmattan
West of us, and we hunker.
Our flaws eat, our chinny flaws.

iii

He tires of verbiage and determines.
Ending sentences, halting.
Nothing in excess of the phrase.
He is a dormer Grammaticus.

In a deep divide
Among his thick breasts
Rumbles a chthonian.
It is Rhea farting.

How she does it doped by planets
Is enough to straighten a dog.
Wall Street trembles nightly
At the deep drum of the Kuretes.

There is a Dorian thrombosis
Lo in the nails!
He shudders rising from the mat.
He tables a horsefly.

Dusty, he calls to it.
A fly is glodge.
There's a lot of it too.
Blake says o simple fly.

He reaches for his genital
And turns, drying.
There are frenesies unspoken
Where the caudal stays.

I see him head for Hong Kong.
His ticket was mistaken.
When he got there he had an arithmetic
To handle by himself.

iv

Why did my teacher, Lachesis,
Warp at my glance, strygil
Ducklings shyly?
I never knew her to say

More than just the needed.
O Peter's pence, extend,
It is mercy, there is a caravan
By the banks of the Charles;

Yes we do smoulder.
We smoulder often and richly.
O flower of richness and forgetting
Hear me drink. I spend.

v

I spend Peter's pence as though
It were mine. My dickey is overdetermined.

I know I have charms, further them little.
They're simply pieces.

I'd hold your hand in the subway, though.
It irks me to say that.
I've a Chinese friend who would not be able.
He would say it is doctrine and point.

I think I understand that view.
I have columns of ancient bone
And they twist. They are stained.
They bear the ashes to ashes.

Come quietly to deliver me
Before the ashes are cold.
I will stand by your side in the winter.
I will tie your tie, twice.

vi

Oh the fervor.
The dreadnaught fervor.
It dictates so many actions.
It gives us paths to swallow.

It gives a plentitude of lunches,
Darkens the silverware with a patina.
We always wish we could be there to charm it.
Is there after all no recourse?

The universe was twice this size
When we began and were young.
Our legs used to touch the floor.
Now we wean our nails

On air-pumped Muslim myrrh.
The imam says go to it
And we wrench in our dainties.
Five times daily we eat stray,

Leaving what tumbles.

Faith is never without its bauble.
Didn't you hear that the Siamese
Father eagles? Like shameless.

vii

There is surely a battered car or two
Near the precinct. Aid it to fly!
Guaranteed landings in San Antonio!
How he stormed the Menger!

From the Church on Mount Tabor.
O scenes of glory, scenes of insolence.
I wonder at your very glory,
Child brides in Iowa, your shine,

The mollusc of paste they apply
To your breastbones. O what fyre!
O what craters banality drives
Under the suburban duplex

Hollowing out the land, a *stupor mundi*.
There turns out more to lose
Than even we imagined, fiery things,
Lace drawn tight over cream of wheat.

O sabotage applied to the dryness.
That would be the pencil mark
Drawn carefully across the preschool primer.
How carefully they hid the retreating children!

viii

Oh no, the next morning!
Always the next morning is fierier.
I sent a robin but he came back with a Pope
Framing doctrine in the withes.

That for sure gave us a belief.
We had from then on a query.
Ain't this the age of queries, deary?

He came down on Stromboli,

Though before breakfast the tourists had done.
One said Easter Island another Norfolk
Until the last of them took Stanley Diamond's
Suggestion and tripped diamond communities.

At the Oscars, though, it was entirely different.
On the red carpet I wove a trajectory
Of miniature overarching tumuli
The celebs followed in jeans, their eyes

Smoking cobalt from the mascara.
The Sultan of Morocco was
Absolutely honored, no gas plants here,
Ansari whajacallit lost his gate pass

In the Andes. Breathing tubes wouldn't cut it.
A foreigner was noticed even before the bar opened
And was eased out. You can tell from the dialect.
There they button their shirts on the left.

ix

A rancid sangoma.
That's the rot of the old dispensations.
Cures can be bottled,
Bark hollowed out into pain's ear.

Tanzania has it forthcoming.
That's where the cheese goes soaring.
The file of medicine men
Walks in and out of the rubber houses.

Have you not, he asked,
A place to put your wounded?
Is there no place sufficiently genial,
And thus appropriate for the ladies?

Seems there was not, for the wounded
Massed at the gates of the Celestials.

They displayed the brick ends of legs
And shoulders filed down.

A body-part smelting plant
Devoured the children as they came to pray.
A March novena was unfolded
Yet it had nowhere to go.

And it was there that we circled around.
We knew how to end-stop.
We knew about legislation.
Our jackboots caught in the feathers.

x

Darling the sea of faith
Is the site of an ambitious new construction.
The foundations are under the water.
They are part of the subaqeous civilization

That continues to pump blood into the whale
And ease it out. No wonder we believe, in spurts
From spouts, and not continuously like oil.
We have so much to be sure of

Yet what little we're not costs rhythm.
We crash against our own sides
Like the Bering Strait, and chunk up
In anticlines of sea ice.

So that being because you think
Is more like stepping into the garden
Then shrinking back at the boa.
We are an ontology, a plain.

xi

There's plenty of insecurity to go around.
There's the dog's insecurity too,
Trampled between paw hairs.
There's the rabbit's unsure nest,

Threatened by beavers.
There's this pinch of salt in my underdrawers
And I try to leg it out but in vain.
Those are all trials of being-in-time.

None of which is to mention the dog-legged
Golfcourse down the road from the sewage plant.
That is sure a nightmare to play.
You come around a bend and you're six

Ironing fecal. The blue Scottish sky
Is flaming in the background
And your hush puppies are squashy as
Fukushima. Their nares are purple.

xii

I don't care if you like me, doc,
But I do like the respect due a carpet mouse.
I muster my whiskers in the outer office.
I go up and down with the market

Like a bulldozer in the sandbox.
I don't care if you like me, doc,
But I think you've got to respect me
For what I've done for the county.

It was there that my beard was tangled
And my teeth came loose. I fought.
I brought a referendum on chocolate
And so I lost, but with honor.

And was whisked away before ...o.
Shit you're not listening, you think this
Poetry's crap on a toadstool, and perhaps
You're right there, for the rhymes are limp

As a...o shit there I go again and the flat
Iron topping on the old Marshall Building's
Vibrating like a massage parlor.
Shoulda kept my mouth shut for

To tell you the truth I'll be dreaming.
Oh-oh old song, my teeth will be clacking.
I've a right arm to support you,
And a pinky for your…ohhhhhh.

xiii

It's a slippery Thursday.
You promised you'd call me
But I haven't heard; oh wait that's my arm
It rings now when I'm sleeping.

I'm told the body can turn to gleaming silver
As did Pythagoras, his thigh of gold,
And the wind can blow through the duodenum.
There's not much to say about loss

When you've been granted the kingdom,
Except perhaps that your slippers pinch.
I was brought up on shoes myself,
Never got the dressing gown hang.

Lovelies at the door, I'd offer em
Bertola, read to them from Kant's
Program for Universal Peace, and stroke,
Ah yes stroke, as though the girl's fur's

Nap ran counter. We ran counter.
We did dextrose. We did glucose.
Oh Fridays after prayers, such rain…
Such a dirigible of MacLeish…

I too sang at Bristol, took rain
Deftly off Piaf's under-score hash-tag…
Ah the wound the acronym…
When a child runs through the garden.

xiv

I'm a deft one with the deaf,
Sitting on hammer dulcimers tied to planets.
Pythagoras was winsome.
Croton hummed like a summer resort.

Down to the shore the young Pythagoreans…
It is far cry to a molar…
Once wedged hard to loosen, dry
Comedies playing across the gum.

He salutes his winsome host,
His fingers tall, bulldogs of dermis.
He has no plane to take him,
Travels stately. Oh tamp him!

He is sure to curl like a mimosa.
Friends he has in the bushes.
A dog was there before it left.
Like Epicurus he tastes death on a mouth

And rinses away the whole face.
That is shocking and bizarre.
Just the possibility of winning,
And the casino was eaten alive with capers.

xv

He knows he is in a wounded saloon.
Nothing will disengage him now.
Quiet he rests, his pillows tuft away…
The boll they remember, how sweet.

Oh lozenge, the glottis, the term
Wounded by the roadside at Gloucester.
He dried it. That mistake grammar makes.
That challenge to infinite wounding.

He withdraws it all the way.
His back is by now a habit.

Nothing is fresh except…that too
He silences. A cheese native to Ecuador

Wouldn't you know he ate it?
He had a muffin for tiffin.
He had an out-of-death experience.
Did he tell you he was courtly?

He never told me nothing.
He was a rogue word.
I tried to silence him with a *hapax*
Didn't know there *was* an end run

Around Gloucestershire or Manx,
Didn't know it if there was.
That was *my* trip you see,
My trip against him, and it went

Like well er then suddenly cliffed,
Notched itself down into the glottis
And remained between the teeth
Of a Neanderthal.

xvi

How I do trust the limbic!
Hard passages from here to our wonder!
Or ourselves as glyphs meeting at cave mouth?
Triage, that's what it is.

I want to be separated
From the toilet paper and the ringworm
And everything between that rings.
But it is all in my face.

I'm a rogue word too, ready
To be pasted anywhere.
See that video snapshot there in the corner?
You can take it to any drugstore.

You can enroll it under any referent.

There will be a place in it
Where paste generates. Touch it.
Sticky, ain't it? Little devil longs to be pasted.

Well, you won't make a world
Out of the past participle but it has a head on it.
Hard-on's only another way to say genitive absolute.
The old teacher settles with his dipstick,

Crosses his legs, and in panic,
Shortly before his children arrive,
Dashes to the trickshop to change.
When he returns he's nothing but a smile.

xvii

You could pull him apart.
You could redirect by a tap on the ulna,
N he'd comply. He's a ready one down deep.
His pants would fit two of you.

Then again, you know, there's the famed
King's English, and he'd none of it.
At Balliol he just ruined tea with a gerund.
That was not holistic.

Used to be an Anglophile.
He loves green clipped grass
And the kind of meat and potatoes
But exquisite logic of such as Ayer,

Or for that matter of Carnap,
Who brought one stingy view of the world.
Course no Catholic would settle for long
With excluding the graces

And for that he sent a son to Ampleforth.
The heavens know no glory like a school boy
In a tuxedo, or the lost world of the heart.
What else took him from Cambridge to Groton

A la recherché de l'immortalité?
At nineses he would sit dining
And display the three of hearts.
He was surely a Bonny Prince Charlie

And had a wound to wipe it with at Culloden.
All that seems provincial when you travel the world
And nothing is provincial except your nail,
And even it is chert and chert is universal.

xviii

You see it's hard to disavow your point of connection.
You can track Modernism only so far
Until it abuts the training wheels of the Classical.
O *myosotis* you dogeared softness

You centrifuge of the power of the architrave,
Turning turning back to you
In no man's debt. I will rave of you.
I will press your case in the Keys,

As though Cuba were within touch.
It is not. Nothing is in touch as long as a poem.
The trailblazed poem can be cut back to size
So fast it is simplistic.

Come now, no hurt feelings.
We simply say what we can.
We read between the lines and we read the lines.
We are literal but we are figurative.

A seal might be a whiskered snout
Or a bond between us. We maneuver
Among these possibilities like zhorns
Or you name it, some word you like

That up to now no thing has claimed.
God knows things are hungry
And an alphabet can only go so far.
Dry mouth was an expression I'd never used

Til last week when I called my dentist.
Who knows what else is out there
Just about to be named.
I think God put special emphasis

On naming because he was half afraid
We'd run out, and *lag tongue.*
He was afraid we'd just say *lag tongue*
Without giving it a chance to mean.

xix

There was a space between the lag tongue
And the things the event wanted to have
Happen to those sounds and we couldn't cross
It just then.

You knew the stupor.
You didn't have to be told.
Everything was right where you had left it
When the sound became more than you could bear.

I would have done what you did,
Fiddled with the dishes,
Made my bed,
Eaten a diet yogurt and lain down in my bed.

That would have been a portal to dreams.
I have come to trust that other place;
And to think it is where I want to be.
I want to be there in dreams

Ready to meet you whatever you are
And to be part of your life
As though between us there could be no division.
I wanted to remove that partition

I had never meant to build
But had become part of the way I walk through
The daylight. I wanted to take it down.
There I knew you would be waiting.

xx

You would find many ways to remind
Me of my head and eyes and face
And the unexpected transitions of planes
That make up a body out of gas and foil.

I don't know whether you knew that I was coming
For it was news to me and my pillow.
The yellow blanket slid down around my ankles.
The chain around my neck tarnished and rode me.

I had several skeletons back there
On that other side where you were
And you held me. I was nowhere near,
I was so near, there were so many parts,

There was so much freedom but it tended,
It had to tend like Lucretius' swerve.
I dressed for it at the partition but took.
I took. That was a rubbing feeling.

That was a charming feeling too
And when it was over I was like the partition,
A separator myself because I had joined.
It was my first team play; I'm an individualist.

xxi

But it did me such good I took.
You were with me at Applebees,
It was well before noon. That I took.
All this I take now, this separation.

All this preparation and partition I take.
I take the border between North Korea and South
To me. I take them. They are nothing, but
It rubs against, it brushes against.

It's like one of my favorite poems it's just called
Against, it's easy to write easy to read.

You just lean against. You just take.
You are in that other portal and you go.

You allow all the firmness.
You are as firmly there as you will be
Your traitor. You leaned at the wall.
Oh how firmly there, traitor, and I took,

I took against the wall the breach.
I took terriers and hounds over the partition
And had no mind to stop.
That was one of the last days

I have seen a partition and I stopped.
Did you take from the well?
Had you nothing more to give when the currency changed?
It would have been a mistake for the rate is flat.

xxii*

She was certainly not the first one I saw
To come bursting off the tennis court
With a steel. And she brandished.
Far as we could get in the bourgeois hymnal

We found little to convert us.
We found a tripod covered with the dust of time.
We saw notes by a Rabbi
Scribbled in a Tuareg encampment.

When darkness fell we were appropriately bewildered
And scquitched up our aprons and ran to our mothers.
The soft flame of taxonomy curdled around our hairpins. That was the day
of the transposition,

Truant lights. A soft broth fell on the Israelites.
We ate a tea made of strangers and walked.
Sometimes each sentence ended. It just ended.
There was a time when every sentence ended

* Compare this passage with *Some Dranster Poems* and *The Sentence*, pp. 98–100

And every paragraph started up and then turned around.
There was a time when the very thought of time
Wounded germane fellows. That sentence ended.
That sentence went backward and was left crawling.

xxiii

We had to pick it up, three strong men.
It was a sentence longer and darker than.
It seemed to. It sounded as though.
Then when the sentence ended it was as though

Falling. I strained at it, believe me.
I turned it in my strong arms and held it.
I made a woven cradle where the sentence
Could lie at night, but still it went on weeping.

The sentence went on slowly...o was it a side
Of the old mutton? We broke down the sentence.
We rode up and down on the sentence.
We made a thing. But it was a thing, not a sentence.

xxiv

Myosotis is a word.
It is the only word written like a flower.
It is relevant. It is topical. It ends with purpose
And begins with the color of the queen's left breast.

Is it an authorization to leave the track entirely?
There is no way a flower can be a word.
A word flies in air, a flower goes to its roots.
There are rules governing flowers.

First, they cannot talk or make sentences.
Flowers are like infants.
They try their wings.
Can a flower urinate?

There is evidence that words can go places
In the ear that have not been explored.

Those places are like the seas under the Antarctic
Ice Sheet, silent since the beginning of time.

Reportedly you can hear a lone sound under the ice.
It is the word that is trying to be spoken
And the place that is trying to hear it.
It is neither quiet nor raucous there.

Myosotis is the sound the ice is trying out.
It is a mouse eared sound, gentle in the ice.
It is a tender sound though you wouldn't know it
For the bearded geeks that penetrate the ice

Sheet as though their drills were all the intimacy
Life decided to afford them.
That is the myosotis tendency
Myosotis is like a wall you go to.

xxv

I never knew myosotis.
They said she was beautiful,
She was like a temple in the old time,
That you would go from side to side.

You worship here or there
And touch her brow. She yielded.
She adopted your prayers in silence.
She followed you from road to road.

She was trim as a pronomial phrase.
Each part of her was a part of speech.
She ran out at either end into exclamations.
It was a silent obscure tussle of grammars.

I didn't know she cared for me.
She didn't know I didn't know.
We kept passing like robust loads of commodities.
One was traded, another invested.

Myosotis was the wide front that barreled.

I always knew about her knee.
That was ice you fell on, baby.
There was an elision, and a nail carved off a tree.

xxvi

Did nothing reassure you this morning?
Did the morn not salve?
Were there no flirts at all?
Had you not a nail to drive, and a bark?

It's not easy to go slow.
Take a tiger by the tail, for instance,
And shake him til he's powder
And he still won't go slow,

He'll run around in circles.
He has a fresh load of gravel in his maul.
That's where he trips up, of course,
Because the gravel is an anchor weight

And holds him to the ground.
He was planning some large construction
Down by the waterfront
But was deterred by masons

Wanting their regular subsidy.
I will never catch up with that tiger.
He's threefold in speed.
A dirigible passed over him

But he outran it, making for the headland.
I know he was supposed to be there
But I couldn't find him today
When I went down to the deck.

xxvii

Did he take one of those traders to Gabon?
I hear one subsided.
If he was on it it will have been an enormous thrashing.

He has enough strength in his ears!

The terror of all this though
Is that the Hellenic masons
Build well and built lastingly.
He leaves them no room to elude him.

You and your elf are dealing in darkness.
Take a look at this road map.
It may indeed get you there.
It may hurt your finger or soul.

It wasn't that we had to be so deft.
There were thrones before us.
We had only to step into shoes already laced.
That's a trick you know, with the ankle bone.

We had to imagine buildings
From the outside in, as margins.
We were what the buildings forgot to include,
Always outside when it was inside.

There was a fragmentation bomb
For every space in the yard.
Our children fed on those spaces.
Each knew a corner.

Trying to stay within the lines.
What is outside is always taking me over.
Can I try to manoever my way?
Can I find a forest to protect me?

xxviii

I did see him raise a shovel
To decapitate a bat.
That was a big to do
And the neighborhood flocked to watch.

Except for that they were silent, too silent,
And didn't talk for days.

There was a hot bottle of provisions
But they were parsimonious.

Now as I look back I can see that he
Fractured a toenail against the side of her finger.
That sure was a hard one
To clean up with the dishes.

Yet it had its way of going around to the side
And being there when we were least expecting.
We all knew it would end, but how?
Not a soul supposed that it would be the dishcloth

That took the brunt of the action
And salted her away.
The chief of police said it was simply a freebie.
And that, he said, overweighed inculpation.

xxix

That was Bill Murray, yes,
In Iris Murdoch's garden by the whale.
How did a whale get into Kensington?
Probably on the tube like us,

Probably wondering why this lady
Curled up over her cigs and Johnny Walker
Was waiting to place her archives.
Why was I silent as a dog those days

As though doubting that the world would end?
I snuffed along with the whale
Did the diddley doo in Hammersmith,
Went over Highgate.

xxx

Okay a duck, we are ducks, we are ducks out of water,
We are sitting ducks, we are firestorm ducks.
Truly I say unto...the train screams into Pisticci...
The road bed starts to unravel.

Scared entrepreneurs emerge from lakeside shops
And speak of Abu Sayyed.
I'm sure glad I stayed at home and dreamed all this.
That's the only way to get by

And for all I know it's also the way down and out
Into the submarine cloisters you drink from.
The one-author-favorite I've become,
Adrian Stokes wrote what inside outside I have.

xxxi

I don't like abortion or wheels.
I like what staggers from place to place.
Whales prefer to doctor me for that.
They know I've a program, and time

Run through with tastebuds,
Rips one dinner after another from the plate.
They knew I wanted to say this
And that I was incomplete without saying this.

I am incomplete unless I say
That an abortion takes away death which is natural.
Even the hibiscus blossom knows what death
Hardly knows, for already it is in the kingdom.

The kingdom of death knows how to adopt
A riderly stance and up in the stirrups.
An instant of target practice might seem enough
But it is less than it says on the package.

The package instructions are perfectly clear.
They leave nothing at all to the imagination.
You put this piece here that piece wander and ten
And sift this over now and it is o sentiment you fine

Tune governing bodies. There is surely a track
Coming up out of my head today.
I know it was not the master sergeant.
A ten-piece band wouldn't have heard him.

xxxii

Speaking of that and the new,
The anthropology of the rubber whistle,
Were you there when they lifted?
O harsh pickings those lots, those shards

Amphorae left in Brundisium.
A foal is there. A foal that tries.
A foal that folds up into a frame,
That reckons it is smaller than.

I know that kind of claim from Giants
And I abjure. I stand back against the rail.
Oh sentient, I trail you, you rode,
You went smiling and crossed.

xxxiii

It was only the Yankees.
Didn't I tell you, doc, their teeth were clumsy.
Something anal said test this shoe, Doc,
For within it festers a stool;

You were really careful to review that language.
You had no doubt at all.
A dream suite packaged us wholly.
Oh it was steep in the country that winter!

It was Horace's *rus in urbe*
Just where we didn't expect it,
Under the bed with the slippers and old
Dust balls and the cream from last night's

Caravan of masculine pigeons.
It was a season when there was
Not much to say for the Dodgers
And the stems on the *arbor vitae*

Were trembling like oaks at Dodona
To get interviewed by Johnny Carson.

If indeed you didn't cast your penny
You were likely to sit there stolen

From yourself by dreadful treks.
The garment factory needed workers
What was Dhaka but Urbana
Illinois upside down and you went.

xxxiv

Seven hard years you sewed hems
On sweatshirts. Did you not cry
Once for your homeland and the sweet?
Well for Horace apparently it was boys of fourteen!

The exquisite scholar squirms at the edition.
Myosotis, he said,
Fingering Liddell and annotating the feather.
There is dross at Didyma, the oaks,

What the fathers in the meadow!
He came down that morning with a trance
And flew from gosling to gosling.
One little chirper fixed on my window

And blew reeds from Smyrna.
That was Ibycus, darling, choosing a sweet spot
By my window to announce the meltemi.
Costco is worth a dram in any country

And there's a price war on bananas.
I'll tell you darling. Your *thiasos* is ready.
Drop by on your way home from work.
Well there will be a trend there you know.

xxxv

In the morning darkness swallows the rain.
Fellow humans swell from their houses.
There are brain scans at the corner grocery
And a dominant third comes out on top.

Darling did you see the turbo prop?
Didn't it whir?
Did Ben Drummond not descend
In a pokey mercury of technology?

Were the very gods of northern Syria
Not present at once for the christening?
The Patriarch drew his robe
Tightly around his knuckle and prayed

Our wonderful father and stepfather
And mad dog stepmother
Be aware of us here in our cleavage.
Let no part of the body drift.

xxxvi

Backward from the central axis,
The tax spine they call it,
Stretches from Carthage to Milan.
I know I am unwilling to spill secrets

But if you only knew what a suicide
Belt feels like from inside.
I sewed them with fiberglass threads
So they came off into the knuckles

Of Sergeant Major Victorian
Who was fully established to protect
The rear guard and the Hussars.
We knew there was threat of attack.

Committing suicide with the Tervinghi,
Well that was one way to feather.
Then of course there was Miami-Dade
And over those dog races

Many an unauthorized shekel was ventured.
Pre-monetization of course was vastly
Simpler with the long Aegean coastline
And, frankly, a trickle of barter.

For a comb, say, you could trade an ash twig,
And for that, metaphor holding,
You could go in silence under the barges.
The new thread diamond wore a closet.

xxxvii

Oh chickens your roosting
Playmates forgotten in the sun by the bay.
May we come in to our anteroom,
Play with your doctrines, and stride?

You know we know the hammerhead's name,
And the cost he charges for a whiskey.
Come dray horse and prosecute us
Leading us over hill and dale to town.

A knife in the summertime
Will alert a community but under
The moon, the sixpence, the knife
Will shudder like magnesium and shatter.

Who wants a knife in his back?
I'd rather have a tenpin
And take it out to dinner.
We could regale ourselves

With sumptuous orations,
Bossuet leading us in a view of the universal.
Lest I shift a hair,
Lest I scramble to defend...

xxxviii

The angelic choirs sport lice,
Infinitely tender babies of filth,
And aspire in their throats.
Going down the road to Orogun

You will notice packing boxes,
The Chinese position on Angola,

Trapping it in my waistcoat
Where it belongs with commerce.

You will be ready and more to admit.
I swear you will find your junior
And be delighted by *dignitas*.
Nothing makes the beard grow straighter.

A feathery obsolescence
Will do a world of good to the tumbleweed.
They for one sure do know how to cook.
They know how to render the low-fat butters

That come in from the Persian mainland.
They are dignified trackers.
Oh yes I keep saying *they*
And didn't *they* say this themselves

They do this they do that
But isn't that simply a way of
Protecting myself from every other pronoun
Like the I of the needle the camel etcetera?

I really prefer grammars like Swahili
That are based on things
As though you could replace not only the pronoun
But the noun itself.

xxxix

That's an exultant oasis, a place
Set aside for Gunderson and Smithson
And Runderson and then for a little dust grain.
I spotted it this morning.

It was on a table.
The Physics Department came out to see it
And stayed for breakfast.
By then they had encased the dust speck

In a transparent pipette

And held it up like a monstrance
To be inspected as perhaps their version
Of ashes to ashes.

No doubt we went away sobered
And unsure of the power of prayer.
Unceasing rogation, as Paul said,
Was indeed one way to catch attention

What with the ominous periphery of
Vatican-monitored prayer, home—
Schooling mantras, and low-keyed hails.
We ended our thinking without sentence,

Sentencing ourselves to three more centuries
Of indifferent labor in the cotton.
Chained gangs of proteins, nucleotides,
Just plain weather in the plains,

It all found a way to get absorbed.
Dress rehearsal found a way.
In between the stitches on the cothurnus
He had tucked bygolly a roll of tens

And when the quaestor came by to check,
Lo and behold he palmed him the green
And got the show on the road.
It was Edward Dirksen I believe

Who'd been the first to open the theater
And who was there rhomboid and fierce,
Clapping with his hairpins.
This is an age when you sure don't know

When your goldfish may become a diva
And the sergeant-at-arms wear that little black dress.
Do I mean that nothing is holy?
Something like that in the finest print.

xl

We're not the first though
To know of the prediction and to eat
Several times a day in case it's our last.
Okay lettuce is not that filling

But when you cram it into the corners
And fix it in the hollows of your teeth
You know yourself better than you ought to.
Yes o feather.

Darmstadt did us in, droll.
We thought it was as in the Postcard
With silt thick coffee in little tuna fish displays.
A dram of Old Forester!

The servant girl brought us a plenty.
She brought us a nope and a yup
And an up your pup and then lay
Dormant as the bryophyllum

On the Sangamon river bed.
It was eros and sedge then
And a whole lot of both,
And to take them in a furry hand,

To ordinate them according to Linnaeus,
That was more than the topsoil ordered.
We were led back to ground zero.
We let things name themselves

For a while, then burped.
When we finished burping the world was
One hundred percent name,
Name here name there, you wanted to talk

But before you could say it
You'd been spoken.
That was sure a hard way to proceed through the bracken.
Did you milden, old fellow?

xlii

The preceptor went to toilet
Down the spine of Isidore of Seville.
It took years to dry out
The driest encyclopedia of the age.

Aristotle of course was as always
Courteous, symmetrical, idiosyncratic.
We started with the *Categories,*
Came out parsing bedbugs.

Monetization they say
Rocked the fourteenth century
With quantity. Everything got measured.
You measured your distance from God.

You measured the difference
Between grace and vilification
As in modern ethics.
How far am I compelled to travel

To assist my cancerous mother-in-law
When every mile of the trip
Causes drought and suffering to my dog?
It was all this or that in balance.

xliii

After the shooting wars we settled
Routinized, into a pond full of geese.
There was a traffic goose
And an urgent cardinal goose,

And three little gooses that ran like acolytes.
Did you goose a goose, General,
At the time of the Battle of the Seychelles?
Did you fire a shot across a bow?

Were there not rhythmic patterns
You were advised to follow?

Come there is a way to see
The Coliseum from the dome of the

Ara pacis. You need to crane.
You'll see a slave.
You'll see an Argive.
You'll go pitta-patta in Belize

Which is still hardly more than a street.
Sure there's a result.
It's totted up over there under the dart board.
It won't hold your skiff.

You'll simply have to take off
From farther up landing
Where the macropedia is being constructed.
That'll be a bit of a journey.

xliv

What, though, is worth more than a journey
To caring, and inside it the remains of the beloved?
We prize these entrails, boss!
We'll arrange for the photoshoot.

This too is an age of the macabre
When the scrolls of decomposition
Are exquisitely painted.
We saw that once too often at Nara.

xlv

Notable among the notables
He leaps to his pussy cat and salutes.
The sergeant major continues playing tic-tac-toe.
I'll tell you it's hard in the army

If you let it be
But if you insist on a video
Of locker room number 65 it's gonna take time
And people'll talk.

Course they'll shut their mouths
When you deliver the goods,
An evening in the mess hall.
There'll be cane breaking for sure

And a rest stop for the anal.
There'll be a choosy team, for sure,
And dry mouth all around—
May I recommend Biotene?—

And a system of micro-organization
Will spray up over the mess hall walls.
When the Chinese arrive
They'll find us diddling and doddling

And playing with our Pac-Mans.
There's inevitably a period of mourning.
Haile Selassie went through it too,
Early in the morning.

xlvi

He'd gotten up fresh to bake,
Some flat bread recipes are too good to share,
And he'd gone down to the stream.
The Lion of Judah had washed himself,

Taken a cholesterol reading,
And was suddenly taken by the vanity.
It was *Ecclesiastes* all over again.
The grass turned brown.

The pride of juvenescence
And the puppy fur of absolute innocence
Trickled away like mustard and cloves.
That was the time when the author of this poem

Who is otherwise unidentified
Reaped benefits from a fortuitous investment
And took off a year
For yachting in the Sea of Cortez.

xlvii

And it was not quite seven
When he arrived for tiffin.
A muffin and a roach, sir?
He lay back and purred.

One for the road was a good thought in itself,
But when you blended it!
Oh he shook a snake at his fist.
He didn't for a minute believe

What they said about the flooding in Delta.
Every word of it was true!
Snakes writhing in the classrooms!
The Ovie's wife taken prisoner.

Well, every now and then he said,
Zipping his fingernail into the coffee,
The world will not be ever the same.
There is always, believe me,

Quite a lot of time for chess.
Grimsey's got the climate
Not to mention the clientele
For a mid-winter Ruy Lopez

That'll dry out your bald spot.
So saying he called his travel agent.
Do you remember the ash storms from Hekla?
Well he ran into those.

He sure did just run into one storm after…
Damn, there he goes recountin' again.
D'bore the teeth off a mole.
He steps back, apologizes.

xlviii

His ring finger's burnin' him.
Sure liked that little black dress.

Aw come on you chicken,
There ain't no room for a blast from the past.

He shuffles back in dudgeon.
They sure don't care for him.
They just left me here in the corner
With a toadstool in my pants.

I'll get my driver and my nine iron.
I'll sure as hell show 'em.
He steps back like Frederick Douglass
As though to debate.

But just then the sirens,
Firing like jets,
Propel him up over the reservoir
From where he can see Bulgaria.

His fall is unbroken.
There's a stage in descent
Where time sucks its own finger.
He drifts there like a whore

Between grass blades.
There comes a view of the Neckar,
But is the Neckartor still there?
And do they still serve coffee?

xlix

He knew he would never make it.
The worm-eaten mountain was too far.
The red streaks of sky were melting.
His right leg hurt.

In his bones there was a tremulo
Of downright. Of gosh he smelled.
This he decided is the hero of our time
As Lermontov depicted him.

But where better for heroism

After all, than in the corner
Where the dogs lie skinning their lips?
Where better to live and learn?

Oh dopey, he says to himself,
Flaying this dog of a text
Will be surely enough to promote me.
He sees himself with a doctoral cap

Standing beside the President of Oxford
If there is one and eating a gum.
He has a hive in his riding crop.
He is stacked up inside there.

How good, he is thinking,
To be as free as this keyboard
And to welter there.
He streams around the corner of the house

Thinking he will meet himself.
What he finds is his simulacrum.
A bony old mutt
With a cheeseburger in its face.

Well there's always a drive-in
He decides, in historicity,
And in them we meet sunset strips
Cut from the sides of Herefords.

We are manifestly not part of the salvation
Planned during the early days
Of carbon formation,
For out there in cosmic space

We have the whole afternoon to ourselves.
Tea in a black hole is a step toward the origins.
He remembers studying Botany
Twice because he thought if he knew the names of the flowers

He would be able to…he shuts
The lip-locked trap on the front of his face.

He endures a breakfast with the man
Destiny bonded him to.

Oh these little feet!
Oh that charming ear with the wash of blue!
Now he is tired of performing.
He steps back into the canyon.

Did you think Nanga Parbat
Slow cream of syllables over the crest?
I know your dressing gown was showy.
We saw three pimples of generation.

The next moment it was extremely still.
The Bactrian was dissolutely quiet.
Without touching a thing we made our escape
Outward into the wilderness of figs and *waadis*.

I know it is possible to wash clothes in clay
Rubbing them directly on stones.
I know places in Ghana
Where they have not seen cars,

And guys in the States
Who simply laugh at the idea of sympathetic magic.
It's a little world after all
And made of little places

Divided into littler places.
I'm not going to whimper
Because you replaced my organ donor card
But I will tell you this—

These belts from Sears.
They ride right up into the cerebellum
And sneak a nap there.
I'm being silly.

lii

I was up too late last night.

The old Lady caught me cadging a snort
Off the closet in the kitchen
And gosh was she…but fortunately the train

Ran right through the station.
I tried to leap out at Back Bay.
The stationmaster spotted me
And called the Humane society

But just when the last slaves
Had been liberated and the Santa Peculiaria
Had tied up tight at Portsmouth,
We had disturbance on the network.

I had to excuse myself and go tinkle.
The Award for Junior Achievement
Hadn't it already been announced?
Anyhow I got honorable mentions

And someone spoke of a chocolate factory.
I didn't wanna go there.
You know my teeth!
Here, he said, is my first bicuspid.

liii

Sure'n yer welcome, Mam!
Feeling kinna seasick myself.
There's a towel drenched with Givenchy
Over there in the corner

But I don' know how to dress with it.
Had too much to drink sir?
No n' bigorree, Officer,
Naysmith's the name, known for sobriety,

The leader in Strabo studies.
Did you view my edition in the Teubner?
Okay okay you cops don't read,
Maybe a little George Sand

But nothing harder than that.
Well your job's not the reading kind,
Rather the skirt-measuring kind.
There I'll go along with yee.

liv

They belt down the highway like brigands.
I predict a collision.
One of them is going to drive into a wall
Or have a stroke. Care which one?

Humans are interchangeable.
Put one here one there kill one love another;
Back and forth they flow these humans.
It's like blocks in a Cathedral.

Or it's like the blocks inside the blocks.
A tender triplet of lambs comes by.
They are not there to support you.
They are there to distract your ulna.

What else is nuzzling an arm?
A lip turned inside out is not a lamb.
A lamb is more like a bracket.
The bracket in a wall supports a wall clock

And a lamb, if it wishes,
Can certainly surmount the shade.
It's about shading a lamp.
A lamb is all about shading a lamp.

In the shade, under the acacia,
He unwinds skeins of remembrance.
Why don't you fell an acacia?
The acacia would be the first to say

Thanks for letting me out of
The prison house of language where I languish.
With the lamb I languish.
I am in the shade of the olde

Areopagus not far from town.
Wanderers come by.
They mull around.
They are simply mulling in the mall.

He hangs back and decides to defrock his lyre.
It was pinching him under the arms.
I know it won't flow like this forever,
There is too much of an orange custard

At the Piggly Wiggly where I had my first soda.
I loved so much the sense of being alone.
Now however there are juveniles everywhere.
I toddle and tip and wet my oyster

Sandwich just as it comes on market.
There's not much left for Bernanke,
I ate it all, and the Feds knew but didn't act.
They just sat there and tipped like crazy.

A catalyst for all this *dédommagerie*
Was the perky saleslady.
She didn't know my address.
She was confused when I said Persia.

Did I know she was from Basra?
No I didn't, Mam,
I thought you was from Oscaloosa.
Not more than an hour later.

Our plane was scheduled.
They went around maintaining it.
That meant a duck or two.
That meant a tryst in Tanzania.

lvii

Oh forests, intention.
Frege says the logic doubles back
On itself like a python,
Like the phrase *quod semper quod ubique.*

That of course was negotiable.
Tell me about it quietly; I'll fart
Anise candy notoriety.
Was Wilde or de Sade a better batsman?

Either could fur you.
Either could go with you into trench
Obscenity. All you need is a coat.
Hide a rubber goodge under yr coat…

I'll tell you you'll be a snappy one
Buster soapy. Yr pricke could…
In spinach. Dexter you scud me up.
I'm ready to dance at somebody's funeral

When the ducks gather on Barton Pond
Alumni sweat obols. They lay aside
Heart shaped diaper patterns.
Quack-quack go the feather beds.

It is a hard row to plough.
It is a hard plough to row.
It is a rule cut straight through quartz.
It is a nobody zone and there is a tail,

Or is it a trail, through cambium.
Oh geez, fur bearers, we smell.
We smell bad in our fur.
We are totally alone in our fur today.

lviii

Let's see, one, two, buckle
My butternut. I celebrate.
Truly I celebrate Golden Pond
And the easy late days of summer.

I follow California girls wherever they go.
They can't go too far from me!
I'll quack-quack up their quack-quacks!
Volatile old fellow, ain't he?

He'll disrobe if you ask him in full plenitude.
He'll take off his socks and put them in the garbage.
He's got a tendency, that's for sure.
He'll bottle up and fly right!

Frisk him if you can, this frisky lamb.
Remember a lamb's for a lampshade.
A lampshade's to control the light
That filters under the dresser.

The dresser sits in the corner of the room.
The corner of the room is getting dressed.
Oh come on, that's nonsense, Norma Jean.
That's pie talk in the country.

lix

He turns away discouraged
By this discouraging report.
He upside downs his little old.
No he don't, he spikes.

See that there nard?
That was cumin, in rolls.
That was flopsy dopsy man,
And an invite to ruckety truckety.

He knows his pants are on wrong.
He put on the belt first and then the pants.
Was there no drool from the cat?
Did a weirdo not squeeze in

N' drive away all the good spirits?
At the Place Macacre he saw for sure a witch!
Her hair was drunk with serpents.
Her toenails were painted by Cardin.

So he approached her in the best of spirits.
Nothing though seemed to make a difference
To the cat's paw circles that had collected
Under her right eye.

lx

Look she extricated her glove from a fence!
Was that her hand or mine I saw raving?
I guess it was probably hers
For mine is so seldom in use in the morning.

Anyhow I drifted past her.
Beatrice, remember, had a fingernail too,
And it caught in the flesh of history.
Come on darling wipe it off,

For a pandemic is coming and it is large.
It will rise up in your pretty toes
And take your legs to the conservatorium.
I wish I could say this was just language.

It would make my uncle feel better.
He has the dominant gene in our cholesterol.
We simply adore the way he walks.
But tell me is he not one of the simples,

Addicted to fireflies and worm bellies?
He certainly knows where the cheese is kept.
So saying he escorted her away into the night.
That was not the last time he saw her though.

lxi

Do you remember the Boardwalk at Frontenac?
That was the max in taking it easy.
I used to doll up and troll.
I used to befriend whelks and sea chicks.

Any gum you chewed brought them running.
Little ones, big ones, they got you by the tail
N'belled you like the other cats.
Oh sweet animal drumsticks,

Our turn will be yours.
Go back to Trenton with a load of carpals

And be careful about the abs.
Oh cheese of the government,

Reek and be polished,
And give us this day...*he surbs*
He floges, he rhodsa, he strigg...
And then he is as near as a cheken.

lxii

I swear it's not so easy today.
People riding bikes on the main street.
Bundles of old cheeses
Left to evaporate on window sills

While matrons shack with grocery boys.
Feathers from ducks ending up in your soup.
It's not as it was in my father's day
When a wart on your nose was taken seriously

Perhaps removed by laser,
N' people lived a whole lot longer.
Who doesn't remember?
Why in summer I used to study Taloass

While sitting in the yard
And nobody paid no attention.
I said it's the notion of a wandering priest
And hardly to be wondered at.

Nowadays it's this kid here and that kid there
And a hullabaloo about kids and their dormers.
The skin seems to come off of just every word.
Oh troll, be gentle at the pass!

lxiii

The young milk troll comes sidling up.
She has a pepper nose and deet.
Lightning bugs shun her.
Oh but she has a smart pace when her fingernails.

You might not have thought.
George Wentworth wrote of her in his memoir,
The Adjacent Country and the Adventists,
And came close to saying she…

There was an old dray stall.
People used to take pictures of it.
They'd wander up and snap it like a sword.
Sure cut those babies down.

You know anything can happen in the country.
The country's where everything happens
Including the weather from North Dakota.
The weather happens very hard in the country.

lxiv

Oh dork and drive by
We wonder at your fastidious eating habits.
When I studied the Gortyn Law Code
It was a chosen talk, mellow man.

My bad, my spin, I rose up over.
There was seldom a chestnut in my path.
I found way easily from mountain…
The chastain blossom is a dog

Dressed like the sweetness of spring.
I simply don't know how to go there.
I do know how to go to the Piggly Wiggly.
But I don't know how to go where the chestnut.

lxv

Fred and his mother went to town to explore.
Hard enough. It was Wednesday noon.
I mean it was Saturday the 12th and jargon.
That would have been the end you know.

In fact though it was not the end but the final
Stage of putting little green bricks in tea.

There was a twist of lemon there.
Afar was as far as we could carry the bridgework.

Say did your dentist? Mine wore a goggle.
He rooted in my face 'til I was pink as a clam.
I drove slowly to his country home.
It was night and there were frogs.

lxvi

In Barnes & Noble I sat by waters.
Lethe ate at my plimsolls and a choir raged.
I sure could taste the pepper on their beans.
I didn't wait to catch up with them though.

Down inside the drains sing the sirens.
A tempest further troubles the waters.
I heartily recommend an extra session of yoga.
Calm nerves and friendly faces charm;

Oh he diddles with his puddles of language.
He is in sixth heaven, chewing and drying out.
He has a far cry inside him like a neonate.
Did you say we are speaking the right language?

If you didn't I'll be glad to help you on with your *chaussures*.
Have you no smaller size, he asks,
Weathering in his gum like an old trashcan.
We are the simple folk and play simple games.

Have you a prescription for simples?
Have you an ardent pimple that will house a dream?
I know acne is recommended for monks.
The trenchant level is the easiest to reach.

lxvii

In a dark cane we will be there to meet you.
In a dark thorn we will be standing to meet you.
Our guylines are wired and tricky.
We have a forest of undone girls, and a rood.

I'll tell you when it's time.
No one knows better than I.
It is surely almost time now
We will be careful to watch the time this week.

You see all this talk about time
Is to illustrate a grammar book
For a language that has never been written
And that will never be imagined.

We don't have time to imagine it.
We are running out of time to say that
We are running out of time.
Yet the new Chevies sell, Ford goes under

And the lemon-colored electric car
Down the street wobbles past the window.
Oh this is no time for deforestation
This is rather a time for plenitude.

lxviii

He takes a cheesecake from the window
And fans it openly with a hot breath.
Dexterous gestures of this sort build.
We know how to snort them straight into the blood.

Oh come on, be careful with licensing.
You get the wrong guy on the road,
You're toast. And marmalade.
But a feather in that spry mixture

Will simply gather up mold.
You don't want more than a little
Of the creature in your sandwich.
Darkness anyhow will be here soon.

Don't you see how that bears on the question of time?
Oh come on now, I won't be wasting your time.
Let's save time in a bottle
And drop it into the Persian Gulf

So that when we are old we can claim it.
You can take a little bit to your ranch.
I'll take the rest down to Toledo
Where I've a rest home waiting.

I know they'll be glad to have time in Toledo
And it's a good place to rest, god bless you.
It's a place where your shoe comes away.
You just know you were there, once.

After Toledo you can always go to the sun.
There's always time for gold in Mexico.
And when it gets dirty
In Patzcuaro you can go further south

To where sombreros are filled with time.
There's time in every sombrero.
This old hayseed will await me there.
He or she will have time for me there.

lxx

It's an awfully grimy patchwork.
You never know where your wheels will take you.
I'll tell you it's fiery hot in downtown Tucson,
And the birds, well, ever seen Byzantium?

There's a trimester every third year,
A whooping colony of ferrets descends on Austin.
Wee little people romp in circles.
Dry wood why do you escape me,

Handily vanishing over the sill of the condominium?
I don't know, snailface,
I don't know nothing.
I don't know the name of your mother

Or of your father's Pomeranian.
I just know I'm here this morning
And the taste of cheese is still on my fingernails.

I know I have a soapy forehead

Made for darlings like you.
I'll lather yee in bean juice!
A night or two later he is seen
Waddling from the creamery.

lxxi

He is surely the hardest nut to crack.
His dirk is florid and saintly.
He simply runs circles around the opposition.
I trust someday there will be a fiery exodus.

Did you not see his aunt?
Did she not bear the significant letter?
Oh, your jaw was always like that?
Come let me bust it in two

Just to see you rake the parts together.
Let's pretend we're friends in the gutter.
You sleep over there I'll sleep over here.
I know we'll find room to despise.

lxxii

Oh chickens, your dad was a dry bed,
Your saintly mother worked all night in the hay.
I am loath to say no to any animal.
But I know that for sure it's time to dry the camel.

If anyone is diseased
Let him step to the back of the room.
He did harm to someone's mother.
I swear we don't put up with such doggerel

Or caterel.
We lay down the law in perfectly good Oscan.
Size it up brother!
Eat it for supper if it gives you pleasure.

I'll say it's late.
Just finished supper and it's time for lunch.
The cat's finished with his dildo.
The dog has read *Justine* twice.

lxxiii

Oh come on now, the world is really burning.
There are tiddlywinks here and cameo soap over there.
There's an acne medicine on sale at Pfizer.
My garters have developed industrial-sized runs

But still I limp along.
Tell me old man did you happen to see a Sphinx
And did he laugh and smile with you?
Was Rupert Brooke by his side?

lxxiv

Sandwiches track the teeth that ate them.
There's sure a deliquescent style in this here snack bar
And an accumulation of dust mites in my toothpaste.
Rub them away fast, sir, lest we all forget to surrender

And go off to Bithynia in chains.
You shouldn't speak lightly of the temperate time zones.
Before you know it will rain on your ulna.
Pepper spray keeps them off, though.

Oh fob, the gunnels need swabbing.
He rolls up a sleeve and pinks.
That stabbed 'em, he mutters.
A trendy little nightclub, and firm.

Not because they deceived him.
Not because they held a candle, snuffed.
Not because suffering came up behind the wax.
But because it was silent, there was a knocking.

The garment district silences came down.
He could see the flame in the pajama.

A finger shot off at an angle.
No trespassing, said the Moor at the corner.

Never mind, they retorted.
It doesn't really matter, they retorted.
It's really alright if you are sure where you are going.
All these things they said and were pretending.

lxxv

Nothing though made any difference.
They might as well have been speaking English
A well-known language popular in the colonies.
That would have cut just as many mashed potatoes.

It is surely Sunday morning.
I am trying to tell you that.
Can't you see that I am trying to tell you that.
My squirrel got caught in a gas main.

Well, last night in Louisville.
And it was not far from Pelagianism.
Okay at Nicaea? There's no stopping death.
No trespassing, death.

Garbage in garbage out
Muttered the aging professor at the tomb.
He uncapped a malt and spilled the ancestor.
Well what's good for the Chinese

May not really work in Tryon.
Course ya never know these days,
So many foreigners and funny tongues.
They exist at the corner of tongue and tongue.

Did you not tell me your German shepherd was wool?
To me he tasted cotton like a little pig
But I know I can be mistaken.
I just simply dropped the ball.

lxxvi

I caught it though when it came up on the other side,
Dripping with parts of speech.
That's when I knew the ballgame had systematically changed
And that the first aorist was playing third.

Anyhow I slid in close
And made it to the top of the Schermerhorn
Where they were constructing a vast palace of windowsills.
It was a delightful afternoon I'll tell you,

The Mariners all over the place to squeal.
A charming oat fell from a bucket around lunchtime,
But we decided not to eat it.
No taking chances when we get a little bit older.

lxxvii

The marbles roll more or less as they wish.
There'll be a blue one over here, a red one there.
There will be pieces of bread under each marble
And the lie of Tennessee will soak up breadsticks.

Oh encourage them, will you Mother?
Will you help them please to find their ways to the drugstore?
Will nothing in you *trend*?
A doll buggy got a trough in its nose

And that was pretty nearly the end of it.
But in a fire truck there arrived a beautiful maiden.
In his pants Mr. Roberts discovered a slit full of cotton
And rode it jimmity-jam-bang.

As usual he was too late.
The furriers had arrived from the Tsar.
Emerald landscapes shimmered on the bay of Tucson.
Oh welcome wizards, prophecy the rope of my name.

lxxviii

Unestablished they put up with this jimmer-jammer.
He hated to be the one who gave away the fort.
A spoilsport will never be the pick of the queen
Though when it farts a good storm does a body...

It was on Washington the burden fell.
Who would have thought of a border made of jackets?
What kind of animal eats lemurs for breakfast?
And so the brain evolved into a chocolate omen.

I am not, he insisted, the one you sought for in Texas.
I am the one they horse-tied and stamped
And mailed to the Tsar in an overheated package.
Take me back to Texas, he said, and put his head on one side.

It's the hot dish summer. You asked for it.
It rode with the risotto up the barrel of your gun
And whew, fired. It fired into the night.
It was as hot as Austin in the old days,

Fifty years ago, the crackling of afternoon beetles
On the walls of the Statesman.
You sure knew yourself old Maccabee,
And strained to put a leash.

lxxix

No puppies were there though to gather.
There's not a chance you were right with the color of your sox.
Billy Sol Estes, you noted at brunch,
Rode up slowly with a stack of well-worn notes.

He had a crawling ant colony on his toes.
His toes were great maggots of...
It was fun being the Virgin Mary,
And wrecking a Cadillac with the spurt of indigestion.

Well, we know that the secret holder
Rode herd on the giants of management.

The little one who saved pennies in jars
Saved an ant. I came home to find it.

I always loved ants.
I love anything that is alone and controlled.
You can come down and sit by me if you won't…
It will be a lot of fun to play.

lxxx

Oh well, the trinket is running down.
There has been enough miscalculation.
Foremost and frontal comes the doctor
Clad in his cotton bib.

I'll tell you we greet him.
We'll take any doctor you send
As long as he is certain.
We are a center that is round,

And a circle that is clean cut and cumulative.
Fall down Mother, I told you I'm praying.
Let me do a little of that here.
I'll put some in the corner.

It was not long before they arrived.
They had put on their faces.
There was a wire between them.
Someone sang a long song in French.

It was easily an hour before they arrived.
Their stomachs were fully eaten away.
They had dark lines on their feet.
I sang a long song in Swiss German,

Enough to break down the borders of the heart.
I had a very hard time breathing that day.
I feel sure it was the smell of the edelweiss.
Our export of horses had been temporarily abandoned.

The long candles in Vevey were sweet as light

And as waxy as the baptized soul.
There were very few places to hide a soul
Besides public transportation.

lxxxi

That could lead you up into Akwa Ibom,
Danger flowers on every toothpick.
There can have been no greater folly than to eat
And to bury the dead in your face.

The little train Thomas rode neatly.
It had nearly made the bend, the soup.
It promised at least to be certain.
Oh how we longed to verify it.

The fact is, however, that nothing supported us.
We were out there on thalidomide
Rinsing our dishes on lemon.
It was a very sad procession.

Ultimately he chose a spot in the sun
And read Albertus Magnus.
That was cute, no?
That brought tsetse flies,

And a sense of the impending firestorm?
You didn't see it coming?
I saw the Vicks on a chest
And a long ad for Cymbalta.

There are so many ways God eyes us.
There are hard boiled eggs and a crust.
Did you chew jimson?
The lane grew narrow toward the end.

lxxxii

Argg. Time for breakfast again.
I forgot the paste but I remembered the teeth,
And I took them along with me to Spain.

How the señoritas loved them!

I rode a bull in downtown Pamplona
Until he turned ugly and had to be reined.
The rain in Spain falls on the bulls,
On the hedgehogs, and on the red

Furry diplodocus that explodes when tickled.
Oh choose me, he bellowed, I'm fine,
I run when pushed, lie when tethered.
Come have a look at what's under my garment.

Well he shat on Wellington Street.
It was inappropriate but hard to avoid
Given the robust condition of his underwear.
He had clean itchy-pitchys in a drawer.

Wow that was saintly to parade in nothing.
He had a galosh in his ear.
That helped to keep him warm in the winter.
He rode a stiff car in Baltimore and stalled.

lxxxiii

Oh my it is hard to be friendly.
So many dangers abound.
There was a tree squirrel outside this morning
But oh how he hopped.

I hope to go closer to the snails in the evening
And to scatter with them on concrete porches.
You know as well as I do about time.
There is just never enough to spend

Or for that matter to make.
Loss glows in the morning cereal.
Chewsticks made of henna dimple the sitting room.
I swear it will be evening before we cross the Simplon,

Then it will be dusk in Val d'Aosta.
Oh sweet honeysuckle Roman I tasted.

Ah chicken there you go, dolled up.
I would have ridden you home!

Nonetheless it was perfectly patent.
I needed nothing but your help to conceive the plan.
When the door mouse came to wake me,
I strode right through the plutonium.

lxxxiv

Me and Justin Bieber, rodents of time.
Oh spill us you macrobiotic Texans.
We're ready to face you.
We have AR-54s in our shirtwaists!

Come little fellow tell me you're just a babcock.
I'm likely to run a slipper through your ulna.
Just gimme a taste o' cheese
And I'll run with the pack and climb the mountain.

It's a fine day for fishing.
Sizzling hot under the pants.
Efforts have been made to check intruders
But you know there is a passage through everything.

He walks around with his hand clamped to his side.
I could swear he has an enlarged, it's a source.
Three-penny operatics settle down inside it.
They are not sensitive, not easily stalled.

lxxxv

Oh zorgg take us to the pure waters.
Help us to lie down softly like elephants
With our tails tied to our Internet software.
Long shots are often best fired over the bow.

Or another way to regard it is this.
A toll is taken at every waystop.
Mints are distributed but hard cash required.
Saltines and Ottoman princesses

Do a lot for the highways around Baghdad.
Their laces come all the way up to their shoes.
Did you not know that your shoes have corners?
Measure them and try them out on rocks.

Rocks won't fit in your shoes.
The *Shahnameh* is that hard to interpret.
Firdausi is said to have composed walking in circles
But the hoopsy-daisy of that one eludes me.

lxxxvi

Oh sugar baby come to me softly,
Windscreen open and butterballs silent.
We have an acreage north of Bangor.
There, I tell you, the summer wind grows sultry.

Juvenilia gather under the law court window,
And there is a shield from some Spaniard.
I know the men who parade here, know them well.
Their doctrines are anti-Pelagian

But Ambrose might have taken.
He was a teacher of the old ways,
Sentinel of the pine of his desktop
Where he had a special file for *domai.*

lxxxvii

Come to me brother, for our toothbrushes
Are calcified and we can share the peridex.
Our doctors are twins?
Say, is that a cerebellum playing chess in the dog pound?

I like the way you walk
With your back to your face
And your fingernails to the wall.
You could carry my cheese anytime.

There is a free lunch somewhere in Denver.

Go for it man you'll be the first to eat
In your family. Don't forget your tie.
You see there's a wooly mammoth in town

And foddering it…well Rembrandt
Shocked the burghers right out of their trade.
Capital is as capital does, and the Yanks.
Oh come petroleum, argument aside.

It really matters what you eat.
Memling liked skinny patrons
And mint-thin hunting dogs against sky.
The head of the CIA hurt bad

And that was why he had to run away.
He was not hard to find in Pennsylvania
Or even Waziristan where the band played.
Did I frighten you with my little sermon?

lxxxviii

Oh come on Jonathan, tap up.
Snap a frosty and be light on your feet!
The creeks in the Carolinas are generous
If you flavor with nitrites.

Just peel a little liverwurst.
The headlines declared he was of no value to science.
They tricked him quickly into signing the papers.
Of yes, old sobersides, be careful with your mantra.

Dry mouth flakes from the inhaler.
He takes his choking body from the barn.
Didn't they leave him on purpose?
Or was the thought process there in spades?

A simple enough procedure, they said.
Rode they not crustacea to war?
Flailed they not like extinct warhorses?
I know their kind in the fat of the rubble.

For the precious these scenes rankle.
There is a drip drip no one conveys.
Tasted grounds bitter the larynx.
Nonetheless we sign Wagner.

lxxxix

Ah my aria soars like a whippet.
Watch as it circles the uncomfortable train.
The gamelon crew sits cross-legged watching.
Farther in, a Burmese chick wags her head.

I'll tell the you Age of the West is passing.
Lemon soup is taking over the subway.
Old friars busy themselves with headknots
And a rumpled dog plays its music.

lxxxx

Is there no harness in this shop to hold me?
I'll bet the last harness blew out with the fog.
We control horses with remotes.
Oh age of Salazar, and the creamy beaches!

Hemp will not have been the substance of favor,
For the marshals banned it.
You know as well as I.
Didn't you say you knew as well as I,

But if so what did you mean by knew?
There are so many ways to know inside a stone.
You can climb from corner to corner.
Hi outside world I'm almost out!

Then you can catch on the ledge somehow.
Your pants leg can snag
On some not quite smelted iron.
Aren't you again a plesiosaur?

Feather man feather man
Come into my quilted garden.

Take a piece of his Columella.
Plant the rape as he suggests.

It's going to be a long, long time
Billy Joel, and you'll eat it too.
There are going to be sauropods
On everybody's contact lenses.

Now don't go around telling me to…
I ain't gonna go there…
I'll tell you when my cheese is ready
Case Solomon proposes a more radical solution.

End of *Myosotis*. Author had to reflect on the propriety of leaving the entire poem intact. But in for a penny in for a pound, and in fact the pennies flow, here, into an ocean larger and richer, I hope, than they. The flow and amplitude of Myosotis are part of the point *Myosotis* aspires to make, that language can create new life simply by reproducing itself. Which means, of course, that the role of character download is subsumed, in the case of this voluble poem, into its stance between naked giving— here's what I am and can say—and a strophaic, liturgical, and immensely oblique cat-and-mouse game with the reader. The game in question is the unremitting share of intervention, of refusing direct statement—mightn't you even think, for an instance of direct statement, the magical language of Walt Whitman, who is if anything clear, forceful, and direct, and who is all those things in the most direct possible relation to the reader? The same probing reader might relate to the fact that 2003 pops up as the creation date for the present extensive poem, but that in fact it has its roots in scratchings and note-takings of twenty years prior, thus represents the staging of its author's various confrontations with style.

***

Minus (1968)

A cat sets off a house.
At the door.
The sill.

It was not there this noon.

The car had been taken
away. The house
threatened
to fall.

I leaned on the wall
Next door, with a bird.
And remembered your promise
Which set me off.
There was nothing behind that
Either but what it plus I
Was. Nothing more than sky,
Frame, lawn, and the gray

And my "knowing."
The removable factor.
The body the car removed.

PL 39

CHAPTER TEN

KIDS' MORBID

An edgy mood is that early poem, "My Room", from Will's first published volume, *Mosaic and Other Poems* (1959), a volume toward which we have crept through the thickets of juvenilia but not, and this is the point, dressed over in the tweak weeds of the poems—from *Guatemala* on—with which we started this book. The early poem was moody-edgy, yes, but it was frankly *me telling you this in good faith.* (Unlike all those midlife poem things with which we started—"Tupus", "Might be Sattiday", "Starlight in the American Stable", "Horses", "Lunch, Paint, Modern Ways", Palamas' language turned into English—in which I turned my face away from you, while addressing you) We will keep nagging at the intervention of interventions, which at some fault line, just at the setting in of the above "poem things," staged a masking operation thanks to which the feeling modes of "Letter Back" or "The Wound and the Grace" would perforce consign themselves to the maker's romantic background, to a place where it seemed right and good to let people know who you are, or at least to pretend to try to do so. By the end of this book, we hope we will have built the model of an archetypal personal development, through language or other symbols, to the point where language as defense has threatened its own vital principle, and the once-friendly guy behind the poem, who has gone through a central hiding stage, re-emerges as older and friendlier, and then as an old guy, and holds up work-sections on Serenity, Charon, and then even "o Gosh," which once more, honest to gosh, aspire to reach you with directness and honesty. As the author writes today, of the poetic transcourse that has brought him to the village in the hills, Mt. Vernon, Iowa or Ughelli, Nigeria—to where he is planning a late-stage reconsideration of his poetic opus—he has to wonder why the poet-maker in him sits like a beached whale on a personal tradition which in the end wanted nothing but endless continuity with itself. Why was there that interventional bleep, and of what value was it to him?

"My Room" may remind the old guy of exactly the pre-interventionist tenor he launched from in his late twenties. (Not to mention the pre-lapsarian condition in which he wrote the pamphlet *Fragments*, 1944, to his dad, at age fifteen. Back to which we will further excavate shortly, when we try a run at the lifeshape make-up of this *entire* poetic character profile.)

My Room (1959)

Nothing has room but my seeing here.
The sofa, the rugs, the books that lie
In their case; they fall to the root of my eye.

Day after day at a glance's wand
(Nothing leaves me alone in my room)
The walls of my furniture, of my tomb,

Converge. The poise of things on the tip
Of my eye is lost, and they drop through my sight.
Til nothing has room to fill but night

Which drops like a fog on the house. The hole
In the world is gone, the globe is tight,
The lid has closed on the last light.

MO 48

The wound present to ordinary life is as decisive here as it will be in the intervention work we began by discussing, but the congruence of character download with available language is sweet and self-assumed in the present poem. Dark the setting, but light and bright the human insight into it. The language summoned for it is everyday language—no oddities à la Tupus, no bent-out-of-shape angles onto reality, like *Epics of America*, no metaphysicals à la "Starlight in the American Stable", or translations of Palamas (that finely argue English into tones and pressures just off the ordinary). The invitation, here, is to join the word-maker in a brief interior adventure, into his tomb (room? mind?). The simple "of my tomb" is enough to jiggle the stakes of domesticity, with which the poem plays its first cards, but "'til nothing has room to fill but night" adjusts grammar—has night "room to fill" or is the room to be "filled with night"? This embedded ambiguity turns night into the death bringer, as well as into the room itself, a part of the diurnal habit of things. We might say that the ultimate digging deeper of the poem rests on a metaphysical conceit—the

masking use of the word "night"—but not on language which has been
forced to intervene on itself, or to render the author incognito.

What will we want to say, about the figuring in of "character" to this
poetic tumbler? How is character downloaded here? There are "me"s and
"my"s, and there sure is what looks like a boy's or young man's room, yet
will we say we know this young man and his response to what he sees as
his world? Eminently not, for the tone is flat to toneless, and even dread
seems excluded by the quiet transfusion of language. You can go to this
poem because you are burrowing and thinking; it will not come to you
with that muscularity of language an intervention poem will batten on.
This is a talk-talk poem. This is you and me having a conversation.

We can as well here as anywhere, then, ask ourselves what this poem
is, and ask it so naively that the poem stands before us as language. Is this
poem a *thing*? Can we pick it *up*? (We can pick up a book that "contains"
this poem, but can we pick the *poem* up? Hard to see how. Poems don't
have that kind of otherness. Can we make a poem ours by memorizing it,
or does its presence as print marks make an essential difference to its
ontological status?) The fact is that the poem is an intricate adjustment in
the noosphere—we all exist as tinkerers in this domain—and not to be
confused with an object-thing. It will never die, but by the same language-
code it will never "live."

***

A final move into the pre-lapsarian should nail down the point of
character, where what would later prove a burin-tipped-in-acid is still the
soft smudgy bristle of the first-grade classroom. From as far back as a
certain long sunny bed in Honolulu, Will has drawn to him the image of a
stark Odyssean/Teiresian figure, bonily scrutinizing the Death Proposition.
(What in that figura, a clip perhaps from what Bergman saw in *The
Seventh Seal*, drew this benevolent piece of mid-western psyche to the
bony cliffs of selfhood, though he was still in the gravy years of youth?
Was it the glimpse of a *danse macabre* which had imagination rather than
experience for its mother? Was it the trigger of the aerial at work here, the
imagination of brine with surf and flinty flotillas in Waikiki Bay, with
their promises of death in the whitecaps? Was it the word-shaped
preoccupation with Mr. D in *Fragments*?

Two panels, from *Four Moods of Our Own Odysseus*, build the
baroque but direct mood we are sampling:

Teiresias (1966)

My thought could not know him better
With the candles low and our chairs at the window
The city was still

Only a cab was heard from one to two
Lovers laughing in their own worlds
The sound of the turning world
It was warm in the room
He went on

"So it will be, choice upon choice gone,
All chance as lost as your ruined limbs.
So it will be in some room, your jaw sunk,
And your nails brittle. But you will leave much.
Stinking with time and place, your genitals
Empty, your fists soft, your eyes mere wells in your head.
So much will be left."
                                    He turned to the window:
Then, drowning the kiting moon in his smoke, looked back.

"And all will be nothing, city on city sunk
In the eye's steep shaft,
Ticket by ticket the world crossed,
The last town as strange as the others,
Its name in a dubious alphabet
And your own name hard to remember.
All will be nothing, lost in the swamp
Of an old man's memory."

Shadows had spread
In the room. I went to the window.
The city was still and crossed with channels of light
A dog was barking, the stars were clear...

PL 17–18

    The narrator, really the figure enduring the figure in the room, then
goes on to listen to the pronouncements of the man who owns death. The

mood is bony, and nothing is communicated except a vision of the end of personal existence for the narrator, who finds himself listening disconsolately to a dead man:

"I saw him smile in the shadows.
His face was still.
His eyes were filmy and dead."

Teiresias—bisexual, omni-conscious, privy to all dualities, including the duality of life and death—reinforces everything the narrator can imagine, about the stripping down death is preparing for him. All that remains, for the narrator, is to take up into himself the experience Teiresias is projecting for him. Upon doing so he too will be one of those who have gone beyond, but are still here.

The course of the narrative is oral, relies little on language intervention to diffract the character of the teller, to stand between the teller and the hearer. We are in the poetry Will had to offer to his *manes* during lively years of lit society, Austin, Texas from 62–64. (He is no longer in "My Room", a private space as tight as life itself, but is now in the "life and death" room of mind, spooking himself, fearing the spook in him.) He is delighted in being there as a storyteller, able at last to draw into the light pervasive memories of all night train trips from Chicago to Laval, in 1947, a *rausch* in itself as he went back and forth through the two-bit half-lighted villages of Québec province; as he passed before himself in the guise of that Eugene Gant whose haunting of the Harvard Library stacks was to trace Will's personal grail three years later, or to enrich his murky Harvard experience with its more than *rausch*, the escape into the night as he fled the Yard and disappeared into Manhattan for a few desperate hours, ending up on parental good friends' front door step at six a.m., or (on many occasions) subwayed back alone to his dorm, from a Scully Square to which he attributed pleasures, darknesses, a forbidden that Hart Crane's *The Bridge* had given him for what he thought his special madness, but for what was really a put-on from inside. To wit:

Odysseus (1966)

The train stopped often that night
In the towns with unknown names
And only a channel of bulbs
On a still main street.

An old man gaping like death, who'd slept
In the seat in front, got off.
I saw him limp with his bags as we left.
The train ground on, field after field lay slack
In the shapeless night.

The others who stayed were sleeping,
A negress and three black girls,
A nurse who slept outstretched in the dirty seat,
A porter who smoked and counted his stubs.
The floor was covered with crumbs,
The windows with soot.

County by county the world went.
I blew my nose and used the latrine.
I stood in the observation car and reaped
The land with a glance.

And stopped at the least of the towns,
Taking my single bag.
There were none to see me go or arrive,
The town was still as a graveyard.
Only the cop was quick,
Who drank his coffee at Burman's
And watched the desirable waitress.

Least of the towns, smallest,
Wood and stone on the ancient plain.
A store, a church, a courthouse square,
Only a stage-set, up for my random eye.
It was half-past four.
The sky was lighter. Orion was low.

By five I had crossed the town
To the first fields. The hills to the east were forming,
The dream of the sun was remembering the long sky.
I walked down the country road,
My back old, my eyes mere wells
In my skull, my hand the clutch of a bone
On my bag. Soon the town was too far to see.

The road was a dusty quai,
The fields a living ocean, wheat shoots
Tearing the humid ground, lines of green
Embroidered as far as the soil's cloth lay.

Nothing was silent: the sun-climb
Deafened from over the chunky hills,
The wheat split clod after noisy clod
And drank the elated dawn.

Nothing was still or held.
I sang with the others,
Caught the preposterous note of beginning
'Til my back grew straight
And my eye whole,
And I entered the road's new country
Younger than any child.

PL 21–22

We're talking here work from *Planets* (1966), in which Will brought
to harvest a lot of the longing tone that had ripened over the prior decade,
that was just beginning to aspire to break easy diplomatic relations
between teller and audience, just beginning to adumbrate within itself the
interventionist or angry poetry we talked about in the first chapters of Part
I; attempting, as we were, to start right in the crackling middle of this
maker's bloody trajectory of phonemes. The town entered in language,
here, is a town bordering on borderless fields, a town at that very time
discovered inwardly in several Will texts taken out of the experience of
Iceland, in which the walker inadvertently heads down a street which ends
in the black silent ocean, a town Will lives today, yes himself the
American Midwesterner lives, in which a good walk north up Springville
Road will immerse you, make it April, in black earth and curried lines of
green shoots, a town, okay okay, I hear you, through which the walker in
the eye, peering from the between cars platform of Trans Canada rail,
down the nippy Main Street of Agathe, Province de Québec, will without
difficulty, hey it's two in the morning, imagine an existentially fierce hike
out into the grainfields to the north, where the ground is frozen, and the
human put on notice of the extremity of its condition.

(And why was this fiery young gentleman, who looked like a local
boy scout troop leader, so fascinated by the peering look back down the

funnel into the great growth power of the *néant*? Nothing comes from
nothing, as Lear and Cordelia discover, and yet that empty black hole in
one's history is ineffaceably attractive. Can the néant-genesis still have
derived from the spatial thrills of two years in the Arizona desert, at age
eleven up, when returning from roundup one would back-shoulder it from
John Barleycorn's back, and see the deep valley's night shadows creeping
up behind? Or can even that experience have rooted more deeply within
itself, back to when it saw itself at seven, stretched out in bed with a cold
and an attractive excuse from school, immersed in reading *Thirty Years in
the Golden North*, or *Within the Circle* by Evelyn Stefansson? The taste
for crossing the border into the night, the other or the frozen was coming
out of the pores of young Will, and so directly grounded was that taste that
the poems stamped with this signature thought no further than that, that
signature, about the problem of character download in poetry. Intervention
was to be a refinement, from within the poetic enterprise, which was still
far on the horizon for young Freddy Fox, an horizon which would in fact
not so much as make itself visible, until far in the future, way farther into
full-fledged marital turmoil, when the harmer guy would learn to tweak
his "leetle problems" into obfuscatory sharpness of language, and say
"back off, buddy," in language calculated, he hoped, to make buddy want
an extra close peek.)

***

The love poem has always been where Will most comfortably invites
the reader or hearer to share with him right where he is. We have an
abundance of these shares in Will's early work, and some in the prose
poems of his later work, but intervention work, which is language and not
soul based, will not thrive on this need for Cupid. We have looked already
at "The Wound and the Grace" (1959), and might have complicated the
argument, just at that point and from the same volume, *Mosaic and other
Poems* (1959), with a poem like "The Word for Love in Danish Is Hard"
(1959):

The word for love in Danish is hard.
I heard it once and then forgot
All of its syllables. How did it go?

Try to remember.
There is the snow on the beach
December. A wind flaying our cheeks

Where we'd stood before in a spring wind.
Odd, tramping the snow on the sand now,

Sea-weed and seashell crinkle with ice;
Waves, surging and slatey,
Powdered with light snow.
Now is it clearer? Now do you know?

Plosh, plosh, boot at the sea's brim,
Hand under hand over hand,
Fingers plaited like winding vines.
Now you are nearer.

The word for love in Danish is hard.
The philologist found it in Norse
and Irish and said
"This is a strong word, crossing
the oceans, crossing linguistic borders."

Her head lifted to look at a boat
Out past the harbor.
Ploshing, plosh, over the wet sand,
Arm over arm, hand under hand.
Her lips, parted and saying,
Dulling the sea's vast churn,

Her lips, saying the word
Lightly,
Making a world, making the sea turn
To flame.

Many a long day since
I have sat down,
Studied the dictionary,
Read 'til my eyes were weary,
Hunting the Danish word for love.
Every search is barred,
Every star crossed.
The word for love in Danish is lost.

MO 6

What exactly can it mean, to say that such a poem puts up as few
barriers as possible between the teller and the hearer? (That would be a
condition opposite to what we imply of the work done in the
"interventionist" poems with which we started, in which the poet
fenceposts himself in with strange locutions and code fragmentations.)
Surely the poet, here even in these earlier barrierless poems, hides behind
a conceit, to keep the explanations literary; a conceit can hardly be direct.
Deeper than that, for the conceit is visible on the page, the poet even in
these early love poems is talking with us in a highly formalized way. This
point is simple, simplistic. In ordinary speech, the speech where I tell you
how the operation on my finger went, or about the effort we made to sell
our house last year, I cannot say things to you like "the word for love in
Danish is hard," or "wounded and bony I withdrew the inoperative digit,"
unless of course you are taking my course in Scandinavian languages, or
my other course on "the metaphorical reach of contemporary American
English," and we are between ourselves comfortable with a word like
"hard" to describe a word, especially a word in a foreign language. The
way the narrator of "The Word for Love in Danish" talks is not the way
we can talk to one another, quite apart from the language in which the
author presents himself revolving around a conceit, the conceit that the
word for love in Danish is intimately related to the romance the narrator is
feeling toward a girl, who *may* be Danish and *may* have walked with him
in the snow. To say that the narrator of this poem has set up as few
barriers as possible, in a poem, to convey his romantic feelings, is to
accept the commonplace that shows of feelings, like romance or fear or
hopelessness, are easily understood across speech or writing borders. The
fact is, of course, that such "shows of feelings" are nothing but the words
that custom enables us to assemble at regular intervals, to characterize our
seemingly well ordered thematics of emotion.

PART THREE:

SERENE YEARS

CHAPTER ELEVEN

SERENITY

Okay we did *intervention*, making a lot of a congeries of expressions that seemed designed to thwart the sentimental, the personal, the "here I am, let's talk" of the poetic impulse and which, more or less, emerged from a life period when the writer was fumbling for a sense of identity and security. The word *intervention* is loose, the time period covered by the effects of the term was shaky—75–90 might be a shot at it, at a time when Will's indifference to the sacredness of marriage, to the fabric of society, to the precious responsibility of children, was wreaking doubled ill results, for two failed marriages were in fact turning in their nugatory report cards at about this time and readying the gent for a prolonged period of trip-taking—but if we are working to define *intervention* as we move ahead, we can do no better than to pair it off against serenity, for with *serene* you ain't seen nothing, we're flaking our way slowly out into the direction of that free boat ride organized and guided by our friend Mr. Charon. And he don't turn back in mid-route. So we're gonna relax for a while, then tighten our belts and look old Mr. D. straight in the face. We trust we will have a rather long ride through the ceiling of life.

Now we're serene, though, we're sailing in those waters where the ship's crew feels like stretching out by the pool and taking a good long think about how they got there, what paths have snaked them along the bushes of misbehavior and finally deposited them, splish, splash, on a love boat headed for the North Sea. We're in the later 1980s, and as serene ones we're going to be sloshing along for a couple of decades. The goodly doc has left the University of Massachusetts—buzz reports that he snapped, one day in his short-fiction class, when a cutie in the front row popped a bubbler right in his face, and he turned and headed fast for the green pastures where they store superannuated profs. In any case the next view we have of him is in Iowa, working again at the University of Iowa, and tiptoeing incessantly around girls like C who would make it most attractive to sacrifice a second marriage, and to invest its fruits in yet another life-inventive kid, in yet another adult errant. (How he hugs those risked kids today, the risk having shifted to his own bitter back!) Then, having been led to the corner where the divorce certificates are hammered out, and pulled back, he was mummified to learn that his wife, his flute-attached-to-the-baroque, has decided to make her own move, and to leave chaos to run their twelve-year-old experiment in domestic relations. It was at this point, as every shit piece hit every available fan again, that the extremity invoked the serenity we now address. Here seem to have been some of the things it looked like, like from the late serene 1980s.

***

Poetry and Philosophy (1988)*

i

Don't matter where I start
It's philosophy.
That is, it's always about being here,
Where…

He hands off the gown
He knows the beat of basic women.
Take off what's inside of you,
Madam, it'll still be the beating heart.

In the forest of anonymity
He tiptoes out onto the verandah
And peruses the deep passages of the sea.
They sing to him like twists and turns in Vivaldi.

It's as though there were some conductor…
Durned sea playing to the bleachers…
Now he takes an old-fashioned settee
And winds a watch…

Elegance in the face of a barbarian has its charms.
But back to you madam, and your beating heart
For that's what makes the gown rise and fall
That you might step…

---

* A later version of this poem appears on pp. 70–78. Differences between the two version are marked in bold.

ii

It's an Edwaard Muybridge
Kind of effect.
That's why I say it's philosophy.
You see it's always about being there

Even when you are there with it.
I don't see escaping.
I can walk a long way
Without sidestepping my flesh.

What I do see is taking terribly seriously
Pieces of fallen equipment.
A whiplash fell off a tree.
Some dogwood broke apart in a vase.

When he walks down the road his body falls apart!
Now madam, you know that's not exactly true,
You know the wind can create an illusion
Of *désagrégation*, as the French say, at any time—

Most of all when your tie's straight and your shoes shined.
That's more of the philosophy, you see.
You double back on yourself
Counting the times you've been contradicted,

Contraindicated, contravened, and just plain checked.
You know you've got the stuff to make a real good soldier
And even a good philosopher.
Yet when it comes right down to it, to IT,

There's always been a doubt.
I ain't the doubtin' type, Mam, rest assured of that,
But I do some philosophy, specially Bishop Berkeley,
And I do like the way a breast parts from the side of a gown.

Anyhoo…you might say I've jes' started now,
Been introducin' muhself, shore is hot in this bar,
Been gittin' ready to ask you round to visit the Department
Where me and muh colleagues piss the time of day.

No, seriously, after checking out the inside of that gown
The thing I want most in the world is to engage you
In a little witty conversation about the endgame
You and me's stuck with. Yah know, PHILOSOPHY.

iii

Edmund Gettier, may his name rest in peace,
Forged the VERIFICATION THEORY for thinking to some purpose.
Maintaining a true belief, and being able to justify it,
He said, was productive thought.

What if you maintain the false, and yet it leads you to the true?
He covered that too, imputing to the false, **like** *there's gotta be a heaven,*
The discovery factor; **f**inding that your belief was wrong**,**
Like finding that inside this room, just next to the bar,

There was a lemon-colored Philipino woman jes' beggin' for it,
Then discoverin' it was an illusion. That mistake could bear fruit.
You could jerk off over it! Seriously, though,
It's no small matter to know small matter, particles and animalcules

And whatever else Van Leeuvenhoek decided to call the minutiae
That hit his lens. Main thing's gittin' there first
With the names, then with the concepts to fit. Concept's the
Operative thought movement, here, **meaning** take it in yer hands

Bud, it's a *concipere, concapio, con Capulet* if you prefer, and thus,
Accordin' to literary history, a bit of a bit of a wolf...
"Aye, you have been a mousehunt in your time,"
Mr. Gettier, hanging up the false in front of the true,

That your real character as fallen, as half a leg,
Son of a gun, howling wolf academic, might be hidden.
Hidin' behind a proposition ain't logic at its best,
When the clean truth is as open as air.

iv

I guess we all have our secrets. "Private vices, public virtues,"
And maybe that's the way to go, blimey, in the dark weeds of
Compromise. I'd rather it weren't so.
I'd rather we could go, each of us, openly to our Maker.

Our Maker would embrace us and hold us.
Stead of that, of course, guy's all the time sulking and skulking,
Envying this man's whatchacallit, and that woman's whatchacallit,
And missing out on the fun.

Measure each breath to its line, and there, maybe,
The breath of individual life will ease you, will drop you like a quarter
Into some slot where you become more. Worth grows.
Holding your place and showing your teeth is a lot of fun

And furthermore, in the end, makes an impression.
That's about all I want, **Man's makin' an impression,**
Which is why I brought that up about getting out of this bar,
About movin' over to that there motel next door where

Although a Philipino chick's already pullin' it down there's at least
Room for a little philosophy. See I wasn't kiddin' about that philosophy...
Now why the hell else, tell me, would I be carryin' Meyerson's *Identity
And Reality* in the back seat? You do? You **really** wanna see it?

v

It would have to be Sunday Morning, wouldn't it, when we decided
No more politics, it don't really matter, my daughter was right
That the earth and our simple humanity on it are what count.
At the same time I was reading this *The Story of O* which my daughter,

The same one, loaned me. It was getting under my skin.
Crudely written though it was, it displayed the same rough energy
I got from *The Celestine Prophecy* and thirty years ago from
A Yaqui Way of Knowledge. It would have to be Sunday Morning

When the sun was cutting out small strips of light from the hostas

By my computer. For Stevens the "complacencies of the peignoir" have to have
Melodies triple-beautied, to outshine a god. My Sunday Morning,

Philosophy having to have it, was some joint between the Enlightenment
And the aura of sacrifice. I knew I had to produce a killing
In order to live, yet that Diderot was there too, a kind of American
Hero, true to what works and Dewey. **I hadn't a sure position.**

vi

When the dog came bounding in I cringed because I knew
Matter brings with it the whole *stofflich* presence of things,
Whereas what I want is freedom from the **polis** and a text,
Scribbled sacred words. The dog though was to lead me

Downward downward to the water, where a trim
Aquamarine sylph slipt out from the bushes.
I stroked her wormy calcitrance and then followed her
Into someplace subaquatic like Grendel's

Mom's cave. To my surprise it was philosophy again there,
A calculus of public virtues private vices, and I gave
From the heart to the antinomy. I've been where
Something I wrote got better as I sinned, or worse as I

Straightened up and flew right up into the sun.
Beauty and goodness ride separate tricycles but on occasion
When the sky is calm and the velocity perfectly tuned,
They can converge in tandem. Silver rims on fire with each other.

Beauty and goodness can meet in the same kind face,
In the worshipful intensity of a child predator
Hardened to the breaking point of love.
There is a wild beauty, in wild things, that will crash

All the barriers of sound. And fly to the moon.
Ah the moon and my love's hands these summer nights,
Walking slowly past the power plant and the field house
And not unaware of the distant out-folding cornfields

That at ten-thirty p.m. seem like coasts of black possibility.
It's not like when I was young young, and would march through the night,
And would find out there, in the steepest over-flowered valleys,
Secrets of the despair in things, or when in Ohio, coming back with my
parents from the coast,

I stood against a cowface across a fence. I'd emerged to piss,
Gone off into the darkness of a meadow, then looked up and seen
This mottled Hereford, the simplest possible presence of the *stofflich,*
Like that dog back there.

vii

Every now and then the curtain of pollutants falls back
And we see the stars. Those times swarm over us, dealing fell
Blows. We know our mortality is for a second, then we fade,
Yet like Kant we know, too, that meeting this dire perplexity

Directly, consciously, raises up our spirit to praise.
We praise our infinitude, like children singing on the way to school.
Dread, awe raises our song! Why not let the little body
Plaster itself silently against the rain? Why not let it fall

Gently without protest? It's because we are callers!
Nothing about us is still. The dry fact wrings us even drier
Until we shrivel in slivers. Yet the long languid energies
Of the American Midwest continue to uplift us.

viii

Philosophy, darling, is what it is all about, even in the bed,
Where the *philosophie du boudoir,* of the place where one "sulks,"
Moods up, is rampant. Love and lust unleash Philosophy One—
Can I this, can I that?—and contribute to our bliss.

I know that the random swathes of longing have carried me
To places that hurt us all. I have no doubt that the equipment
God gave me to make wide spaces in the gene pool
Has at times led me astray into pure pain—to me and others.

Now that I am older I want to heal and let heal but with the intensity
Darn it of a heel, for only a heel can do the occasional harm
That explodes beauty from its chest. I see power rising from the chest
The way an Olympic athlete brings a lifetime of rigorous practice

To a minute and a half of explosive efficiency in the hundred meters.
It's the way a poem line that works replaces decades of drossy gleck.
Those who were truly great with the line, like Oppen and Eliot,
Filed and filed. The clean bone they came down to whistled in the wind.

ix

Oh soldiers remember on your way to battle that the stars
Will for a moment align, maybe in your passage through the moonlight,
And in their crosshairs will be framed, for a moment, the fine thin
Purpose that drove the Neolithic hunger. We are never far from our
sources.

We are still the same tragic lovers of beauty that fell in the Long March
To the Sea, that brought Xenophon and his men home. Only now it's
Probably the kitchen sink where we will be standing.
The water will be running, down a drain that leads to the city sewage plant
And above the drain we will be administering the last rites
To an organically grown carrot. Never mind. Time and circumstances
change.

No two moments are alike in their passion. Keep cutting, boy.
When you rinse, rinse like a sacred butcher, washing the sweat
Of the labor of the world from your arms, and standing for a minute pure.
Stab wounds all over you.

x

Sunday morning, in any case all agree, is a time to take stock.
Laden with achieved learning, all brain cells activated,
We stumble downstairs to the all too familiar.
And at once it is the unfamiliar. It is the life we left.

We are in the far place of reflection and abstraction.

Neither a child nor a dog is the animal of yesterday.
The house of the neighbors is like a long ship
Dug from the peat at Sutton Hoo, and philosophy,

Attired like a Mediaeval schoolmaster, is standing where
Mr. and Mrs. Dockeson used to cut their lawn.
I have said that philosophy it must be, in the long run,
That makes the spheres interlock. It's Dantesque this world.

I cannot imagine it not spouting from my ears in canticles
Like the Canticle of the Sun. You go out into the lawn.
There is a patch of brown grass. It fell victim to Roundup
And you nurse it daily. You inspect some bruised tendrils.

xi

Would not Saint Francis have taken the whole passing scene,
Rioting wood squirrels, squirmy mushrooms,
And replaced them with the love that moves the heavens and the other stars?
He might have. But he was flesh. He might have gone

Down on his knees among the spores and praised gray,
Which is after all the color first in potential.
From gray you can make white or black or shades.
From gray you can make a suit that befits a businessman

Or an Ampleforth schoolboy. Gray is beyond all
Question the brightest and strangest color in time.
It is the color of the feather that the King wears in the summer crown
Made of fillets. The feather came from a mockingbird.

The feather is nothing to mock, but came from just over the tail
Of the prettiest mockingbird as she knelt to a worm.
Out in the bay there was one less worm to fish with which meant
Salmon the size of your arm escaped, and so it went, the world

One filament of philosophically interconnected possibilities, the kind of
Fabric of causal nexi, Aquinas said, which in itself proves God's
Manifest presence. I don't know about that presence.

Fastened-together events, like causes and effects, might be the work of a
devil

Anxious only to seem. *Post hoc ergo propter hoc*, after all,
Can be exploded by any Ampleforth schoolboy, and once that's
Been accomplished the network proof of God gets shaky.
When I said there's always philosophy, then, I meant that

Sometimes, when it appears that the world is making sense,
We might well suspect a trick. **Why should our cosmos make sense?**
Why should we not grow more than that?
I take a stain to my Masters and am taught how to fly!

***

For the author, eschatology comes close to the daily, on a parabola
which leaves only micro centimeters of breathing room, between god and
the kitchen sink. Mysticism of endless postponement? In a sense, yes, the
miracle we threaten to become is forestalled only at the last minute—by a
ringing doorbell or a glitch in the network. And then when it comes to the
next world—as we put it, wearily surmising that we are about to do it
again—we find that we are at last entertaining its parallel nature, turning
with a smile to the thought that the next world is doing itself as we live this
one. So eager are we, to become the meaning a drama perpetually
unterwegs becomes.

***

Love Me Love My Dog (1990)

My dog was in my coat
And didn't understand it was time for a change of position.
I hurried him through the door alone.
Your dog was shifting its position.

Our animals often tell us about the world,
What is changing. A louse stains my dress.
I figure it's time to be ashamed.
Or a fried maggot slips through the car window.

All these signs from animals test us.

It is wise not to move quickly.
There will be roads uncovered for us by
The movement of animals.

If you take those roads it is faster.
The animal swells up over danger,
And flows around masonry;
Simple creatures touch danger with hands.

I'm not sitting here while the road bends.
I've placed a dog there. He could blow.
I think he'll move a little.
All he needs to do is to move a little.

I'll let you pretend you were not present
When I made all this clear.

Let Your Voice Ring Out Loud and Clear (1999)

Let loud your out clear ring voice
And see whether it works that way
As though trying out whether syntax
Is only housekeeping applied to primitive sounds.
Get rid of the Os in Tiepolo and say Tiepl like a Jew.
Vowels were invented by the Italians, anyway, and for all I know, just think of your
Latin, they invented grammar too.
My people were always touching things
Or throwing a word like a rag at a thing
And asking me to clean it.
When things were clean we put labels across them like banners.
The thing we call an egg lay in a dish with a label on it saying *dish*.
Mistakes arose when the labels fell off and we used names like banana for the now unnamed dish.
Calling an egg a dish and a label a banana was alright until we came to the banana
And had to name it something else because banana was taken.

In the Furze (2000)

In the furze, along the river Bettchen, crowd the dogs of the camp.
They had simply followed their masters over landlocked plains
And here they were driven like herds into the pens of their masters.

The dogs took turns growling at the sentinels.
There was always someone nasty to growl at.
There were women sentinels and there were dog sentinels, and all the
same they were to the dogs in the pens.

In the furze the frost grows hard and impenetrable at night and alights on
the dogs.
There are pellets of frost on the necks of the dogs.
The sentinels gather in little groups to praise then blame the dogs,
shouting at them.

A frame can quiet any picture, and so the tintype of a dog.
For a dog is not a silly being.
A dog is not a creature to berate in a picture.

A dog will go growling out into and across the furze
And will stand to face you and the guards.
Women guards are bad to dogs.
Dogs know it and snarl.

In through the furze comes a dog red in the eye.
You noticed him coming from a distance over the landlocked plain.
And you followed him to the place where the sentinels were rounding on
him.

There you stood in the furze in your shoes and socks.
Meanwhile, not far away, more dogs were coagulating out of the furze and
mist
And were coming in packs to the pen.
Those were drifting dogs, dogs steeped in lore.
There were ten of them
And they didn't stop there.

Figuratively Speaking (1995)

Some speak directly,
Listen to my huge voice.
Others sneak up, Oh by the way sir.
There are ways to be present.

In foreign countries we do our best
To be as silent as the natives.
You look at me,
I see a configuration of settlements.

We would never ever tell.
You go this way, I'll go that way.
You see the dry weather makes words
Dry. They skip away from the lip.

A chest of sentences is buried.
This map shows the way.
When we get there my how we will talk.
Quietly now we are near.

The whole world has been said.
I read here, go home, relax.
A tree gives me a withering glance.
Not going to talk about me?

I practice the silence.
I'm not gonna be a tale teller.
If a thing is too lonely to be
It is a sad commentary on the forest.

I Have a Silent Childhood (1987)

Could I be your silent stepchild?
Could I be the reason your dog was moody?
I have this silent childhood inside me
And it is there in my shirt.

I can't strip to deeper than that childhood.

I am its skin and its face.
I am its mother and its face.
Strip away this silent stepchild.

You will feel easier and fly from me.
There will be a place for your longings.
Rocks will jostle in your trouser legs.

Let other stepchildren replace me.
I am only one among many stepchildren.
I think I brought it with my dog.
He was a hero, a saint, he read.

I am glad to be so silent in your company.
I am not worth more, even alive.
As for death with dignity I am your dog,
your father's stepson.

He was both a loser and a winner.

This book is not about literary analysis, nor, really, about a guy's life as what he writes is embedded in it. How I constructed the present book probably counts here, though I was afraid I would kill you with boredom, if I autobiographized again, and you'd have run away screaming. Maybe this much is okay? I started with the interventionist stuff, rather with a nub of it, the *Guatemala*, where I had always felt I'd hit the nail on the head, as I had with *Epics of America*, and then I posted some of my favorites from that time period, second half of the 1970s, first of the 80s, favorites that clustered around that for me generative time period. That cluster method became a way of construction, as I ferreted out texts from the past that I felt I could live with, and came on others that I thought who wrote that, ain't too bad, and all in all as I realized that the criterion of publication—what had gotten into journals and books, and what had been excluded—had been a pretty jackassy criterion, and that in the end, in order to let this book sail, which I wanted to, book thing and all that, I would have to do some more *ab ovo* creating like that you do by putting together a fresh book in the first place. Like for example, because I am myself always changing, I have to recognize that my—and it's gotta be the same for you—whole aesthetic choice grid will be continually reshaping itself. So this "I have a silent childhood" is something I never saw before.

Just picked it up. Privileged it this morning, as I was rummaging. Put it first here, in the serenity list, on the simple luck bet—it felt good. And so you go back and look at it. How do you know? It's got that sadness, that wryness, that belong to the flow of the discussion here. And so you let it sail. And is there any way to come clear on an absolute value of the piece? Of course there is not. The poem is a thing you work with and not something with a value sign attached to it.

***

Serenity may be sounding like a pretty goosy term to use here, for a description of the years of descrescendo, the 1980s, early 90s, when though marriages unraveled and children fumbled, the grand tetons of tumultuous commitments were over, and the soul started quietly to walk down into its shoes. Having chanced it on the stepchild, I wander into the kind of good-natured-enough quirkiness I laud, as decrescendo funny stuff, no hard edges, no intervention IN YOUR FACE.

Return Ticket (1990)

I give you, wench, your
Ticket home to Borneo and a pass…
You got a pass in signaling…
You got a B in tickling and a…

He goes on vacation.
He sits down with Nora, says…
Aw c'mon he says, tain't that…
She sniffs him like a cocker…

In Borneo they fear him.
They lock their houses.
What he says of liberation…
It is too too small

To match the liberated condition…
On the beach Torvald smokes…
Cheerio old chap he mumbles…
I pull off my thong and whistle

Til Nora well, let's not say that…
The oil can spits lubricant.
The door slides quietly on hinges
Carved from pure honey.

Why is Nora so still
Was it the mai tai?
Was it the soft green sorbet?
O my children, the wonder!

In the flat time of oaks a jurist
Pronounces a man dead.
A door flies open and a blind
Carves sight diagonally

                          ***

A lot of that stuff is going to slide in under the cover of serenity, for
to stand the already puzzling world on its head seems balm for this back-
corner affirmer, who is learning what it is to say yes to, and winking there.
It is to the elusive, intricate wave of the soul into the music of things. It is
the geometry of high jinks carving small pieces out of the flesh of its time.
Post-intervention this is, but no longer the *take me here I am a gift of
character* granted us by the range of earlier poems—from "This Autumn's
Progress" to "The Word for Love in Danish"—in which the face of the
lover was minted on every coin. To note: the wrinkles and furbelows of
space raise many a head in the serenity poems, which may wish to relax
into the condition of a Braque still life, lambent and succulent. Has
serenity then to do with the sedentary, the sidelong, the angular, the
"standing inside or into" in which Will hunkers and in which he tries to
pre-live the life this life implies. (Back to page 1, the superscription, boys
and girls!)

                          ***

The Side (1985)

I have long been absent from the side.
I love the way they say it, worn.
I love side as part of resting.

It was there when we went further.

Something lonely came around to the morning.
It had stillness in quantity, and left it.
We felt the stillness in a place.
We were doctrinal, fiery, chose...

I didn't know first as side.
I knew it as portal. It was a dome.
Driving from Portland on one side
On the other the dishes, hard ones.

There was always a corner to brush.
You said it is a time lock.
On the side dole was eruh created.
I went around, it was over, timed.

***

Side 2 (1987)

You said there was an easy, it wasn't.
There was always still a place.
There was no way there was no side.
There was a drift, and a stain in the ocean.

O you who know my heart!
Quickly lest I am at the mercy of...
Row, the side, oar traps as specialists.
A winding path along the mall.

There is a table mat beside the table.
It is all there is to hold.
Did it but know, then leave space.
It made no gesture of yielding.

A rarity in a stone lay there.
You and it knew it was careless.
You and I could read a sign on a wheel.
It was that the chandler was dying.

We made baskets, claimed
The side was too small to be contented.
Did you see the young man fall?
His death by bird?

***

Side 3 (1988)

I fell so in love with the side.
It didn't charge much.
I bought it on credit or I er...
Well, anyway, there it was.

It sure looked like the side I loved.
But it had a little crack in it.
I forced my hand in at that crack,
Like a foal, or a gymnast.

It didn't seem to matter where I went
With my protruding.
The crack was a monitoring.
But inside I was not on the side,

I was in the place under the side.
My love for the side grew hot.
I browsed over the crowded places of the side.

Why does Will, turning and twisting in the efforts to stabilize life, to make it settle, to take it easy man, serene, take such interest in the side? It is where character can fall away from itself, into a geometry, yet still maintain a controlling right? Put it all on the line, the geometry, the angularity, sandwich it in an autobiography, as though Mr. Chap had not already written enough of the things. (*A Portrait of John* stands out, but what is not autobiography in the sequence of love poems, despair poems, exaltation poems that dust the extensive poem opus that Will traces behind him?) Those serene years can be time-marked, by a quick shot. A first shot across the bow—way back early in intervention days—had surely been the first affair. Becky, the University of Texas Union, way in the early 1960s, when the act of infidelity had only begun to shadow the lobes of this midwestern enthusiast. Back in the time of *Mosaic* (1959) and *A Wedge of Words* (1963). Will had worried that bone for many a year before even character intervention had begun to seem like a possibility, before the hardest edges he knew could be applied to the name of the maker of the poem. *Zee fall. Zee dealing with eet.* The palpable moment of desire, after which yielding will forever be easier…until many struggles later it, that yielding, becomes the exhausted cat's-eye figure of loss, and the brink itself, the pain done to others. It grows, this fall? It grows in us all, but incrementally, dependent on the stages our maker decides to adopt in making us. Of course the chasm under the guy's feet grows wider, and the tap dance across the minefield of time grows ever more grotesque. His character becomes him so carelessly that for years he just tires into being an actor in time, and finally knows somehow that it is time for personae and for poems about stelae that are told by no one, and that themselves puff like cysts on history's throat. His intervention poems date in from the mid-1970s to the early 90s, from the guy's age fifty-five or six to seventy or so, just the delayed bad-boy period to be expected from a sibling-less, word-crazed, slow-growing youngster, who needed time to know adequately how to hurt and be hurt, how to enjoy making people wonder who you were. If anything won for him a longish chat with Charon, the "final poems," it will have been the trickle-down economics of death, which made itself full and felt, from, say, that famous third marriage, the marriage to Julie in 1995. From that date on, our buddy has walked the line in pretty steady concourse with Charon, and even before that, in the last years with C, 1988–1995, there were serene chats with oneself—we'll play a few of those recordings—and the tiniest hint of an easing down into the easing against in its essence.

***

The period of serenity follows the period of intervention: in other words, the guy who cut loose with Becky, in a 1962 Austin bedroom, who threw off the traces and the guardrails, who ran from security carved into experience, and who hurried into the arms of the unknown, this very guy, maybe thirty years later, began to think that nothing could be nicer than a good supper with the wife, Andy Griffith on the box, and the comfortable feeling that none of his children had decided to act out in his fashion, though more than one had scraped against the rocks of depression and aimlessness. What in those already antique days spurred the thirty plus years chap, driving through midtown Austin with the pride of his heart, a luscious, married, undergrad thing, with every moment inviting the world to shriek that horror, *scandal*, which was sure as rain to bring down chaos and dark night? What broth of hatred broiled in the thin soul of this dweep, as he fought through an outburst of beauty and passion-love? Was it the hatred of the expected, or of the seemingly ordinary, which had driven him to that shore of passion for passion's sake? Was it self-destruction, and if so—back home with you, discussion!—what kind of character-download was the fellow priming himself to configure, in "life and art"? Was he fixing to be a guy who likes to be known for what he is?

***

You Said (1986)

You said there was an easy, it wasn't.
There was always still a place.
There was no way there was no side.
There was a drift, and a stain in the ocean.

O you who know my heart!
Quickly lest I am at the mercy of...
Row, the side, oar traps as specialists.
A winding path along the mall.

There is a table mat beside the table.
It is all there is to hold.
Did it but know, then leave space.
It made no gesture of yielding.

And so he keeps on going, and we are in the early second millennium of our time. See him search for ways to be himself right onto the paper, no interventions required, but plenty of sideways?

Like a Geometry (2001)

It didn't seem to matter where I went
With my protruding.
The crack was a monitoring.
But inside I was not on the side,

I was in the place under the side.
My love for the side grew hot.
I browsed over the crowded places of the side,
Hoping there would be a side to love.

But the fact is the side kept being away,
Kept being of another who was monitoring.
O side, return in front. Be of other
Yes, like a geometry, a stele,

Be a hand at the outside.
Go drench your self in a side.
It is the place to be given away.
Of course there is a fabric.

The fabric and the side may fight.
There may be a quintain of fire.
Go there to the side.
Be careful, fire. Be chosen or smart.

You may take away what is left.
There is a place where you can leave the side.
Put it in a corner.
Let it stay there, on the side.

Such an assertion of indirectness, blended with the same kind of willingness we saw in, say, the real old "My Room", 1957, where off-perception gulps up the daily. The character download, here and throughout these serene work pieces? It is as though the voice writer had stepped outside the traditions of making poetry. He is not imagining. He is not intervening. He is virtually not talking even to himself, but he is calculating in language, a funky mathematician ausculting a wide intersection of ratios for being in the world.

**

It's the Figueroa Principle (2000)

It's the principle of reciprocity.
If a stone falls in jungle peat
It will rattle on down,

Rattle through the tubers.

If the tubers are not tightened
Up daily old antelope old boy.
So the stone goes on settling
Carapace of moss, dribbly tooth.

The Senator will have a throat
For this, for he is dumb.
He wants American things
In American jungle not in Philly.

Authors on cards stick to the table.
Each sure wears a beard stuck on.
There's fodder and nestling there.
A rope of cheese is sent down

To show the stone the way to drymouth.
Oh *Novum Organum* yourself
You soufflé of Enlightenment metaphors.
Drab, drab, drab, they chuckle,

Watching the terminal fall.
Drabber than a night on the moon.
The rich phlox of butter and jelly.
I said reciprocal and meant it.

The stone thuds against the Tomb of Lenin.
Sparks jerk their ways through the moss.
The training wheels on the President's
Perambulator are removed.

He slips from his carriage.
Before they catch him he slips into the ground.
His face is a mudgy peat too.
He is surely trying to convince the Senator

But it's too late.
Driftwood stacks up in his smile.
He treats a subordinate wretchedly.
Come, Spirit, dumb the rink.

***

Please Take My Truck and Drive It (2002)

Please take my truck and drive it any direction.
When it comes to rest you will find a door and a troll.
Turn off the ignition. Close the doors and lock them.
Please bring back my truck and drive it in any direction.

Drive my truck into the shower.
Take a shower made up chiefly of my truck
And my littoral. Let a sandy beach replace the truck.
For an hour you can wander, avoiding the waves.

Give my truck nowhere to go and it will follow.
Read with me in the corner of my truck door.
Bring the truck back full of illuminati.
You will be of the cognoscenti

Driving my truck in any direction
And at any door walking away from it.
Come inside I am in my truck and we are.
It was a long drive but we made it and are here.

Doesn't matter if you have a license; drive.
A truck in the west is just another boulder.
It will steam until you…go right here, west.
There is a door on the far side, a window.

Enter if you like through the window of the truck.
Make yourself part of the tumult shower.
Go in at a careless entrance and thrive.
A door is only a door if you allow it.

The last time I was in Kansas.
Didn't you breed then, somewhere around back?
Custom had it that breeding was of the door.
A generation tottered from there.

We had a wing and a prayer to travel.
Not having a skeleton though he rested at the door.

From there they transferred him.
He left the building in terms of a door.

                              ***

You Will See My Point (2003)

For all I know you will see my point.
In one sense it is a door of mine.
Sleep in that archway and thrive!
Only two ways to revise a view,

A door and an arch into the door.
No one had suggested the roadway.
The roadway was far too sharply.
There was strain on a bird.

At Amritsar the temple began to dissolve.
A flow chart is in an artery.
It is a staple of the locals.
They keep a chart in the door, a corner.

Moan carefully if you like.
Door, door or window. All the same.
You enter here, then go west.
By the door there will be a road.

You will see my point.
You will go a long way to tell me.
There will be a sign there to tell me.
Had I a chance I would stop by the door.

If I am absent go west.
There you will find me, and no door,
No closure, just hills to follow.
I will be a seed of parsley.

Come back to me slowly from the door.
You know how I can reduce
From a bone. Eat some carefully.

The door is loosely open and afire.

Yet a clause in the contract wrote me off.
I had to explain to someone.
Oh come, blaze, be total, not anxious.
Stand by me, weather the door.

***

I Am Dog-Tired this Morning (1999)

I am tired as a dog this morning.
I didn't sleep well. My hand hurts.
We will try cheese on it first.
When you pass the fire hydrant.

On the left there are dimes.
Farther beyond them is a whirligig.
You can go to the side with a cheese.
Labels are misleading.

Are there flames in the west?
I thought I saw a figure at the door.
There is another window open.
It is rarely the time to don a wig.

Cherubim, to the door.
Enter with your flames.
Go around to the side where there is a door.
Labile choices ride away.

In the wind a small voice.
I tore it from the mountainside.
Ants came out from the cracks.
Did you go to the door on the left?

He comes out of the door with a care.
I will take him away to a door.
He will go in, there will be an allée.
He will walk in loops up the allée.

Nothing but a fyre will remain.
Its ash will not give birth.
There will be a door to be closing.
Meanwhile he is far up the road.

He will come to the door first.
Please be patient with the road from the door.
In winter the door is of treble power.
He is clearly there, beside the door.

***

Argg: Time for Breakfast (2007)

Argg. Time for breakfast again.
I forgot the paste but I remembered the teeth.
And I took them along with me to Spain.
How the señoritas loved them!

I rode a bull in downtown Pamplona
Until he turned ugly and had to rein.
The rain in Spain falls on the bulls,
On the hedgehogs and on the red

Furry diplodocus that explodes when tickled.
Oh choose me, he bellowed, I'm fine,
I run when pushed, lie when tethered.
Come have a look at what's under my garment.

Well, he shat on Wellington Street.
It was inappropriate but hard to avoid
Given the robust condition of his underwear.
He had clean itchy-pitchies in a drawer.

Within poem-things there are any number of statemental differences.
"Love Me, Love My Dog," and "Please Take My Truck and Drive It"
affect development along a narrative line, while "I Am Dog-Tired this
Morning" remains content with largely disjointed articulations: cf. lines
three and four of stanza 1, or lines three and four of stanza 3 for the
"paralytic" argument of "dog tired." Reduced to some blockage into its

elements, poetry of such stripes has no truck with the comforts of character!

Okay, you get the serene bit? Isn't it somewhat screwy stuff, curling its tendrils over the feel of the daily, the kind of *hey that's it* that you get from or while reading Merleau-Ponty's *Phénoménologie de la Perception*, and you zap know that is what being-here-in-the-world is like. It's not like there's nobody writing these serene poems, and telling you that he's there and that he's the real human personal thing, and that he is willing to share with you but not sure whether you are there, but it's that he's not doing the conversational talk-talk thing for you. Serene sure is one kind of name to give this angularity which is the best antidote to behaving bad, losing your family, losing the love that sustains you, and learning how to drink (a little) before breakfast.

Bad boy phase marginalized, *el poeta*, now topping sixty, both enters the gamezone of *The Modernist Impulse and a Contemporary Opus; Replaced by Writing* (Cambridge Scholars, 2017) with its thrusts at the novel, but also freckles up into a first, the toneless dramatic monologue, in which the character download is slowed to a molasses. Dry as dust and hurtful, the banner is flying over the following escapade from the backyard in Iowa; but this time statemental sequence and rigor, and an abundance of rope, pay out into the audiosphere.

Anonymous Assault (2007–14)

*

It was late.
He'd been combining, first time with the new engine.
Powerful stuff.
He'd done half the soy beans between four in the afternoon, and now; it was nearly eleven.
He'd taken a shower.
She'd demanded it, ever since she came out to him from town, and wrapped herself around his life.
And he'd been mighty lonely, time she got there.
He knew it was hard for a woman.
Getting up every morning quarter past four just soon as they heard the sparrows in the trees.
They'd roll over against each other.

He'd be horny, but it was nothing to her, she shoved over onto her side
and slept a few minutes.
He'd get up.
Go out into the first half light.
He'd feed the chickens.
She'd come with hot milk.

*

It was late.
He cleaned up and turned over.
She was there, all he wanted to know.
For a minute he smoothed her hair.
Then he dropped off, heavily.
He snored and twisted.
Damn, she said, the noise.
They'd gotten a party line phone.
Two months before.
It rang when anyone on the line made a call.
Never knew if it was for you.
She pulled herself up.
Her ma warn't too good.
Some kind of growth and nobody understood it.
Could always be her.
She pulled on a woolen wrapper.
The house was cold, sharp early fall,
A threat of frost.
She went down carefully.
No way she wanted to fall.
Not like caring for one, nope,
Caring for two.
She lifted the receiver.

*

It was dead silent.
She thought there was no one there.
She listened for the operator who usually came in after the silence.
No operator.
She was about to hang up when she heard nothing.
Nothing? Nothing is something isn't it?

She listened again.
Someone was breathing?
Was it the dog?
She looked around quickly.
He wasn't even inside.
He must have been left out in the barn.
She listened again.
Someone said are you there?
Instinctively she answered yes.
Someone said are you there and stressed the there.
I said I'm here.
Back up.
Back up?
It was a man.
It was the rough voice of a man.
She was confused.
Back up?
The phone went dead.
She put it back on the hook.
She was upset.
She sat down on the edge of the settee and looked at the wall.
Her heart was pounding.

*

Next day her husband went into town for feed.
It was sunny.
She went out in the yard.
The weeds were growing in her vegetable garden.
She bent over and pulled up handsful of vetch.
The soil was damp and clayey, and her fingers stained.
She went in and washed her hands.
She ate some soup.
She sat down and looked at *The Saturday Evening Post*.
It was full of advertisements.
She would have liked living in a city.
There were interesting new things there.
She had been raised in Comstock.
A few thousand.
It had seemed big to her.
Her dad had gotten a car.

She'd gone to school in it.
She'd been admired.
She'd had friends.
Sooner or later though she'd gotten married.
Her husband was a farmer.
She'd followed him to his acreage.
She was sitting in his parlor.
No she was sitting in the parlor.

*

It rained the next few days.
Her husband was mostly in the barn fixing equipment.
She washed and canned.
Her half-sister came by once from her farm down the road.
The two sisters ate together.
Then they separated, to their own parlors.
He came in for supper.
He went to the phone.
He called his Dad in town.
But his dad wasn't feeling good.
They didn't talk long.
There was other folks on the line.
He always relayed something.
Mrs. Hansen was expecting.
The pastor had been out fishing with his brother.
There was a horse loose from Whitbread's stable.

*

Not long after he went to the field the phone rang.
She was reluctant to answer.
But she did.
A bright metallic voice, woman? man? who knew? asked how she was.
Could be worse she replied.
She wondered if she should have replied.
Nothing's ever perfect.
The voice had become a person's.
What do you want?
Back up.
What do you mean back up?

She began to get that feeling again.
But did she want to live in ignorance?
I'm standing in my parlor.
Are you alone?
This time it was the rock-hard voice she had heard before.
Let me get my husband.

*

The next day she took the car into town to see her mom.
She told her mom about the phone.
Her mom was perplexed.
Phone service was itself not second nature to her mom.
Comstock got service when Mom was in mid-life.
She never called.
She just went around the corner.
Or she listened on the party line.
Her daughter was plainly worried.
But she didn't say so.
Mom just knew.
George okay? she asked.
Sure, same as ever.
Liking the harvesting? she asked.
Sure, a little lonely. Sure.
Mom was determined to understand.

*

The harvest usually took about three weeks.
What with combining, baling hay, getting the soybeans to town.
Lots of little things too.
Welding a tractor hitch.
Calling around to grain elevators for the best price.
Checking the moisture content.
His mind was full of these things.
Neither he nor she exactly noticed the other.
Not exactly.
But when he reached over in the bed at eleven
He found that she was asleep.
Seemed different.
She noticed she didn't sleep much.

When she did she dreamed.
That was new.

*

The harvest came to an end.
The grain elevators were filled.
The nights were turning chilly.
No frost yet, but chilly.
He was in the house a lot more.
Or out in the barn.
She kept the house immaculate.
She ironed the curtains and bashed down the cobwebs.
She didn't sleep as she used to.
They did make love sometimes.
Owls hooted in the barn searching for mice.

*

One day they were sitting in the parlor.
It was nearly time for supper.
The dog was sleeping by the artificial fireplace.
The phone rang.
He got it.
She there? the voice asked.
Who's she? he asked.
The phone went silent.
He didn't hang up.
Who the hell are you?
He thought he knew the voice.
He kept on talking.
We got the moisture content down, he said.
Should have the load ready next week.
But he was talking to himself.
He hung up.
What was all that?

*

She had to go to her sister's.
She had been away four days.

It was no fun traveling in the fall.
The roads were bumpy and dusty.
The old car was falling apart now.
She had thought of her husband.
She had missed him.
She knew he missed her.
She tried to make herself prettier.
Her sister, who was expecting,
Always had beauty secrets.
Put your hair this way.
Over on the side.
Tuck your blouse in.
Did you ever try a touch of color on your cheeks?
She was excited by these ideas.
She would be glad to be home.

*

He was glad to see her.
They prepared a dinner they liked.
They listened to the radio after dinner.
She could tell he wanted to go to bed with her.
They talked a little about farm chores.
Should they buy a couple of new hens?
Should they start mending the fence around the house?
That was for prettiness.
She said yes.
She wanted to live well.
He wanted her to want that.
He pulled the curtains shut and turned off the light.
They went upstairs.
When he wanted her she was shy.
Unlike her sister.
She envied her sister.
She copied her a little.
She touched the rouge pad to her cheeks.
She saw him going into the back room.
He was going to undress.
They undressed in separate rooms.
She got in bed.
He turned off the lights.

*

In the early morning the phone rang.
He turned heavily.
She snapped to attention.
She went to the back room.
She lifted the receiver.
At first it was silent.
Then a man's voice spoke.
She knew it.
Back up it said and hold the phone.
She wondered where the party line was.
Where was the operator?
Should she yell?
What would her husband think?'
These thoughts took only a second.
Already the man's voice was repeating.
He said to back up.
What did back up mean?
Pick up a piece of dust.
A piece of dust?
She almost laughed.
She was in her Penney's nightgown.
It was cold in the back room.
Even in Fall they had frost.
She was shivering.
She felt she was being hurt.
But she had reserves.
She had strength.
That strength had given her determination.
How else would she have left home for the country?
All this was in her mind.
All the time.

*

For days she bore these secret events.
She thought of telling her pastor.
What could he say, though?
He was a young man.
If he had a secret life it was buried.

He was busy.
He had church members night and day.
They had problems.
She thought of how sensible he was.
She tried thinking in his place.
Some woman called me.
She has gotten anonymous phone calls.
She is disturbed.
Then she thought how he would speak to those issues.
You must tell your husband.
Why don't you tell your Mother?
You must pray.
You must not go to the phone when it rings.

*

Days went by.
It had been a year since the phone calls.
Twelve months.
The first buds of spring were appearing.
The land was softer looking.
Her husband had sold seed corn in the winter.
She had knitted.
She had read the books of Mark and Luke.
She read Revelations.
She had been joyful thinking of a Golden City.
A wren had played hip-hop on her window eaves.
That was even in the coldest days.
Now she could go out in ordinary clothes.
Just a shawl around her.
Did she feel pretty?
She didn't know.
What did pretty mean?
Pretty was what others said of you.
Her husband was no talker.
He was a worker.
He cared for her.

*

Her husband was called to jury duty.

He took the car.
He would be staying at the county seat.
He would be hearing a case of juvenile murder.
This was very rare.
He told her about it.
She was shocked.
A child kill a parent?
He said it made him sick.
He drove away frustrated.
He hated leaving her.
He hated leaving the fields.
He might be away a week.
His mom would call in on her.
So would hers.
She wouldn't be alone.
He drove off.

*

After he had gone she thought about him.
He was not handsome.
But he was strong.
The way he lifted a hayrick
All by himself.
Or the time they asked the young fellow,
A beefy teenager,
To help off-load the soybeans.
They started working at four.
The kid fell asleep in the tractor.
Her husband left the kid off at the house.
The kid slept all afternoon in the back room.
Maybe he was sick.
Her husband went on working 'til midnight.
And got up the next day at four.
That's the way he was.
Strong and wired.
Her dad had screwed around a lot.
She'd learned this from her mom.
He'd had other women.
Who could even find him now?
Her husband was strong and reliable.

*

Her body was her secret.
It was what never got said because it was there first.
When she thought that she thought about the Foundation of the World.
Didn't Jesus say he'd been there before the foundation of the world?
To her that fact was the fact of her own life.
It had been there first, the body she was, her presence,
Long before she thought about it or named it.
These seemed to her deep thoughts.
She thought them and thought about them.
They were what made her feel dependent.
It was not her husband.
He labored for her food and shelter.
He gave her clothes to put on.
He did little things for her too.
He had given her a kitten in the hard winter.
That had kept her nerves steady.
She cared for him, as she had been told to.
But she'd had an early hint of problem.
She'd thought marriage meant forever.
She'd thought if you loved someone
You would be with that person in heaven.
Her husband had said no.
That was not how he saw it.
He saw it that each of us is alone in their faith.
The end was a terrible and overwhelming
Meeting with Jesus.
A personal meeting.
She'd been disturbed by that.
It had choked something that had felt like love.
Maybe it had been the loss of a sense of dependence.
Her body was her secret.
If he wanted it that way.
She and her body,
Or she following her body,
Would go to meet her maker.

*

These thoughts deepened in her.

She was a Bible reader.
But more than that a Bible thinker.
The third time the phone caught her off guard she thought it was a voice
from on high.
Her husband had been down in the barn.
It was a cold autumn day.
The birds had been flying in all directions.
She knew that because she had gotten up in the night.
She had relieved herself.
She had walked around in the parlor for a few minutes.
There had been something uneasy there.
But she had heard nothing.
And her husband had been sleeping heavily.
He was tired these days.
She had tried to let him sleep.
But he had waked when she crawled back into bed.
They had talked about the winter ahead.
Should she go stay with her mom?
She had pushed aside the idea.
It was not the right move for a wife.
Should they keep trying for that child?
He held her as he asked this.
She was tired, trying.
Eventually they had gone to sleep.
Rolling around on the stiff mattress like a couple of eggs.
Touching, separating, moving back and forth.
Dawn had come.
She fixed him a meat sandwich and coffee.
Now here she was.
God's creation.
The day was going to be long.

*

When the phone rang she was drinking milk.
She still had her gown wrapped around her.
It fluttered when she hurried to the phone.
She rarely heard the phone ring.
When she did it was party line stuff.
That was sometimes juicy.
Usually not.

But it was words about her world.
That was like an extra friend to talk to.
The voice was brittle.
How're you doing this morning?
It was directed to her?
On a party line you weren't sure.
Until you got into a conversation.
I saw you in town, near your mom's.
It was an epicene voice.
Was it for her?
Did you hear me?
She still didn't know.
Me, you remember?
You? Who are you?
There, she too spoke,
She was drawn into the human vortex.
Now it was silent.
Except for noise in the background.
Did she know how to pray?
She knew how to pray.
Knees on the hardwood.
Her head bent.
She knew only too well.
Who asked her?
She spoke again.
What did you say?
Did you ask if I know how to pray?
Were you asking me?
There was something like a clatter of dishes in the phone.
Get down and pray.
Stay there til I tell you.
She stared at the phone.
Pray right there in the cold?
Before dressing?
Before getting her bible?
Did you ask me to get down and pray?

*

Her husband was cold.
He was not old but he had arthritis.

These autumn mornings killed him.
Especially working with cold metal.
He cleaned shovels.
He straightened teeth on his wood saw.
He replaced some worn bolts on his tractor axle.
Every time he changed one he had to thaw out.
He'd go in the house sometimes.
Just to warm up.
Sometimes he'd take a glass of warm water.
They would make a wood fire.
He would sit close to it.
Then he would go out again.
His knuckles would hurt him when they scraped on the edge of a table.
Now and then, at work,
He looked at himself and thought, I am not happy.
At those times he had a glimpse of the oddness of thought and language.
Thinking something was not the same as being something.
It was like you could say anything.
He could have said I am happy.
It wouldn't have mattered what he said.
Whatever he said he'd be either unhappy or happy.
These aporias flitted by him now and then.
He was used to putting them right to work.

*

She had never before been told to pray.
The wood hurt her knees.
It was not like cleaning the floor.
When you clean the floor you move.
Her knees were bare.
Get down and pray.
Pray what?
What did you say? she said into the phone.
The voice came back rude.
Now urinate the voice said.
Urinate?
There was a noise in the background.
Was it in the phone?
Was it in her own house?
Was it her husband?

She was very silent.
She was what she thought was good.
She had always been.
Do it the voice said.
She was alone with the order.

*

Her husband's parents were not well.
He had not known life was going to close in this way.
Like his wife he had been brought up country Methodist.
He believed what the parson said about heaven.
There would be rejoicing in the kingdom.
People who had never danced would dance.
God's throne would be golden.
We would all be able to touch it.
This vale of tears was sad, true.
But the future trumped it.
Now his dad had heart congestion.
He'd been rushed to the local emergency.
His mom had been beside herself.
Sisters and an uncle had come from another county.
It was just hard.
It was just the news to deal with.
It hurt like the cold bony fingers he woke with.
It hurt like the discolored toe he'd dropped a drill bit on.
He figured he'd better call on Mom again.
As if he hadn't called the day before.
He'd rather have dropped it.
But she'd be desperate.
He'd go on in and call.
Maybe drive quickly into town in the late afternoon.

*

She dropped back on her haunches like an animal.
She was alone with herself and a voice.
The voice was up there in the phone.
Or was it in the room?
She was a simple woman.
She had desires.

She had no fear of death.
She did things one at a time as she had been told.
To her surprise she rose to her knees and peed.
It was not much.
It was really just a few drops.
But she was behaving like an animal.
This could not be good.
She felt the secret her body was all around her.
It wrapped her like a cloak.
She was trembling now.
She thought she heard a voice on the phone.
She rose and as she did there was a little puddle beneath her.
Hastily she wiped at it.
It was like wiping up after a puppy.
Done it? asked the voice on the phone.
She went back to the little puddle and wiped it more.
Did it, she said to her horror.
Outside she heard a clattering.
She put the phone down quickly.
Her husband was coming toward the door.
She cleaned the puddle again.

*

What we call quality time, today, is fleeting but precious.
A husband and wife, or a boy and his dog.
They sit down and talk or just share being here.
On the Iowa farm, a few generations ago,
People didn't really strive for quality time.
It was not a concept.
Work was the concept.
And making new workers for the farm.
Still people are people.
And when they are put together they live in terms of each other.
Her husband was that way.
He was sensitive and even thought about his feelings.
We have seen that he thought about what went on in his head.
We know he was concerned with the difference between language and thought.
When you are interested in that difference you have to be interested in what other people sound like to themselves.

That interest is a kind of being in society.
He was concerned with his dad.
He was concerned about his fields.
But right up there in him in front of concern was awareness.
He was aware, as he fumbled through the cold into the house that there was a feeling in the room.
It didn't feel the same as when he had gone to the barn.
He kicked off his boots at the door.
He looked around.
The room was warm.
You there? he called.
She answered from the kitchen.
She was drying dishes and shuffling around.
I am here Mr. Brown she said.
Ummnnn he said.
Cold out still?
Ummmm he said.
Cold as the twelve winds.
This was an expression his mom had used.
Cold.
He went to the phone.
Calling your dad?
He picked up the Bakelite receiver and had a feeling.
Was the phone warm or sweaty?
Probably not.
Probably just the contrast with his cold hands.
He spoke into the phone.
He called his mom.
He arranged to go into town.
When he had finished she had gone up the back stairs to her sewing nook.
He called to her.
He said he was going into town.
Could she come down and pray with him before he left the house?
They often prayed when one of them was going out.
They prayed to be well.
She said she was a little busy.
He asked again.
She came slowly down the back stairs.
She acted nervous.
Are you well, asked Mr. Brown.
I am well she replied, taking his arm.

They knelt down together facing the reproduction of a painting of the
Virgin and Child.
Now she was wearing the simple gray housedress she had sewn.
He was wearing rough faded overalls.
They knelt on the floor.
They took one another's hands.
It was cold on the floor in the parlor.
They prayed and then they were silent.
He got up and went out.

*

Toward autumn
Bugs sought shelter in the house and whirred around the lampshade, or got
into the clothes in their bedroom closet.
In the damp cold, fungus formed around the feet of the bathtub and clung
to the work boots they lined up in the back hallway.
Her mom had taught her how to soak a brush in lemon caustic and scrub
the corners.
She was glad to know how to do this.
She was good at it now.
It made the house smell good.
She cleaned the house thoroughly this day after her husband drove down
the lane.
It would be hours 'til he returned.
Before she finished her scrubbing she went quickly over to the floor where
the little puddle had been, and polished the floor there.
She didn't want to be hurt again that way.

*

Her husband was from a large family.
They knew everybody and everybody knew them.
They were gregarious and friendly.
They were in real estate and insurance and the police department and it
was possible, she thought, that one of them was the one who played a
phone prank on her.
She thought about this as she went through the hen coops, scattering seeds
and guiding the older hens back into their pens.
It had been a risk, calling on the party line.
Anyone could listen in.

Thing was though, not many people used the phone line, especially during the day.
Some ladies listened to the radio in the day.
Most guys were at work.
Oddly enough, it made her feel better, analyzing this situation.
While she was doing that she thought of another kind of move she could make.
She could just never answer the phone.
At least when her husband was around, for sure.
This made her feel better?
She thought to herself I am feeling better and clearer and I have a kind of control over my feelings.
She left a bowl of slightly soured milk in the barn for the cats.
They were good mousers.
She saw them lap it up.
She went back toward the house.
It was a beautiful day, gentle.
There was the first soft blossom of the leaf buds.
She liked that.
As she entered the door she asked herself what she would do if she entered to hear the phone ringing.
It wasn't really a ring she feared, like a bell.
It was a staccato shrillness in the air.
She didn't hear it, hadn't heard it for days.
Her husband never used the phone.
She only called her mom.
She thought about the phone.
She went in and sat down.
Was she *waiting* for a phone call?

*

The party line operator knew everything about everything.
Or rather she knew just enough to know too little.
Let me explain.
All calls began with her.
You rang her up at zero.
She answered.
She asked who you wanted to call.
Then she rang you up.
While you were talking she was right there.

She could hear your conversation.
So could everyone else who picked up on the line.
When they picked up the phone there would be the conversation.
They would have to wait their turn.
They could of course listen, while waiting.
Many did.
So did the operator, some of the time.
The rest of the time, though, the operator was fielding incoming calls and prioritizing them in a queue.
Everybody couldn't speak at once.
Only one conversation could be going on at the same time.
The system was an invitation to eavesdropping.
Many townspeople eavesdropped a lot, though some, by a natural instinct, hung up when they heard a conversation in progress.
The same with the operator.
She was as interested as anyone.
But pretty soon she fell into a job is a job mode.
She didn't pay much attention.
Naturally gossip was generated, and based on supposition, like most gossip.
She wondered whether anyone had heard the call she received and that was on her mind.
A few people had picked up that day.
A few of them had been struck by the mixtures of silence and command and crisp almost military tone.
And by the fact that there was no response from the other end.
Her end.
They had thought directions were being given.
There were three or four women who had noted.
They talked about it over Bridge that week.
That was about it.
They had other fish to fry.

*

His dad was doing better.
They had put in a stent.
That helped
His breathing had evened out his heartbeats.
The old guy was too precious to lose.
He was a joker, he was a responsible dad.

Everybody liked him.
When he got home neighbors came to visit.
George was there but he didn't know a lot of these people.
They joked with his dad.
Then they decided to let the old guy rest.
They went into the parlor.
His mom brought around ice tea.
There were eight or ten folks.
He sat with them and rocked.
It was the first afternoon he had rested for a long time.
It was relaxing to be with his own folks.
His wife was a wonderful woman.
But he was a little afraid of her.
She always seemed to him to live around secret spaces that he could not enter.
That was exciting.
But it made him feel on the outside.
Made him want her too, like something different.
It was good to be on home ground.
He listened and didn't pay much attention.
Then the phone rang.
His aunt hopped up and listened.
Then she put it down and sat down.
Funny thing, she said, May told me.
May was the operator.
They all paid attention.
The operator was like the Delphic Oracle.
Said she put a guy on the phone.
She heard him say a couple of words.
Nothing at the other end.
She didn't know whether to cut off the call.
She took a minute away from the phone.
Then she went back.
All this recounted slowly, with gestures, *muy intensivo.*
And then what happened? his sister-in-law asked.
Not a lot.
She heard more silence, then a couple of commands.
That was her word.
Commands.
How did she know they were commands?
The tone of voice.

What did the voice command?
Silence.
No answer.
Hey, the operator has her conscience too!

*

In the dead of winter farm life slows.
We all know that.
It is two years since the start of this story within a story.
I heard it from a man who had weathered an Iowa winter.
He had been alone that winter
Except for the phone.
None of the other stuff.
No TV.
No radio.
But he'd gone near nuts.
He'd been wanting to finish a book about Africa.
It had been slow going.
He told me how he'd go to the phone sometimes,
When he should have been working.
He'd listen.
Maybe for an hour.
Then he'd go back to his work.
It was terribly hard concentrating.
There was no distraction from concentrating.
Hence the phone became a matter of preoccupation.
When he remembered that winter it was the phone he remembered.

*

She was getting that way too about the phone.
It wasn't just the memory of the disturbing event.
Lots of friends called her.
Or she thought it lots.
Her grandma called.
Her aunt called.
Once she had a call from a guy who had been sweet on her in high school.
Maybe two or three calls a day.
Her husband got calls too.
When the phone was for them it rang four times.

That was their signal.
They could listen to other calls.
We know that.
But when it was their number it was their call.

*

One day in late March she had a call she couldn't interpret.
She wasn't even sure it was for her.
When she lifted the receiver the man asked for George.
That was not her husband's everyday name.
His everyday name was Tom.
George Thomas Jones.
When people asked for George it tended to mean they didn't know him.
She said George wasn't at home.
That was true.
The man seemed unsure.
He said I want to reach George and then he gave her husband's last name.
It was the right name.
You have the right number she said.
But he's not here.
The man seemed satisfied.
But he didn't say anything for a minute.
She wondered whether to hang up.
She didn't like to do that.
Then he asked her when George would be home.
She didn't really know.
She said he was in town.
He would be back by dark.
The man again seemed satisfied.
Then he asked her if he could ask her a question.
What kind of question was that.
Nobody asks you if they can ask you a question.
She didn't know why she said yes.
She supposed later that she had been brought up that way.
She had been brought up on the idea that if someone wants to ask you a question they can.
So she said yes.
Can you remember that I called you before? he asked.
Then oh my God she knew she remembered.
She remembered how she had complied with that voice.

Now was the time to replace the phone and call someone her husband the
police the operator.
Who should she call?
And if she just hung up the phone and kept a silence?
Would that work inside her?
It was surprising how fast all these queries and options went through her
head.
It was also surprising how habituated she was to complying with requests.
From childhood on she had been brought up into that compliance.
Yes Granma I will.
Yes aunty, I will go the store for you.
Yes Miss Perkins I will turn in the math homework by noon tomorrow.
It had been that way when George had "asked for her hand."
It hadn't occurred to her to say no.
She didn't exactly not "love him" but she automatically obeyed him.
Yes I remember she said.
You remember what I asked you to do?
Yes. Why did you ask me to do it?
No response. The wind was roaring outside today.
There was a big storm.
Have I asked you to do anything now?
Who are you?
No response.
No you haven't.
I want you to be drenched in waiting for me.
What?
She shifted position.
She looked out the window.
It would be hours 'til George got back.
She didn't want to try to understand what was being said.
I have to go.
Go then.
She hung up.

*

Many days went by.
Life took its normal course.
The same things at the same time.
Only there was time.
In the light of time everything looked always a little different.

Her husband looked tireder after work and she felt tireder.
But they also had fun.
The most fun they had was Parcheesi.
She had learned the game with her grandmother, and they had played
endlessly.
It was a good conflict, with room for spurts of winning and ways of
blocking the other person.
Her grandmother had loved the blocking.
It was punishment but in the spirit of the game.
Her grandmother had also liked croquet.
That was for the same reason.
She adored trapping her adversary's ball and hammering it out into a patch
of thick grass.
It was a benign kind of fury.
She and her husband played Parcheesi in the evenings.
That was something they did together.
Did they make love?
Sometimes.
But you know what she felt about it?
It was like two giant turtles.
This was how she would dream about it.
Clunk clunk.
Prehistoric.

*

She supposed that although she was not in the world of crisis still she was
not in a stable world.
She was too much alone.
The phone call business had been disturbing.
But it was intermittent.
She wasn't sure, from the last call, what the tenor of it was.
She knew she had felt compliant.
She remembered what she had done on command.
That response had been powerful in her.
Was giving in what she wanted?
Was it perhaps a pathway to god?
Or was it simply a desperate response to loneliness?
She was not extremely introspective.
She was intelligent, like her husband who had thought about language
even while using it.

She wanted to know herself.

She was like a mediaeval mystic who was waiting for some claim on her that she could not resist and who was not beyond accepting a lower body response as the locus of the power from on high.

This set of historical anxieties blended, in her, with a fear, which was part of her time, of the power of anonymous mobbing, the assault of unidentifiable personal presences, stress *personal*, to whom one could not say no but did not know any way to say yes except raw compliance.

*

It had been over two years since the first alarming call, *the* call, and while she had not forgotten *it* she had lived out over the top of it.

There were no big waves on which she rode over the top of that memory. There were just little waves in the sea of life.

No baby yet. No wealth yet—in fact not much more than decent poverty, grounded in a couple hundred acres. Was she pretty? She was the image of herself. She had nowhere to go with it. She was usually at home on the farm. She cleaned. She prepared meals. Who was she?

She was asking herself this in early June.

Her husband was sorting out seed corn and setting aside the consignments he had promised to neighbors.

He was a DeKalb rep, in addition to being a full-time farmer.

It was a way to earn during the winter.

These were times of repetition and heavy skies.

*

She was fixing a cake for the birthday party of a neighbor child.

It was mid-afternoon.

The phone rang.

Three jangles.

She instinctively hurried to it.

The voice she knew was there.

She felt alone but not alone.

The voice seemed part of her.

The voice told her to be silent and humble and take the power of the world on herself.

The voice told her to lie down on her face with the phone and eat the phone.

She tried to eat it.

She tried to nibble at the Bakelite.
Later she could not believe that this had happened or that she had taken it seriously.
She had been that alone.
The voice commanded her to vomit.
Suddenly she did.
She retched across her plain apron.
She retched and retched.
When she was able to rise the voice was gone.
She stumbled back into the kitchen to wash her face and take off her apron.
At that moment the front door into the parlor opened.
It was her husband scraping his boots and coughing as he did when he came in on cold days.
He called to her.
She had sprinted up the back stairs to their bedroom.
She was distraught.
Her hair was dripping with sweat.
Her breath was foul.
She was hardly in herself.
He called again.
She didn't answer.
Then she thought that would be worse, not to answer.
She called faintly to him from the bathroom.
He was confused by the smell in the parlor.
It was vomit smell.
He went over to the phone and smelled it because it too stank.
Was the floor damp?
He had not forgotten, though he thought he had, that moment years before when he had found the room sticky with the sense of the phone.
The phone was a kind of mouthpiece to the world but a big fellatio to the world too and he was not comfortable with phones and now he was deeply uncomfortable with himself.
He was the type, anyway, to stand away and to breathe the air.
He stepped out for a moment.
He adjusted the latch on the barn door.
Just to make sure.
Then he went back in.
He called her again.
No response.
He went to the backstairs, but as though knowing it was not right.

It was not the way to move forward.

*

She had been devastated by the call and especially by her own catastrophic response.
It was one of those undoing responses that seems to set your whole life back.
All you had determined to be, in yourself, was undone.
She felt helpless.
And transparent.
In the last months she had built places in herself where she could be self-sufficient.
Perhaps if she had loved her husband it would have helped.
But did she love anyone?
Even herself?
When she saw him standing there she dissolved.

*

Such a scene drove him mad at once.
He stood there at the top of the stairs.
But he was not really anywhere.
He felt he was in a house of sickness.
He had been turning the party line issue in his head for weeks.
He went back to the conversation he had heard in town.
There had been such talk of the party line.
And of its dangers and of its dissoluteness.
He was a strict and jealous country Christian.
He was not really a loving man.
Nor had his wife given him much to love, as he saw it.
They had fun sometimes.
In bed, infrequently.
And then pretty mechanically.
At Parcheesi.
That was fun.
And he had been working past his strength to build an acreage that would care for them both and for the children he wanted to have.
Now he was sure she had been talking to another man.
He didn't know how to handle this emotion.

He didn't know how to handle her stink, her disheveled clothes, her wild look.
He stood there looking at her.

*

Despite the seeming foreshortening of time, as both husband and wife experienced it, more than two years had passed since the first anonymous call, and the event on the floor.
It would have seemed, to an observer on the wall of their house,
That these anonymous attacks were infrequent and fell into a pattern much discussed in the surrounding culture.
There had been an era in America when loneliness had been the highlighted peril of middle class existence.
That had been the time of Riesman's *The Lonely Crowd.*
Big cities, alienated people.
The Sixties had been a cry for community.
Then the Internet came along, but deep down inside it came something else, the hollowness of a true wasteland.
Eliot's *Wasteland* had been a park compared to the present one, made up of shrinking values—not just religious but human—social complexes in and around power and hurt and territorialism.
The voice that belonged to no human was everywhere.
Our wall-hugging observer would have seen all this here but would have seen the tweak too.
The terrorism of the anonymous lay cheek-by-jowl beside the deranged.
We are all on that edge.
The curve of life is disturbing.
The search for consolation from others is perilous and uncertain.
It has to seem that recourses to order and inner discipline, like we see them in Seneca or Marcus Aurelius, are where we have to go.
The people in this little story had no such places to go.
They were barely Christian.
So they plunged into the vortex.

*

It is probable that he was jealous.
I say probable because in a world where trust is at a minimum it is as though mistrust, thinking the worst, is the default position.

Jealousy is the default position, the desire to hold onto what you have
annexed, so you can carry it with you across the threshold of death and
hold it, the annexed, to you as a viaticum or a sleep toy to make those
unsure billennia easier while the cosmos is deciding its own fate.
So what he did, does it matter?
Two individual destinies, a damp phone, a vomit-smeared apron, the
hovering flight of angels above, it all just lay out and played out as it had
to.
Add your ending.
He killed her.
She killed herself.
They went downstairs and played Parcheesi.
He went out and bought her a television set.
Who cares?

*

The phone, and the room, and the apron, and the long lost angry hours of
isolation sat in the house and would never be expunged.
I am not a great imaginer.
I like the view of this story that is the way it worked out.
These two people looked at each other.
She flew at him.
With six-inch nails she drove into his flesh.
I also don't mind his beating her.
Keep it language though.
Don't get the cops involved.
But while I was thinking of a third thing I liked
She wandered out of the room and out of my story.
She left me here with my own lonely desire to break free of the unclarity
of life.
I suddenly wanted real bad to know what kind of story had brought us
together.
I was being honest.
I don't feel old but everyone says I'm old.
Every time I open my mouth I lay words on the table and walls.
For sure I'm trying to say something,
And that is why this story is here representing me.
I'm so anxious to make something clear.
As was this woman alone in her farmhouse.
She put in a lot of time there alone.

I haven't been able to even suggest the nature of the time when she was there and there was no event.
If I could do that I could say how the creepy waiting for an anonymous phone call and the debilitating overreaction to it were much more important than the call itself.

*

They got back together.
They held on.
God knows how.
They were country, and closed in.
Waiting for wounds to heal was no new thing for them.
It was the definition of life.
Life was all about silence now.
But that's what it had always been about, silence and waiting.
If you hang in you make it through.
The telephone became for them a symbol of dangerous potential.
It can have been that that brought on their withdrawal from communications.

*

What mattered to her inside she could never explain
To herself or her husband or her mom.
It had two parts.
She shuddered to think of the anxiety promoted by the other.
We are very fragile to one another.
I can call you a dreadful name to day and that will hurt you.
That will hurt you even though the law protects you.
We say that you have a thin skin.
She had a thin skin.
Things went right through it.
So have we all.
Prisoners in jails are especially vulnerable to comments that diss them.
Omertà makes whole cultures function.
Monks on the Isle de Lerins refused even to own their own clothes.
They wanted the threat of the other, upon them, to be reduced to zero.
All this she could never explain to herself, her vulnerability.

But the other thing she couldn't explain was other people and how willingly and complexly they hurt you even though they too were paper-thin underneath it all.

It was as though hurting was a way of forgetting how easily you yourself can be hurt.

*

You know there was a real end to this story.

For it's a story about the threat from the anonymous.

That threat which is part certainly of the language of our time and perhaps of the language of being human at all times.

We are naturally afraid of the unknown, and especially of the unknown voice, for the voice is what should be a whole person addressing us and when it is just a voice without the person it can be terrifying, especially if we are alone and vulnerable.

PART FOUR:

ARGUMENTS WITH CHARON

CHAPTER TWELVE

ARGUMENTS WITH CHARON

Who knows when first the shadowy image of that dark oarsman floated through the floaters of Mr. Will's inner eye? Pretty darned early, no? This guy speaking thinks he has been close to the dark unthread since the start, for it was the hump forever presented to him from inside as to-be-climbed. It is not that life put him in the midst of death, as it does the victims of war or domestic violence, for the penner of these lines was long somehow *innocent* of the great boundary, and its play out in the daily; his first corpse, as he has said elsewhere, asserted itself in his thirties along a country road in Austin; he can still remember passing that almost waxy figure on his drive home to lunch. Mr. Death was playing a subtler evidentiary game in the formative life of this fellow dier. In his earliest Hawaiian epic, in *Fragments*, in "An Emphasis for Easter", wherever Will left his traces against himself he left his sense of being up against the existential wall. Climbable though it seemed, and worth the bruised knees, it was nonetheless a permanent wall, and is, and remains so; a permanent wall. (Much as he has tried to soften the escarpments of time, by prayer, gestures into faith systems, latterly into a "leaning into" internalization, which brings death into the game plan, and maintains with Death a bracing sportsmanship, the ready at hand menace crouches where least expected, where most the daily seems to say *ok man, go go.*)

So in turning in a final section, *right here,* to the pretense of an end-stage coverage, yours truly is in effect prolonging this entire poetic character book into its permanent form. He feels that form around him, the end game against which he is playing, and which he forever is. Deep within, he knows this end game is about being about and against. That much seems to be disengaging itself. Why else would he be so eagerly proclaiming, from page one on, what came to him only recently, in a formulation *tout fait* in his year 88, the mantra: *I live life as though it were, in itself, a standing into a future condition, in which orders I can't imagine will recapacitate me, assigning me to the rights of place.* He looks for precisely the about and against he knows implicit in the passage, and must settle for the inside (or into) for indeed he need only secure a description of self as in action towards, to meet what seems to him required for salvation history. In one sense, never give up, never stop leaning against, never stop making it possible for what is to let more of you become its stuff.

And this *against* takes on a dustier but more penetrating cast with the accumulation of years. Because it is this guy, a trove of sardonics are no bad place to herald in some of the pinches of language that belch up in the years between, okay let's say September 11, 2001, and whatever macula of time *this* is from it. (Macula, yes, for the twinklings up of time, which rise from this lively stew of decomposition, are forever slicing the daily thin.)

***

If you attended closely to the very inception of this book, you will have found that the act of naming seemed to the author a primal self-definition act. The names of the world jagged out from it in Hawaii, in *Fragments*, in "An Emphasis for Easter", while the author's first publications in the prose act—especially those in the *Giornale di Metafisica*—wrapped themselves tightly around the exploration of the naming act. (In *The Review of Metaphysics*, 1960, he thought it useful to argue that "man is a participle, half-noun, half-verb.")

***

The Medical Transcriptionist at Aigues Mortes (2015)

The waters pull back from their names
As do the small brown ponies of the Camargue.
Watching I sift the treacly sky and become less.
Things are all happening to me.

Did time slip a bone from the pocket under my rib?
Did space-treacle nag my shins into formlessness?
I know what slipping from a name can do.
Try to get with the word Camargue between me and that coast.

The Medical Transcriptionist at the End of Time (2015)

From every distance came things in search of the words they were called.

Were they dragging their labels like rats from the depths of his body?
Were world-things stripping him of the descriptions that lived by him?

Song from the Dark Ones (2015)

To the west a star
Mounted time's thick glue
And reigned. We fell full length.

Blackthorn hedges
Closed me in dumb.
I blurted dumbly.

What west furrowing fox
Scrambled past us?
Had he a leg?

Had his ruff ice?
Flame haloed him?
I stumbled like a beetle

Trapped in a circle of mucous.
Time meanwhile ended.
It was a relation things

Had to me.

The Medical Transcriptionist Books Passage (2015)

The transcriptionist is a dollar carrier, no cards,
And if possible would lay down cowries.
Homo symbolicus he hates to be,
For this reason takes the names of the body's parts and diseases
To where they belong.
In a pinch he'd drive a name through an organ
Until they are inseparable like the liver and "liver."
"Le Foie", for instance, takes up the same space as "the liver,"
And the addition of the two makes the organ space tight.

Can all the words for "liver" in all the world's languages, make it inside
there?
He's busy at stuffing!
Finally he finishes "naming" the liver, but then there's the rest of the
body.
He thinks about God, the Name of all the Names in the world,
Stuffed into things.
Could the end of the world be the unpacking of all the named crevices,
The freeing of everything from what we have called it?
The transcriptionist takes stock.
He is but a crowder of the given?

Paths (2015)

It cannot be strange to go down a path
That is nothing less than the path you climbed.
You turn for a minute and the stones are descending.
But they are the same stones you climbed.

The same stones go down in a path
To the river you walked through to this story.
You winter this story like a comrade
High on the path on the path down.

At path's end you are already returning.
You have been greeted by old compañeros.
The path climbed together is the path
Life took with all in all directions.

A path is not a motorway here.
A path is the same way up or down, turn.
This is nothing less than the path you climbed.
This is nothing other than the door you entered.

Now step back onto the path itself
You are walking the path they come to find.
You turn for a minute and the stones are ascending,
Then as in an Escher they are going down.

The right way of any path is not where you chose it

But on the long road. Others come toward you.
You walk behind a crowd, until you walk into it.
Who is crossing? The path slips off its edges
Then straightens. Another person is there.
The other person would have been known yet is not.
Who can the other be, who is on the path upward?
The path is formatted to go down, there are others.

There Must Be No Limit (2015)

There must be a way to get around the side
When the front door is blocked.
At the side there are other choices.
Other choices though are inside the house.

Inside the house there are locked doors.
At the side there is a key you need to find.
The front door is locked and there it is.
You go around to the side and look.

Inside the front door there are locks.
The way to open those locks is at the side.
You go around to the side and look.
There is a road on that side; you go.

The road though is what you remembered.
It leads to the house, a village away.
You cannot see the village from the house.
It was locked in a corner of the house.

You go back to the side;
There must be no limit, and then.
You take a long breath at the side of the house.
Last winter you were beside the house.

When you came to the house it was locked.
You drew a long road leading to it.
Then when you came around to the side
It was darkness all over again.

That was enough, you thought,
And locked it. The side was closed.
Afterwards you came to the house again.
But this time from another village.

There must be no limit.
There must be no further to go than the side.
You hurry to the locked door.
You rap at the window.

Charon indeed. We are writing this semi-final section from the later moments of the author's eighties, and though he still sports the track and the bar bells, and shouts out through the mist at passing ships like his, and rereads that splendid poem of Kunitz about sailing out alone into the North Sea, to give yourself over to the whales as a final cargo, though he still does all that he knows that he is playing a game of maximum interest now. Guy who has been spared the face of death far more than most, and allowed, far more than most, to eat at the table of life and to do so with appetite, reverts now to the languages of the Angelus, and prays that the party continue. Around him the party forever stops in its own tracks— think of the inhuman violences we do one another these years in sectarian conflict, schoolyard acting out, lonely abnegation—and yours truly fights a daily battle against refusals. The very figure of Charon—the Greek folksong has it that "I fought Charon on the sill of my house and we wrestled to the death"—provokes the strongest strike back, yet strike back we do with a readiness to yield. (What good boxer doesn't fight over a deep sense that he might himself take the real blow on the chin?)

Did serenely go with the side; were they of a pair? Nothing is more quiet, more willing to meet itself as indirection, than the side, "the side." The poetic character downloaded by side work is far from interventionist, is in fact ready to take you by the hand and sidle with you, almost as had the voice of, say, "This Autumn's Progress." Can we go further and say that serenity can walk you a country mile, spin you a long tale that may or may not lead to the cemetery? The notion of "long" is our slide into the diminuendo, or is it also the epicization of the final stages of Will's poetic opus?

Novelization of experience—Will's three African novels appeared with Mellen in 2006—*The Male's Midlife Rite of Passage: Three Imagined Lives*—plus an easing into the rhetoric of exploration, minute inquiry and narrative tension; these were components of various paths outward from the story work even of the earliest of Will's poems—"Four Moods of Our Own Odysseus", "Long Day", or "The Word for Love in Danish is Hard"—all of which *esquisses* gesture toward the sniffing curiosity of beginning, middle, and end. (Picking up, were they, on the internalizing of the life-curve, each stage of which frames within it each of the other stages?) Are we then moving, in the downloads of serene and charonic texts, into final tales to tell? Into the area of accounts to resend to the maker?

***

The World of John Holmes (2014–15)

The Zikist

***

Have we not prepared
Make that a refrain carved into the os maximum of brain
The charge for failure rises in drought years
And there is a rectangular corner in every gunshop where hunter-gatherers barter for their lost weapons

The fine for disasters is set by the county
As in the time of Charlemagne,
Who founded counties on the basis of lodgings
And who in sackcloth paraded his clowns
Over and over while the horns whined…

***

He sweltered and dealt a blow.
My, was his hand a stick!
He rose with it in a menace
And was contributed

He was a Zikisk, a Kropotkin fiend,
You name it, no stroller in the streets.
My was his hand a stick, fibrous!
At midnight they broke into his room.

But he was a tennis player too; that was
Nothing to him. He soared, I tell you.
He had an ancient signboard, vulgar.
I'll say I distanced myself!

Oh for sure they'll come slashing.
They have sleeves, made of iron.
Fly modern man before…
Holmes knows quite well what I mean.

***

Howl,
Creatures set loose on a shore so strange we find no trace of ourselves to
lie down by.
It hurts my right leg to think of it under a bench twisted backwards
Like the bewildered forces Xenophon addressed.
There was no counting their dispensation.
Xenophon had to dream.

***

He was a human wilderness,
Every part of him militia.
What else would a grad student do?
If at Goma the M23 circled

The small Pole Institute?
He determined he would continue his studies
Of the Eastern Congo where the road
In and out of town was the same.

That was not an easy decision
For someone with simulated
Gongorians on his arm and a sling.
It required all his strength to bend

Before the Germans and their herd.
Cameroon had been a better place
To swallow *njambe* and grow fat.
The spirits ducking there ducked

Duck duck and flapped around.
Over the area where the stool meets the tile.
New décor they muttered,
Exiting by the transom, roundly.

***

But the thirty-seven-year-old shopping center had problems even before July 20, when a gunman opened fire at a midnight screening of The Dark Knight Rises *in the movie theater that sits adjacent to the mall in its parking lot.*
    In recent years, shoppers have fled the aging mall for fancier centers like nearby Cherry Creek. Management, seeking to weed out what it perceived as undesirable customers, set a curfew for minors and enforced a dress code for shoppers. In 2004, a mall leasing agent was caught on audio tape explaining that the mall wanted to attract more whites and reduce negative aspects like young, black customer(s).

***

Augustine turns inside his black leather of skin
As though he knew my guilt and prefers to look at the floor.
I don't deal with prophets.

We went out to Orokpo in the afternoon.
David's house was grounded and mouldering among the mud huts and sweet shops.
What had that friend to do but die,
There in the desolation of a village doomed by potholes and COPD?
His village festered.

***

Is evil real in our time
Or simply the copy of the copy of the apparently evil?
The invention of evil without a universe to thrive in is the surface of evil.
Milton and Goethe locked the principle of evil into a universe of values or into a Manichean war of values.
The joker is media evil, and media evil can kill.

***

But is media evil evil?
The slickness of the virtual, the *mysterium tremendum* of the moment in
the technical garden,
When all hell breaks loose around the trackpad
And runners with metallic toes climb Golden Arches into the eroding
Mississippi?
Is that evil?
What about a navy captain riddled with ammo;
a downtown Denver gunshop?

***

There is a hard stupor that gathers around the minds of men and women
who are about to leave this earth.
Forgive us our sins as...
The Chinese longshoreman at the quai in Hong Kong
Turns slowly to his abandoned past and plunges it fearlessly into the
gunmouth.
They are dredging for the pasts of the fish that have eaten the fish that
have eaten the fish until they fell like dust pellets through the bottom of
the ocean and came up only this morning as that light faint trickling of
dust from the Sahara that is landing on the desiccated Iowa cornfields.

Can that too be evil, that falling apart?

Names of Things Eat the Things

***

This poetry is magic like all poetry.
Names of things eat the things, eat the hand
With all its rings. It is good to be startled.
Sometimes, when there are dogs around.

Dogs take the sting out of surprise,
Howling. There's a bitter for dogs.
Didn't you heal one once, feeding it?

Oh well, dogs and caterpillars and heads
And toes of state, they charge. They charge a lot.

Like all things created they move in circles
Among our legs. We tender them.

There is no currency in legs but what we put there.
We simply don't know the price of a leg.
Words fly off. Did you see?
Did you see the word fly?

We scraped if off. All of us scraped it. It came
Off in shreds, on the floor.
Oh man, how we had to route it then!
Our sciences failed us!

***

None of us is anyone, including John Holmes,
The letters of whose name could be creatively rearranged, Hohn Jolmes,
and who would still be no one, as we are no one, a gross and elaborate
chuntering of atoms, Lucretius' weave with valences, points where the
rain of basic particles shlurps up the land.

***

We fall apart at the mention of our names and yet we can pull pieces of
steel out of one another, in the spring when the earth upflowers into the
airy graves of the soldiers who are gone, of us all as soldiers, unremitting
and talented. And when we fall, our name tags flutter in the wind behind
us and we tremble, touching the earth, as though in love with a rent so
hard to find, some passageway back, and no GPM but only the lonely
psychopompos never too far from us, his wand tearing up the subsoil.

***

What it is to kill yourself
In the tangle of self and other and still to have the self left.

Greek science passed to the Arabs in Northern Italy.
Galileo and Brahe and Kepler mechanized those skies that Babylonians
and Greeks had peopled with figurae, hyperlinks, narrative structures, as
the Aboriginal in Australia, walking and feeling and thinking the Song

Lines, places himself in the organic geometry of the sky. Even Marcus
Aurelius felt the whole on his skin, and shuddered.

The truth does not come in splicings or quanta, but in the webwork of self
with the other that wove the self. The Olympics are part of that webwork
and as I watch/listen this morning, China and America, women at
basketball, I soar with the text of the mass, the manna that dropped like
dew to the perplexity of the Israelites. They had to settle for everything,
whole gifts, not snack food, and like snacks Lucretius' particulates spread
on the air, dispersed.

***

So imagination is dead!
John Holmes, I suppose, has stolen Wordsworth's *Einbildungskraft*, and
masked himself up into the dactylic of the fiery screen.
Did his head not split at the neurons, building inside it the file cabinets of
a personal apocalypse?
Columbine and Virginia Tech, were they not our Treblinka,
Hammering at our ear drums?
Nature hath ample power to chasten and subdue?
Or is nature just the fish skin on which we scroll indecipherable
predictions?

***

An Alexandrian Age you say,
Plotted by a stigmatic tactician,
Globally colored?
Or is it the Age of Anxiety, that blossomed between Marcus Aurelius and
Augustine, centuries when Gnostics and Christians and Marcians and
pagans fought to conquer the turf of accounting?
Who had the words for the soul?
Who could name the whole?
Is this the Age of Perplexity, of the melting away of value
Into ways to name value, of ways to do value?

It is a quest age and throws up the nostrils of instant salvation to
neuroscientists in gas masks.

His saffron hair will lie in tangles on the ocean.

A Wall in the Imagination

***

We have come to a wall in the imagination.
It was there before we imagined
It was gone before we imagined
But then when we had forgotten, it was once more before us.
It was a wall made of all we cannot do and all we did not do.
It is a wall made of our sorrow.
It is a wall made of this summer,
Which found us surrounded by Olympic athletes,
and with our pants hiked up and our neckties buttoned and our buttocks
lavishing themselves on the strange Iowa harmattan.
And at our sides whatever it is that makes us feel stronger, perhaps a dog,
or a piece of garbage,
And on the road ahead of us lorries going northward
And on the road behind us G-men, hungry for a little of the activity.
Yes we were northward to the wall of the imagination
Where we would find
The shredded face of Mr. Holmes cut this way and that in the morass of
visibilia.
That would be the end of the road of the imagination, and simply to stand
there, like Romney at the Wailing Wall,
Would be absolute folly,
Like pretending an understanding.

***

John Holmes' fetus could be mine or yours, it is soft and egg-like, a
jellyfish, same extra planetary eyes same paper-thin bones same chalky
toes same broad flat nose thing same little ditsy pecker with such a future
and yet I'm sitting here this morning—just eaten lox and bagel—and John
Holmes is sitting in Deadwood having brought to an end many lives and
ruined many more and who's gonna say why I'm here and he's there will
it be a question of innate morality not on your life man or of the luck of
gene sequencing which after all joins us all at the beginning of human
time or is it something in between like tweaks and valences given and the
mode in which we live them and the "construction" we frame them with?

***

It took Augustine to discover the soul, or Marcus Aurelius, or maybe Paul,
But it took the socio-economic, the master/serf in the field of cassava,
The church bells at Perpignan in the fields,
To bring to birth a community of persons.

A person is what kills, or loves, and the same person kills that can love,
for love is but the ultimate in finding the other, and so is the bullet of the
gun which finds the other because it is needed that the gun may not be a
lie.

Tell no lies, they told us,

And going to the cinema hold your breastplate before you, and jostle for
the security.

There is no place inside you that is safer than your rifle, and no wound
deeper than a hangnail.

***

In the winter it grows cold,
The children attach to each other.
They are legless and face the wind.

In the churning summer
There is a tailwind hungry for the Rockies.

I ride often on that wind that tore
The side of my face from my children.
How can I pray for what is made of rock
In all of us? And how can I not

Answer to that other voice that crowds me?
Mustn't I feel that there is a jar in Colorado?
Something there had to be without form or motion.
Something there forgot to wear a face.

***

What is not lonely is what is left here.
The drainpipes seem to be in order.

I smelled nothing around the toilet basin.

I don't know why language like this
Has to fail its target
And instead of morning reach ever farther for the face.
Don't know why being sad is silent.
In any case the harmful ones just vanished.

On the eighth day there was nothing but silence,
And Jos Plateau rang out with mission bells.

***

Did you have a hard time hearing what I said?
That the priest chosen for the ceremony
Had been summarily discharged?
He was somewhere near the border when they spotted him.

His jerkin was polychrome.
He pled the weakness of all who simply substantiate.
I would darn his sock in the emplacement,

Finding with him a way to diminish the tales.
Yet where he was going I was going and we never met
Except then in Aurora we met going opposite directions.
He was headed for the high charged screen,

The intricate wire works in place to enable the show.
I was grunge, an old fry, let's say, and labored.
I had no idea when he fell, no take.
Seemingly the language that defined us was over.

Things that are over don't make much noise.

Mercy and the Countryside

**

Herr's *Dispatches* hurt to read,
What if he'd been writing from Aurora?

He might have occupied a seat on the aisle
Leading to terror, and bent over for a view.
That's how we discover we are in the soup.
That's the way he was, the things in Danang.

I could go around the block and see a lot of squirrels.
I could dig up the earth of my yard
And display the foreskin of the gods of humus.
We are never far from the discovery of someone's pain,

And often of ours. Horace found an antidote,
Rus in urbe, a spot apart in the sun.
Integer vitae he lived with an enviable body
To carry him. Eased off on sex, by forty,

That he might turn new forms of the epode.
Catullus' *apud me cenabis bene* was nothing to Horace,
At his best serving simple dinners of hare and oyster.
He had nothing but death to touch with his fingers.

                                   ***

He took a turn in the square,
His face faced this way, his shoelaces,
He took them off and showed me, faced
Well square up toward the clock tower.

That was when I knew him best, last year,
And it was the test. What we tentatively and then
Didn't was so small, so modest a test,
Oh how we roddled. He took a turn.

We roasted an ape, there was a symbol
And we rang it Nepalese style, prayer turn,
And fabricated smelly ancestral. It was a clan.
I took my servicemaster to the ball. It was summer.

                                   ***

Language, you see, puts its fingers round the event,
And squeezes, until the fingers turn white.
He emerged with a gas mask, battle gear and an uzi…

What can we do with language like that?

Can we attach it to a number of things, like the mask itself?
Or the plimsols the guy was wearing,
Or the dog-eared bible he wore under his frock coat?
Let's see, all we would need would be glue,

Permission to view the evidence,
And a surface to glue it to.
(As I say this I name some things in my room
To make sure of the procedure:

The door is acquiescent, a sticky tab in its corner,
And so is a bottle of milk. They are named.
All systems go.) After viewing the evidence,
Naming it as I go, I get permission to visit the killer in gaol.

He's in solitary, so he has no name, but still I give him one,
Backhanding it to him as I leave and watching him glue it
To the nightstand where he keeps his bible.
Nothing, you see, but does not have a name.

(Evil has a name and my dog has a name and my children have names and
my penis has a name
And all of these things can be named by gluing and by sticky tabs).

The real trick, you see, would be to slip a tab into John Holmes' brain and
glue it to his medulla, and then to find a name for it, and then to name the
parts of his brain, one by one, until you had a total account of that two and
a half pounds of neurones and rubber.

The Lyric We Are In

***

The wall came up against the fyre, and it.
The wall came up against it, and it was it.
It was the color it was and you rode it.
The color it was it did or what heard it?

You see we can go on at length being here in a word.
Think of all the chips in all the brains and all
The computers and the chips in them.
Could you do more to be them?

A little bird and a little package of floss
Flew away to build a nest.
They had a dream that one day...
But no sooner were the results videotaped

Than the dream turned to lox and cream cheese.
Oh my that is a delicious eventuation!
But the mentally ill man down the street
Can barely enjoy it though he has the money to enjoy it.
He clips his pomegranate tree and barely says hello.
I know you can make a nest out of floss I tell him
But there is something about his rejoining smile...

                              ***

The world of John Holmes is this world.
This is the world of John Holmes.
And of the persons who attacked at Columbine.
And of the guy who shot Gabby Giffords.

This is the world of the Sikh temple massacre
In Milwaukee and of the killing of Kennedy
And then of course of the roadside killings in Iraq
And the drone killings from offices in Army Bases

In upstate New York State and the killings of Christians
In Churches in the middle Belt of Nigeria
And of the killings of thousands of citizens in Aleppo.

The value of life is as precious as ever, he said
Counting the days of his existence, and thinking with exuberance
Of the joy of eating well and drinking a martini.

How he dreams of traveling again along the banks of the Neckar,
Or down the Rhine in a Volkswagen Beetle,
From where he could see the ridges of light over Bonn

And arrive after ten

With gables wrinkling the sky
And rise the next morning to a market full of
Shiny globes of fruit and greens
And hear the Schwaben

enjoying the purity of sun
Against the Fachwerk of the Rathaus.
Days those were when he could not imagine
That the world would stop, and now,

For the seventeenth time, he is making his will
Again, and fingering his chin bone.

India

***

Am I too old to travel to India?
I feel this morning as though the banks of the Ganga
At Benares were part of another world where I have never been.
Corpses tucked into saffron-colored napkins,
Children playing with cotton candy among the dogs,
While their mothers tripped once more with another body
To the filthy cleansing waters!

Take me again, take John Holmes with me,
His hair on fyre with the permanent revolution of the mentally ill,
And leave us beside the windy discoveries of the spiritual capital.
Take us with the psychiatrist from the University of Colorado
Who dealt with Holmes and the trado-magic of his mind,
And was not so close to magic.
May the River of all cleansing be the point where we gather ourselves,
Threesome grotesque, to finger trace metals,
And to yield in a hailstorm to our half-conscious edges.

***

Under the heat of the great moon I froze.
It was too romantic.

There was too little room left for error.
I tried to wash away the error.

Oh Father, what roads.
The criminal vanishes.
Time is acephalous.
I know how to talk. I know how to be straight,

Plain, accurate as a willow. Climb my branches.
I am a branch of the *acrophileton* tree.
If I smell bad smell me again for I am hot
When I am smelly. I will come off in your hands.

You will mutter, have away with this imbecile.
This imbecile is putty in the old god's hand.
No one smells him or says ashes to ashes
Or reads over his grave.

***

Turn down the heat, I am scorching.
Summer in a drought-struck Iowa takes the tongue
Our of your pocket and lays it panting
By the icebox door.

This is where we trust each other because we are alone.
No one can take us from ourselves and there is nothing else to take us
from.
On hands and knees I make my way to Mt. Horeb,
Fortified like Elija with hearth cake and water.
Less than that could feed a nation
Thirsty for the truth which it undiscovers in its *scientia*,
Overly analytical, minimally interpretive, feather bed of facts on which we
are lying,
Telling ourselves we can come, through medicine or calculus, to the core
of the matter.

***

Lo and behold it is raining feathers.

They are coming down as though a pillow on which the gods slept has
been opened, or is it manna
Dropped like dew or is it snow,
An early touch in the Rockies?
Whatever it is we know it was here before us and we are just catching up.
Our kind is all about just catching up.
What matters has already just happened.
We were born before we were born, and we are forever trying to catch a
glimpse of what we just missed.
When a guy kills there are many souls left out not yet arrived and not yet a
plenitude.
That is the reason for our sense of the incompleteness.
For the schoolmen perfection lay like a germ over the course of a life.
The dead-as-infants go skyward in the form of their perfection.
The dead as aged, wrinkled and useless, go skyward in the form of their
perfection.
What an assault on empirical science!
The *empeiria* is abandoned as a bastion of simple technique,
Of that *technologia* which to the Greeks seemed manual labor, the
abortive work of the hands.

   In the chert of a fingernail

***

Have you a killer inside?
I have been where nothing like death was imagined,
Life was a way of walking carelessly,
And time spilled like custom-made rivers down the sides of my body.
Today I have others to measure,
And by them to read terrible temporal teeth marks,
And yet when I go inside to where it is as always
I know what Emily Dickinson meant about notices delayed
Past the time you died to them.
Somewhere you received them.
You read notices in the air of your incandescence
And thought you left the site of your attention.
You were *it* now in a new place
And took yourself with you.
So I guess I had no killer inside or left him behind me
Where nothing that mattered would observe.

I died when I was born, but the barrels of energy refused to desist.
Lifetime was borrowed time, a battery flaring fitfully,
Damage to a mouse here and there.

***

If I were to go out now and try to name a thing
Like Aurora or John Holmes or the navy veteran who was killed in that
theater I would weep like a fountain over them all.
I would see nothing through my tears, no trace of a profile or genetic
marker.
I would say hell with it, in a voice razed by the human. Or rather with the
voice inside that I come to when I come to the wall and find there nothing
responding except the wall that wants to talk to me but is not responding.
I cannot say I would write this poem were it not for the desire to make a
lucid statement
And here I am blubbering…
If I were to go out now and try to name a thing
The thing would catch fyre in my face.

***

Julian Assange is a standard bearer of an age where John Holmes can be
seen as just one more shuffler of information.
This is the world of the Russian sociologists for whom a datum is just that,
Clear light shed on a table.

***

We are a nation of bloodthirsty angels flowing in contrary directions
inside a roomful of hurt.
The Hurt Locker was a show about war and being hurt there. War is one
way to be hurt and to hurt.
Another is to shoot up a midnight cinema performance.
Mustn't there be a meaning?
Can hatred blossom on an act that is *pur*, an *acte gratuit*?
Nonsense language runs and runs until it arrives at a wall.
At the wall it may climb.
But does it ever come out and over, does it make the sky part of it and the
earth a transparent sheen to walk?
Or does the wall simply stay there as part of the end of the sentence, and…

Unsaid languages are there but have we time to say them?
We are a nation of angels and we believe in them
War being one way to be hurt.

***

Faced with tragedy we have many ways to turn.
In *The Persians* Aeschylus portrayed the defeated foe with their pain, and lifted from all, victors and defeated, the onus of our common disaster.

The early Christians—and Gnostics and pagans like Marcus Aurelius— fought for the best account of the topography of going beyond, to a place where there was peace. The Christ said, *my peace I give you*, as though peace could be handed over. I have spent this summer thinking of the difference between peace and freedom; I prefer the latter.

The contemporary fallen, you and me in our time, face the random disaster of killers in this land devoted to law and security, and yield to the fate of brutes. We take it in the face. Rilke: *ich habe kein Dach ueber mich, es regnet mir in die Augen.* Since Arnold we have been watching the tide of faith go out. What do we put between us and roaring despair, or even the gentleman cynicism of Krutch's *The Modern Temper*?

***

Philosophy and theology are the names of the sciences of what we have, to replace despair.

Philosophy is just language. It is the effort of the namer to arrive at a formulation of what is being named, while at the same time to endure his/her language's doom. Can we take philosophy to Aurora, and feel better? Or Columbine? Can we endure to say that we find the situation unendurable?

Theology is just language. It is the effort of the namer to name what sucks his/her breath away with the power of anticipation, of having said all before it could be done. The ongoing force of language absorbs this effort, and yet the power of anticipation, to pre-be the statement of it, remains in the speech. Can we take theology to Aurora? We can endure theology at Aurora, here because it was there before us.

***

There's no assurance.
Nothing he strove to do did he do.
There were blocks against every streetlamp
And he fell, and his shoe too, his shoe.

Much as he had tried to achieve, striving,
He strove in vain. Things curled at his feet.
He kicked a duck from his toe, and charged
Too much to see it. You see he strove,

And when fyre caught on he eluded.
He eluded and he strove, for he feared.
He took on the past tense fearlessly,
Eating his heart out with strive, and strove,

And Itchygumi and Kitchygumi.
His was absolutely a fiery line,
And he followed it straight up. He strove
Manfully to…his cheese softened,

It was a dreadful canton, and in the pepper…
There he strove. Gruessli said the mountain
Women on their way down, he choked.
He buttoned a desire in a tooth, and ran…

It was well past midnight.
He knew he had acquired a power, and strove.
Whatever it was he strove, and it was smaller
Each time he rode. He felt the domination.

In the shadows of the streets he held.
He went through dark green corridors.
Grave markers ribbed him, he strove
Though until they said yes, darling…

It was a stone like none other and he rode.
Hail to me, diamond, did you not strive?
Did you not bear me? I bore you
And it was a wound, so I strove, strive.

***

There is always the tradition.
The tradition we find and invent on our shoulders,
Carrying it like a piece of pie from diner to diner.
The tradition unites the Pope to Zoroaster to the Buddha
Watching the ravens.
The tradition is where we are genetically one,
And belong to what we were as carbon.
I beg you to belong with me to the tradition,
With me to take the mass of the elements
Into my shoulders where strength is tucked away.
I beseech you in a thousand languages to let the tradition take over at the roots of our hearts
And make us one among the animals.
There is no reason for disunity
Among this small band of organic wanderers
And there is no reason to step on each other.
Why not, as do the monks at Kyoto,
Eschew strenuously the treading on insect life
Even among the finely chopped pebbles of the walks?
We can endure a shotgun shell to the face but can we endure an environment that says we no longer belong to it?
I don't mean green, for I hate the cult of attention to nature
Or for that matter the "sensibility" of the Romantics with their picturesque cult of generosity to the wild
And indeed I hate anything like the idea of a cosmos that is friendly
But I mean the tradition of *being here* over and above the velleities and the incorrect pronouns and the so adorable little black dress that every guy slavers to raise;
the oldest fashion tradition, so old it doesn't carry a cell phone or set up weather stations on Mars, but roots in the lichens atop Mount Chocorua.

***

Saying

I have no more to say about China

After the Olympics said it all about synchronous backflips and choreographed hurdle running. I only feel I should ask how my own hit-and-miss country matches up to the dragons over there in Asia.
Have I a clue?
I blame it on the Native Americans.
Some group to extirpate was what we required
Before we could figure out a society afresh for ourselves.

Back home in England and Germany, we had no autochthonous population to slaughter and so we slaughtered one another in say The Thirty Years War or the Invasions by Gustavus Adolphus or later the Revolutions that made us bite our ancestors' ankles and dance away into a wilderness made up of Seminoles and Algonquins. Killing, tricking, displacing those folks was one way we brought ourselves together, sharpened our knives, intensified our powder, and even learned to live in communities showing flickers of respect for others. The respect had our stamp. We valued survivors, who could make it in our landscapes. We became as rough and fiery as the Indians we replaced, but we were cannier by the addition of our roots back home in a Europe turning modern. No wonder the Indians fell and we went on killing, and we broke their backs.

Belief in a reasonable god.

***

Again this morning a bullet left a gun in the hands of a malcontent and sliced away a life.
The children of children are growing up blowing themselves to bits.
No one believes in our condition, but we are driving ourselves out, making the land an infection.
Will we survive?
Will some Esalen nut import the Mayan secret of the end of all days, and match it with *Revelations*, and free us from our day-to-day calendars, in which a breakfast with Dan sits beside a warning that the West has invited abominations?
I hate these excursions away from the "formalities of history," which, though I erode them in book after book, form the axis to erode,
Like the laws, which are there so there can be something to be broken,
Like belief in a reasonable God which can be there to give substance to doubt.

Only Plato then knew that we err, mis-measure, mis-see, only because we know what we are trying,
And are defined by our ways of failing it?
Yet with the nut from essalen, or Benares, or downtown Jackson will come irregularities of overall schematism,
Will come worlds doused in their own chaos,
Tiny shrinking murmurs of indicators of the MEANING OF ALL,
and we, though hating to lose the sleep, and hating to wake up early to play ping-pong by moonlight, will assemble in clusters like Jonestown, and though neck deep in folly and forgetfulness will proceed to annihilate THE FRAMEWORK.

***

The door post is clumsy and walks into Chuck's eye, which bleeds.
The ironing board has high cholesterol and comes apart in the nursemaid's apron.
The chimpanzee has a bald spot in the middle of his cutaneum and goes around showing it like a Purple Heart.
Woe to cultures in which the signposts of hilarity dictate the future to provincial governors.
Milestones like these will only end up streaming blood in Rockefeller Center
Or depositing poop just warm for Master's plastic glove.
No doubt, my hearties, we are floating on a surface of apricot nectar which we take for urine,
And a God or two envies us,
But short of that panoramic perception there is little to rejoice at
Save the certainty of supper.
Speaking of which, would you step to the snail farm and bring me a couple of dippers?

***

Love, the sea of Faith is receding
And we are walking in our bare feet.
What's under them is water and mud and run off but we don't care as long as we are touching the earth forbidden to certain *obas* or the Sultan of Sokoto.
On hot summer afternoons like this I go down on my kneebones and whistle.

The Gods come together around me and tease me with photos of the life to
come,
Which is more like Sunday noon in Topeka than like a tropical oasis,
But nonetheless the notion of continuing is Hoechst OK with me as it was
for Odysseus until he decided that staying with Calypso was going to be
boring, though to Achilles, hovering below a disclosing pit dig, life itself
seemed the only game in town.

California Girls

***

The Beach Boys used to sing under my window.
They were wispy in New Hampshire, the air thin;
A bear once crossed my stoney back yard.
A file of parakeets drove down the line in a Ferrari

Bright'n sassy y'know, like Italians,
Each one talking. I swear I heard one of them
Address me in Tagalog but God knows I'm not sure,
Having majored in Home Economics rather than Linguistics,

And having forgotten all I knew about peppercorns
N'canned salmon.
Anyhow California girls became part of my sub—
And I slept on and dreamed of a place far away
Where I could be half nude and academic,

And plaster the sand with esoterica.
All that collapsed in the War before Last
When my dreams took me down a mountain.
I had a load of coal to deliver to the outliers

But they were cagey enough not to be at home.
I carried the whole thing back on my head,
It carved a runnel in my caftan.
It broke my sense of the real California.

***

The Chinese in Angola.
Did you make a baby face and tie on a pigtail; then
Afterwards go downtown to bowl?
Oh these immigrant settings!

Immigrants swarm through this small Iowa town.
Most are named Holmes, John Holmes,
Because we thought it would be easier
And in some ways it is, easier

Just to call everyone the same name.
John, meet John, meet John's friend John.
The Holmes was sort of an after thought
Especially with the L in it, but

A specifier always helps so that we can know
What in the end we are, all one, a family
Shlunking in gas masks, rifles in our pockets.
I always thought Chinese too clannish to bowl,
But in Luanda there were rows of them,
Miners and accountants and lorry drivers,

All there for the yuan and a break from
Autocratic capitalism. I was surprised they too
Were all named John, and most of them Holmes,
Although at the bar I met a guy in a swimsuit

He'd been underwater on rigs, who said his name
Was Johnson, John Holmes Johnson, although
He and his wife were from Chang-sha in Hunan,
And he looked for all the world Chinese, except

His hair wasn't bright orange.
I talked with him for hours before I realized
He was an outsider, a rogue sweetheart,
The killer I was too strong for.

***

There is a water shortage everywhere.
Crops are dry, prices are soaring,

The wind gets caught in the boojums and flaps
And someday soon nine billion thirsty people
Will up and rend garments, and leave this world.

The strain is more than we knew.
Two thirds of the Arctic has melted this summer,
Islands off Bangladesh are swamps full of flies,
The head of the United Nations has been asked

To walk slowly on the very idea of development.
The watchword is sustainability, and even that
Presses too hard against the little guy's program.
Parties and politicians have intemperate backbones,

And put up with any excuse for carelessness.
Somewhere in the Sahara a magnificent black
Sub-group is polishing ritual items and making
Minimal gestures toward freedom, if not peace.

Freedom is what they are cooking up
As they begin quietly to draw together.
They are the first of a new *civiltà*, devoted,
Private, uncertain. They are for the most part

Tentative, like the Ottoman Empire, trembling
On legs unsure of their history.
Walls of rock will protect these quiet initial denizens
Until they emerge, labile, fractious-to-count,

To parse, to unearth the beautiful debris we leave.
Their freedom will be visible on their hands
Which run out in all directions into things,
Which are emulated. No one can suspect that a

New history will be written with the words of the old,
That time will be rewritten but with the same
Symbolic pressures. There will be nothing like ease,
But perhaps for a while their guns may be solid

Stone, too heavy to carry, and they will have to kill
Even game in parties of gun lifters.

It will be sweet to see the planet regular again
And its edges pumice smooth in the evening.

May these friends of different eases
Gather and speak of us in our hair
And masks and long thin penises
And though their *hair* be long and matted

May it be its own color; may their scars, wiped onto them
By invaders from other oceans, peel.
It is that peeling that will mean so much
And cave settlements given way to steeples.

Unlike our world, theirs will peel to display
Parts of their bodies inside it and games
Children delight in. We small ones will remember
And dance backwards in dream into the sharp

House sand made of us on our wanderings.
Our fingers are shrunken and our time
Too lonely to die for. He makes a sandwich.
He cuts cheese. He drinks a beer, a native beer.

***

Every movie I've seen has ended like this, in drought.
The movies I see you pick up off the humus,
Dry them, spread them and perhaps sleep under them.
Movies are really good for household protection.
Or did I say the wrong word, movies, did I mean to say blankets or
coverings?

Or should I say they become detached from their things
And float around capriciously and all I can do is grab
One as it passes and *try* to attach it to something?

Though half the time I screw it up, like I might say
I went to see the blanket last night and the ending
Was, wow, knocked my sox off, and later we went

Out for rainbows and ate and ate. I would in that

Case have meant we were eating hot dogs but the
Trouble is I needed something for rainbow to mean—

There was one in the sky—and all I could find was
Hot dog and even with mustard it didn't look like…
Oh you know what I'm talking about

And how little I have to contribute to linguistics.
Not though as if that was my purpose. I don't care
What you call me as long as you append *roan*

Or *siege* to my formal moniker. I'll be happy.
Siege will do just fine if I'm
Attacked, and can remember what you called me.

I'll be happy to shoot up a cinema, taking careful
Armpit at the last, and oh the British raj,
And Telfer, and his sister, and Tompkins.

***

The fly headed for his ointment
Landed square in it and failed.
He of course was the fly and history
Was the ointment he landed in.

Dull adages these, buster.
The guy turned to *techne* and fabric
To cobble together an imperium of power
He needed. He'd failed an exam.

God knows what else he'd failed, curled
In a routine bed in California.
He knew what the ceiling smelled like
And the color of decayed bacon.

He knew what a window could be
If it was never opened. A place
Trash fills to the brim.
He knew what a dog knows

When it is thrown into a corner.
I know that too, and so do you,
And so I suppose we too could be
Killers in mediocre cinemas

Prior to mediocre showings of films
No more insightful than a drive-in window.
"I don't have the energy to kill,"
Or "where is even the handle of a gun?"

PART FIVE:

GOSH, AFTER ALL THAT?

CHAPTER THIRTEEN

FLYING TO BYZANTIUM

No, of course we have not forgotten our title theme, the nature of character download in poetry, and especially, in these last two Parts, in fact reaching back to the *Anonymous Assault* of Part III, the modified nature character assumes after all, in the longer narrative poem. In the briefer poems of Will's early books, *Mosaic, A Wedge of Words, Planets,* there was an easily identifiable Imagist/Symbolist ploy, directly linked into the expression of feelings of the Romantic movement, and we knew where we were in the tradition. We were "expressing emotions" with inherited verbal material.

What kind of character and character download should we ascribe to the maker of the *Assault* poem, who has no tricks up his narrative sleeve— as did the workman behind the interventionist materials—no intent except to be himself and tell a story in the simplest language he could manage. We found that same pellucid mindset in early poems, or even in "serene poems," where we seemed to impute that modest intent to the maker of the "just me" poems. But the story of Will's poetic development was more complex. Take in your hands and compare the voice behind the *Assault* poem with the voices behind "Letter Back", "My Room", "Three Snow Moods", "Circe", or "This Autumn's Progress". There is of course a difference imposed by genre—the compassable lyric versus the played-out phalanges of the discursive and apparitional long poem. But there is a more substantive difference. The short lyrics in question invite conversational ripostes from a reader (perhaps simply a reader inside them) implicit in them, while the voice behind *Anonymous Assault* is dry and self-contained, presses itself toward the condition of pure digital narration, and in that fake Homeric fashion does what *The World of John Holmes* tried to do, to stall the world in its names, so that the denomination of time may remain intact and unyielding, and no reliance will be given to the corresponding cooperation of a reader (whether in or out of the text). The same mock-epic strategy plays out in what follows, the *gosh after all that stuff*, which simply gives the refusenik to the seeming closure of the materials of this workbook, and tries its version of the endless ending that Kazantzakis settled onto his *Odyssey*, with the chortled discovery that Odysseus' journey has simply been a preface, and that, as Homer himself had it, the old guy is off in search of some ignorant hick who can't distinguish an oar from a winnowing rod. We will listen to the below, the last hurrah thanks to the mercies of digital printing deadlines, and then "wrap up" our many wrap-ups of commentary on the location of the poetic character in the poetic making.

***

Flying to Byzantium (2017)

Puff-cum-fluff cloud packs,
Stars turning red over remote Adana
The landscape of northeast Turkey rent stiffly.
Yr finger yr soft eye weeping…

Hog-ruminant agents
Invent assaults. You edge them in tight.
A wrecked 4x4 steams by the chop-house;
Fetch sleepily, Lou, we ream.

Soapstone figures, carved from day's glass.
We align their simples. Haven't you eye,
Tooth, dreamscapes to hallow?
Can't the Sultan dry the wood of dream?

Gather these pieces of the airless flight,
As you live within the long wail of bisque time.
Child you, and hungry; whassap world.
Beige glows off gynecological hot spots.

Wreck me, wreck me, I will settle!
Fearful boys we tracked, our teeth burning
For cut. The Golden Horn blew.
Turhan widened an office window.

What I had to know!
There was a steamer waiting. We boys!
Say did nothing split but the dogface?
Did Egypt not welcome our toes?

1951 December American School of Classical Studies Athens

Three boys will fly to Byzantium,
One two three.
Only they will fly by the overnight boat from Piraeus.
They are another trio that has gone their ways, Spiros, Dmitri, Fred…
Board them, they will move with your fingers, give them passports, sleeping bags, *paximadia*, and move the keel like a giant sausage into routes scattered over the bloody insulae—Delos, Tinos, Lemnos, Lesbos….new discovered worlds for the three going east…

1951 December 26

He takes out the Horae and measures.

Sixty-six years roped out as if by Inca quipus over the years in Virginia Woolf's *The Years* each with its density, the flavor of brougham, the Hyde Park thematic, the banners of the headlines, King George and Queen Amanda, and down with the tea and rum.

He counts one two three, sleeps, counts again, enters by stages into the shipping lane Turhan discerns this morning from an apartment over the Bosphorus

After which in his mind the Long Wail is heard once again, the wail of and for history, the wail of time in the pasha's window, the night coming down off the steppes, the Mongol hourglass.

Then he too sleeps, matters not in what part of the globe, but at an angle to a rudder, to a crowded poop deck, to the first gray dawn of the Golden Horn with its rubbery barges of Black Sea Crude, and its payload (today) of IBMs.

And the character downloaded onto each shelf of wine in the captain's quarters, onto every brass button, onto the waves moving eastward, onto the waves running westward, onto the bodies of seven-year-old lads, is the mind of this endurer turned inside out into the outwaking glamour of the Horn from a distance, and it is eight in the morning everyday, and three guys descend the plank, might as well be the plank of time.

1951 December 27. Eis ten polin, *Stamboul Rose, Constantinople*

Yeats still treads this ground.
Where is life more intricate than in the breaks
Between lines?
Where is Homer except where the absence of continuity becomes the
enjambed kolon?
We part each line of wave like the hairs on a centenarian,
Making our way to Byzantium.
Making our way through the small streets of time.

We're in the artifice of the map of experience.
Crowd you not all that you know onto a ridgeline of fingernail?
Athens, Poros, Paros, Smyrna, Bursa, and the Golden Horn.
A sweep of the finger, a gesture that slices east into west.
Character download now onto the drunken wholeness of the sliver of
Historical Intervention.
Time and meaning drink the smelly fish of Faustian insight.
He twists like a truncheon.
He directs the kaiki toward the shore of Rheneia,
the silver dead at his side,
the wind a ticket to the dams of the erotic.

To the East the waves rumble against the coast Agamemnon slew his
daughter to assault. Priam looks down through the ring of fire that drove
him fierily to his knees.

December 27, 1951, 7:30 p.m.

Travelers to nothing but themselves they tread streets narrower than their
erupting pulses down allées unknown except to the other.
What, guys, does your brainstem say today?
Whores, chicks, filmies at every plate glass window,
Our pockets full of fear and semen,
Our eyes mere wells in our heads.

We dwelt on the outside, wandered from palace to palace,
Longed for the explosion of time to take us in pieces.
Then returned to our hotel like sheep in a meadow.

The next day we visited the finials of the Greco Muslim, and tied ourselves in the wind's history painted green and purple and scripted with the pastiche of Arabic.

July 2016

Now it is news from the marching orders of a brutal season.
The clumsy arguments of pain sweep the latter years of the three kids from Athens.
The waters we crossed to the Golden Horn are crossed in reverse by the flotsam of war.
Hang up Paros and Poros beside Lesbos,
Take away the Sappho who wrote here and leave us the wreckage of bodies in transit.
A child speaking Syrian Arabic crawls on the beach where Sappho read with her age mates.
The waves pock indifferently against the mole of cloven contracts.

A new continent

Zealandia grunts with its Atlasian sea weight,
The ancient mariner thrills to his micronometer
And small boys like me, somewhere on the floating surface,
Add a continent to their wall maps.
So it's under us, he thinks, placing his butt
On a hot spot in Illinois.
He's a homeboy, middle to upper,
And from his sebaceous flow longings
To be one with the noosphere.
Teilhard de Chardin is the driver into that mountain
Where oblation is the figure of Mongolian gneiss
And the whole is if nothing the name of our dream.
He has traveled widely in Mercator and his underpants,
And drafts *voyages à l'intérieur* which he will turn back
This afternoon with interest onto the eastern corner of
Mare Nostrum. Was it Christ or Athens?
He grew up into Arnold and out the other side,
To where the Gnostic midlife spilled from him.
Goodenough pointed as carefully to Alexandria as the finger of *eli eli lama sabachthani*, and then, with Cavafis' *eitane k'aute mia kapoia lusi*s, he lay down for fifty years in the ideas bed of this washing *thalassa*.

And now he's flying to Byzantium!

And all the old coals are burning in the furnace,
And there is a double-barreled shotgun
Hanging in every pharmacy,
And though winter is trebling its force in the country he comes from
He is nonetheless doubled up into the mind of the muezzin.
Is this but an old jerk's flotsam
Or is it the long trip home into the breaker waters
Where the incision of history cracks?
He hears the wail in his gut,
The passion of the labor of childbirth in the exhausted Mediterranean?
The archaic Atatürk fled across the barracks of Adana?
Military positivists chasing the Enlightenment back to Constantine,
The reason of the Romans?

His heart travels again with the Stamboul Rose,
Dreams weave the rose,
The subways in and out of Scully,
His particular *rausch* planted against the late evening blood moon.

And now he and the boys are flying to Byzantium!

February 2017

History wells up in chunks.
We live it from a distance and then are the smell of the abbott as he craps
a soup cut from beans.
We are the fingers on a pussy on a back street in Adana

When the moon is rising and the pimples on a teenager
Flash in the gummy twilight.
We are the genuine prayer of an anchorite made of wholeness
Begging the roaring deity for a piece of the cake of eternity
In some bastion of longing.
History wells up in chunks and lays us again,
Three chumps from the Agora,
Against the side of the plane leaning westward into the Fayyuum,
Flying flying over the *mare sacrum* where blood and the Dome of the
Rock coincide in the afternoon sun.

Organisms

All flesh is a single crawling organism
Cilliae beating against the drumskin of wonder
As we pile out neurotically onto a beachhead in Palau.
From far did we come, o brothers in cytoplasm,
To where the Mongolian Turkic meets the
Patriarch in the offices of the PLO.
And yet we are here today, shoes all polished,
Brilliantine creamy at the edges of the scalp,
And we are in negotiatory mood like the *Nations Unies*
And will stand in for parties who are too busy hating to remember the
pleasures of being here.

Did I say that?
Let me touch something elementary.

February 28, 2017

My father's birthday.
He gave these days to my son, to treasure and spend.
Dad was a Montaigne rationalist,
A foe to time and its flow,
A namer of spades for just what they are.
In his own son he bore a harvester of hours,
Wretched on the wrong side of the clock,
Forever undarning the sock he was wearing,
Cutting himself back to the eye's dumbest innocence.
That's the me on this trip
Through the holy lands of Jehosophat
Origen Sirach Melchisedech Ali Synesius Mardonius and Pericles
And other guys in hat-shaped hats
And universe-shaped palaces.
God left his print.
He left his mark on the frieze at Bassae
And on the Temple Mount and on the language of Cavafi
And on the cesurae in Herondas and on the footsteps of Flaubert
At Baalbec.
I am at home in Iowa but I am at home in the *kulturwelt*
That was opened by others wherever it could support itself
Could be Buenos Aires or Novosibirsk.

Sons, Suns

G of expression.
I am panting behind the joy of making it new and the joy of providing employment to the tragic.
I am the sun.

What of the son that became one with the father
And spread wings the size of golf courses down over the eastern Med?
What of that son who ached with each plank-sized crack up along the coast near Smyrna, or each Land Rover whipped onto its back by the roadside device that snapped it near Adana?
There was pity out there where the Greeks and Turks had battered each other to pieces in the desert,
And there was pity yesterday
When a Russian plane crashed in a wheatfield near the border of Kurdistan,
And in splintering destroyed a colony of ants.
Nothing was too small for the pain of it to radiate.
The pity of the son and his father drooled like hard rock candy over the tangled surfaces of the bituminous rock.
The mother and her father bent into escarpment-shaped wreckage
Over the shattered columns of Palmyra.

The Long Wail

So the Long Wail
The three young boisterous heard
As they boiled over onto the Anatolian plateau
Was the very long wail of the Copts in Cairo,
The German tourists going topless and breastless at Sharm el Sheikh
The filth of the refugee camps in Gaza.
And as we fly to Byzantium, dangling pieces of a Yeatsian mosaic
In the webbings of our fingers,
We look down onto the finials of basilicas sharpening mosques
Against the gaudy sunset, and we turn to one another once again,
The three of us Oedipean in failure and desperation,
An architect an historian and a poet,
And we caress sixty-five years like fingers of grass in our fingers, and nibble in loneliness at the time that was loaned us.

And then suddenly again it is night,
And the wall we broke through to enter this arena
Is staggering backward into the wall it too yielded to
And there is an inner shelter of light,
There where the doctrines of Maronites, Gnostics, Animists of the Desert,
Lilith and her fiery descendants, pulsed and roamed,
And the light is once more overwhelming,
Brimming like a fiery syrup over the edges of our eyes
And we are being sucked back into the sources,
And hand in hand tumbling backward onto the rubber mats
Of the soul we stumble and are gathered.

Historical is the Ground

The ground beneath us is historical.
I write at it today from the tripodal axis of cultures
That brim up formlessly from cuts in the landscape.
Ughelli, Iowa, and then that stockyard of insights
Flaming up instructively from the *Achzenzeit* of Jaspers.
I am on fire with what I'm given
And dance in the mornings over the hot coals of my masters.
What I do not own I am given, from the light bulb
To the practices of control, from the internal combustion engine
To the amplitude of the sleeve on my jacket.
I can dream and when I dream I am the silver bullets
Of the human adventure firing at random over the Gobi
I am as practical as a lever and as on my own with death
As any sailor before the discovery of the azimuth.
Come take me by the hand and lead me to the strange places
I connote simply by eating among them and holding hands.
Help me complete that list scribbled over the fortune cookies of time
Then to write it again as though I had never started.

To Do

Committed to it simply for the sake of commitment on a sinister day among the parks of the Western Hemisphere.
The to-do list of places, the romping grounds of soul.

Give me food for the hunger to eat off every plate and read by every light.
Give me the imagination I wasted in a tool store
In West Des Moines when my eye fell on the wrenches and I realized, as
each of us knows from *handedness*, that
There are ways uncountable of addressing the surfaces,
Of taking another person's hand as though it were a rope.
World tools surround us giving us places to hold to,
Giving us ways to pull ourselves up or shift to the side,
Mattering to us constantly as we design our living space
In the corner of the side of the package our lives are.

The ground beneath us is historical, from the flint to the adze,
Behind those, even, the *zuhandensein* of the rivers to travel and the
darkness to hide in and the sunrise to be astounded in...
Nothing you see is not for use, from that Eastern Mediterranean
That marked your life with stipples from decade to decade,
Or the strident noises of the hurdy-gurdy man at Rock Creek Park,
Keening to a baboon's tune in the loneliness of a city corner
Or the man in grocery attire at the door in Chobham,
Bringing milk and wheat bread and the Manchester Guardian.
Not that it is all good but that it is, and that it is good
To accede to every thing in its name and place,
Even though you know that the heroes of low cholesterol
Wake at night fervent, their bodies trembling for cream
And their chins narrow rivulets of slobber and candy corn.

We are designed and ready, and far though we fling
Coats of dreadlocks over our exposed white organisms,
We will keep on climbing until we reach an Everest
Taller within us than our chins, and the inside we present,
As feelings, to the establishment of clothing.
We know our heights are them climbed,
Nothing wasted but the storms history frees at our step.
And now that we have bowed to the pirogue in the flashy sea
And peppered our text of Pirenne with accounts of the interior of time,
We return to Iowa or Ughelli, to our bodies as placeholders,
And once more stand within where we were never not.

Africa!

World as placeholder, slippery against the turmoil of landscapes.

The figures against a landscape, King Hussein, Marco Polo, Ariel Sharon
and the apes they all were against the Drakenburg Range…pencil smudges
of the passage north we are all in our genes.
Can you not behold me this morning at an angle in a corner,
Sneezing like a fox with the harmattan thickness, surfaces heavy with the
pock dust of a Sahara I had known from the north?

Where had I crossed to the south—through Chenini, Tamanrasset, Luxor,
N'djamena? To be sitting like a flower at a stool,
On a porch become sacred for the window it gives me?
Ughelli pours by in Rivers on the Federal Express flooded with goods.
Dangote Cement, sharp sand from the river, cattle from the north,
Lumber from the border with Niger, the implosion of the fragmented
goods that add, one wishes, to the good of the whole?
Am I not eyes to bathe in the flood unceasing, as a nation,
Framing its purposes, responses to responses, without knowing the
question?

The question, for certain, will print itself against the red earth.
Someone will find it there, incised, or muddied against a plimsoll,
The question of where we are going, which of the arrows within
Guides us here directing, as we fumble through the leaf mold
Parting this or that fossil to find the gene that is its silence.

Are we too not rushing, at the speed of our spinning planet,
Over valleys carved into the silence where asteroids tangle
With debris from Kroger's?

Back to Being Historical

Ultimately you are back to being historical.
You take your own hand like a lover
And wonder at the touch that is not the touch of another.
It is your own touch touching you!

You take another's hand, a hand you know well.
It is not your own hand but your hand returned to you from time.
You shake that entry into time
And a friendship is formed between figures of flesh.

Between you and you, wringing your hands or self-caressing,
There is nothing the clock can measure,
You are alone on a cliff in the Drakenburg
Or eating a burger in downtown Cincinnati,
It is all the same.
In the body it is always no time.
There is that freshness of now in the body,
And we may pray that within the lawn where we fall
There is a simultaneity of ourselves,

Ourselves as it were holding ourselves
In the condition we have become
beyond sickness, underneath health.

That would be a body that no other could take
Though we ourselves cannot have it.
It is the body given as gift,
The right foot, the left shin,
Body as handedness and body as thinking.
Immense wholistic stars
Nestle and nip in that body as it lies on the grass
In the little country churchyard
Or marabout wilderness in Algeria
Or among the joss sticks in the small Buddhist temple
To your right in Hunan Valley
Or on the snag-toothed promontory in Jutland
Where the sea is beginning.

If it is there that we begin our journey it is there
In the history our two hands meeting have released
From things as they generate us.
We cannot go back, we are forward,
Always ahead of ourselves when least we care to advance,
And picking up our pieces.
It is at the point where you no longer find me that I find you
Just where you were when last we became historical to one another.

And the Long Wail is where we become one another,
Meeting in the ever-present lounge on the edge of the barely available.
It is from that Wail that we listen to one another
And then listen to ourselves listening to one another.

It is in that Wail that we are bodies at all, and one,
Trespassing with lonely faces on one another's visions.
Can't you see us passing one another
Crammed together into a single city
Accreting at thousands of citizens a day?
We are coming from somewhere.
We are coming from inside ourselves
Into a light we make by establishing a place inside
Where pebbles can be rubbed like flint.

We are still and always doing things over.
Are you my neighbor? Am I your friend?
Have we not rather scrubbed one another into existence
From out of the plain? Haven't you flint in your shoe?
Haven't I a stalactite hanging from my ear?
We are starting a community and in it will be three
Twenty years old boys setting out
And Granddads recalling. They will be the same
Person knocked up into a form and from within them,
Figura humanitatis, will emerge a single figure,
The golden human of Leonardo, and society,
Globalized and fearless to inspection.
Society as a whole, in Borneo or the Bronx,
Will rise from that image of the golden human.
We are all the possibility of all of us,

And what you may become I too may become.

We are all becoming?

Having said that, I emerge onto a street,
Any street, and make fulsome gestures of acceptance
For the merest fact of being in this world.
I am no longer afraid here, no longer a teacher
But for the last fucking time a learner,
With a slate and a notepad
And in the distance an horizon I scope
On which to sketch the highest plateau in Chile
And its pertinent folds.
I would call the skirt of the goddesses of the world
And the air they generate a tapeworm of dynamic parasites,

Swirling in the air like churns this morning.

I know there is an end and a beginning
For we are both of them. I feel both of them
Rising where I slept last night
On a pillow of silence and daring,
Faithful I hope to the clumsy fears and primeval longings
That roiled with the Greatest of the Glaciers,
Opening as never before near Mattoon and Peoria.

POSTLUDE

CHAPTER FOURTEEN

END AND BEGINNING

This book has been an autobiography written through poems and commentaries. We have been tracing the beginnings, center point, and later developments of one guy's life in his poetry, and at the same time, inevitably, raising the central questions of what created literature is, what role art has in forming and responding to personality, and the very *raison d'être* for the creation of poetry. How different has this text been, from an autobiography in which the discussion has revolved around the writer's place in his *race*, *moment,* and *milieu*—Taine's formula for the coordinates by which to calibrate a person's or society's development? Goethe observes that the exact date of one's birth can be determinant, for the social/cultural milieu he develops through, and we have tried to spot some landmark culture stages, through which Will's work passes, but on the whole the attention has been on artistic or download development, that latter smart phrase denoting the stages of the passage of the author's personality from beginning to end.

This, then, has been a character-download type of autobiography, in which all eyes are on the way the poet retailed himself in language. In that kind of study, which ours has been, autobiography is measured out in style issues, and may well veer incalculably away from the writer's vulnerability to his time. In the present book, for example, there is a gross national product type autobiographical thread: sensitive kid in Hawaii; asthmatic nerd in the Arizona desert highlands; wunderkind talking dramatic poetry with Hartman and Bloom at Yale; young prof with a quietly passionate fury to write a life; a morally weak kid-guy submitting to the female form in midlife and screwing up his family; a gradual subsidence into serenity, cooling it by century's end and a sharp marital equitability; approach to the Mr. Death thing that gives an edge; a panting *au revoir* to the reader tracking this narrative. There's all that. Then there's a parallel autobiography which will intersect with "all those events," but which will play itself out in the language of style development. That autobiography will track the loose-flow Romantic narrative of an Hawaiian harbor, the "here Dad look at me!" of the gift of

Fragments, the honest-injun love and romance and narcissism tonality of the Penn State and University of Texas early volumes, where social constraints were pinching the toes to the screaming point, the high-narrative translational outpourings of the late 1960s, along with that flowering of academic globalism, the game-play hard-edge interventionist self-evasive of the late 1970s and early 80s, the sides or dranster poetry of the 1980s and 90s, angular and retrograde alabasters of the play self, the long-narrative winged tale, from a spooky anonymous assault to (in sharply harsher mode) the teeth-gnashing (I hope) John Holmes stuff, to finally, maybe just to show he could still run the mile, the flight to Byzantium, earnest money on the one-thing-at-a-timishness of language.

The difference, then, between an ordinary autobiography and a biography in terms of style? Considerable. Style will involve the ways the guy settles for, or is able to handle, levels, tones, visionary poises of language. Style is how the guy is disposed to lay himself on the table, and as such rolls itself out into a semi-voluntary choice history, which autobiographizes *de sa propre manière*. A history of style is not a history of folks, although it sure derives from folks, from their individual manners of eating, drinking, scribbling, self-projecting, belly-laughing, or belly-aching. Will's style history, the way he has changingly downloaded himself, sure is a history of Will, but an edgy history lending its own stains to the woodwork of his life structure.

POEM TEXTS AND TRANSLATIONS

Mosaic and Other Poems **MO** (University Park, Penn State Press, 1959)
A Wedge of Words **WOW** (Austin, Univ. of Texas Press, 1963)
The Twelve Words of the Gypsy (Lincoln, Univ. of Nebraska Press, 1964).
    Translation
Metaphrasis (Denver, Verb, 1964)
Micromegas **MI** Iowa City, *Micromegas* editions, 1965–70)
The King's Flute **KF** (Lincoln, Univ. of Nebraska Press, 1966 Translation
Planets **PL** (Francestown, NH, Golden Quill Press, 1968)
Brandy in the Snow **BIS** (New York, New Rivers Press, 1972)
Guatemala **GU** (Binghamton, Bellevue Press, 1973)
Botulism (Amherst, Micromegas Press, 1975)
Epics of America **EOA** (Amherst, Panache Books, 1977)
Selected Poems: Our Thousand Year Old Bodies **TYOB** (Amherst, Univ.
    of Massachusetts Press, 1980).
The Sliced Dog (Seattle, L'Epervier, 1984)
Emtering the Open Hole (Seattle, L'Epervier, 1989)
Recoveries (Lewiston, Mellen Press, 1993).
Trips of the Psyche (Lewiston, Mellen Press, 1993).
Textures, Spaces, Wonders (Lewiston, Mellen Press 1993)
China, a Modern History (Iowa City, *Micromegas* editions, 2006)
The Long Poem in the Age of Twitter and *The Being Here Site of the
    Poetic* **LPAT/BHSP** (Lewiston, Mellen Press, 2011)
*Being Here: Sociology as Poetry, Self-Construction, and our Time as
    Language* **BH** (Lewiston, Mellen Press, 2012)

Poetry Editor Work

Arion: A Journal of Classical Culture, Austin, Univ. of Texas, 1962–65.
Co-editor, with William Arrowsmith (initial volume) and subsequently
with Donald Carne-Ross and J.P. Sullivan.

Micromegas: A Journal of Poetry in Translation, Iowa City, 1965–70.
Editor

INDEX

A Yaqui Way of Knowledge 72, 221
Adolphus, Gustavus 302
Aeschylus 299
Africa 38, 61, 117, 264, 282, 322.
    See also individual countries.
America 4, 49–54, 72–3, 94, 97,
    135, 206, 211, 214, 222–3,
    230, 238, 271, 288, 315
    American exceptionalism 4
    Native Americans 302
Angola 170, 305. See also Africa.
Aquinas, Thomas 14, 76, 225
Arabic 317. See also Language
Aristophanes 123
Aristotle 173
Arrowsmith, Bill 134
Assange, Julian 298
Atatürk, Kemal 318
Augustine 285, 288, 290
Aurelius, Marcus 271, 288, 290,
    299
Aurora, Colorado 291, 298–9. See
    also Holmes, John.
Australia 287
Autobiography 144, 230, 234, 329–
    30
Bangladesh 306
Barrès, Maurice 4
Baudelaire, Charles 3, 29, 114
Belize 174
Berkeley, George (Bishop) 70, 219
Bible, the 254–5, 293
Blake, William 146
Bork, Robert 4
Brahe, Tycho 287
Braque, Georges 232
Braun, Richard Emil 134
Brooke, Rupert 192
Brooks, Cleanth 1

Buddhism 87, 301, 324
Bulgaria 130, 177
Burne-Jones, Edward 136
Byzantium 190, 313–26, 330
Calvin, John 36
Cameroon 284. See also Africa.
Canada 211
Carnap, Rudolf 155
Catullus 292
Cavafi, C. P. 317
Celestine Prophecy, The 72, 221
Chardin, Teilhard de 317
Charlemagne 283
China 83, 113, 118, 288, 301
Columbine, Colorado 288, 294, 299.
    See also Aurora, Virginia
    Tech.
Congo 284
Constantine, Emperor 318
Crane, Hart 1, 29, 209
Cuba 156
Cuchulain 77
Dickinson, Emily 297
Diderot, Denis 72, 222
Donne, John 114, 128
Douglass, Frederick 177
Ecuador 154
Egypt 314
Eliot, T. S. 1, 42, 74, 135, 224, 271
    Wasteland, The 42, 271
England 302
English 2, 38, 125, 127, 155, 193,
    205–6, 214. See also Language
Enlightenment, the 72, 222, 238,
    318
Epicurus 153
Eschatology 226
Escher, M. C. 280
Europe 82, 302

Flaubert, Gustave 55, 319
Fragonard, Alexandre-Evariste 91
French 60, 198. See also Language
Fukushima 151. See also Japan
Gabon 162. See also Africa
Galilei, Galileo 287
Ganga River 297. See also India
Gaza 320
German 38, 196
Germany 302. See also Europe
Gettier, Edmund 70–1, 220
Ghana 179
Gloucestershire 154. See also
    England
    Gloucester 153
God 8, 13–4, 24, 60, 76, 81, 101,
    156–7, 173, 190, 197, 223,
    225–6, 254, 257, 265, 267,
    273, 280, 302–4, 308, 319
Goethe, Johann Wolfgang von 285,
    330
    The Sorrows of Young Werther
    11
Greece 80. See also Europe
Greek 2, 25, 126–8, 282. See also
    Language
Grenier, Robert 27
Guatemala 24. See also *Guatemala*,
    under Will, Frederic, Poems
Gutenberg, Johannes 55
Hartman, Geoffrey 12, 329
Harvard University 209
Herondas 319
Holmes, John 284, 287–9, 293–5,
    298, 305, 330. See also *The
    World of John Holmes*, under
    Will, Frederic, Poems
Homer 1, 36, 313–4, 316
Horace 27, 66, 137, 166–7, 292
Hulme, T. E. 36
Hussein bin Talal, King 323
India 295
Indians (Native Americans) 302
    Algonquins 302
    Seminoles 302
Iraq 294

Ireland 77
Irrationalism 5
Jackson, Mississippi 303
Japan 84
Jonestown 303
Jutland 324
Kant, Immanuel 73, 152, 223
Kazantzakis, Nikos 313
Keats, John 11, 80
Kepler, Johannes 287
Korea 158
Kunitz, Stanley 282
Kurdistan 320
Language 1–3, 5, 11–2, 17–8, 21–3,
    26, 37–8, 40, 44, 49–50, 55,
    58, 60, 65, 82, 85–6, 90, 97–
    101, 109, 112, 114, 123, 125–
    9, 131, 140, 166, 182, 185,
    188–9, 193, 203, 205–7, 209,
    211–2, 214, 237, 256, 258,
    267, 272, 274, 278, 280, 282,
    291–3, 298–9, 301, 313, 319,
    329–30. See also Linguistics,
    Translation, individual
    languages
Lao-tzu 86
Latin 1, 15, 38, 227. See also
    Language
Leeuwenhoek, Antonie van 70, 220
Lenin, Vladimir 238
da Vinci, Leonardo 325
Lermontov, Mikhail 177
Lewis, Wyndham 37
Linguistics 2, 4, 37, 50, 97, 213,
    304, 308. See also Language,
    Translation
Linnaeus 172
Lucretius 158, 287–8
Mallarmé, Stephane 21, 23–6, 36,
    102, 140
    "Crise de vers" 21, 24–
Polo, Marco 323
Marot, Clément 128
Merleau-Ponty, Maurice 243
Metaphysics 29, 44, 68, 111, 206,
    278

Mexico 190
Meyerson, Émile 40, 55
Middleton, Christopher 27, 134
Milton, John 1–3, 21, 62, 285
    Paradise Lost 1–2
Montaigne, Michel de 55, 319
Muybridge, Edwaard 69, 219
Mysticism 226
Native Americans – See Indians
Nicaea 193
Niger 323. See also Africa
Nigeria 205, 294. See also Africa
Novalis 11
Odysseus 304, 314. See also Will,
    Frederic, Poems
Olympics 288, 302
Oppen, George 26–7, 74, 224
Origen 319
Ottoman Empire, the 306
Palamas, Kostes 125–9, 205–6
Palau 319
Pericles 219
Philosophy 5, 12, 14, 40–1, 49, 57–
    8, 61, 63, 67–76, 78, 218–23,
    225–6, 299
Physics 129, 170
Piaf, Edith 152
Pindar 27, 114, 137
Piraeus 315
Planck, Max 129
Pléiade, the 3
Poland 4
Pollock, Jackson 37
Priam 316
Prosody 4, 76, 34
Pythagoras 152–3
Quine, Willard van Orman 40
Rabelais 55
Raine, Kathleen 1
Rembrandt van Rijn 201
Renaissance, the 3
Rilke, Rainer Maria 299
Romanticism 5, 11, 137
Sabatini, Rafael 133
Sade, Marquis de 183
Sand, George 180

Sappho 317
Sartre, Jean-Paul 55
Seneca 217
Seychelles 173
Shakespeare 2–3, 11
    King Lear 2, 84, 212
        Cordelia 212
    The Tempest 2
        Prospero 12, 36
Shelley, Percy Bysshe 1, 11, 135
    Alastor 1
Shostakovitch 34
Snyder, Gary 27
Spain 16, 35, 198, 242. See also
    Europe
Spitzer, Leo 2
Stefansson, Evelyn 212
Steinarr, Steinn 123, 125, 127
Stevens, Wallace 42–3, 72, 222
Strabo 181
Sweden 15. See also Europe
Syria 168, 317
Tagalog 304. See also Language
Taine, Hippolyte 329
Tanzania 149, 182
Teiresias 207, 209. See also Will,
    Frederic, Poems
The Story of O 221
Theology 11, 299
Translation 40, 123–31, 206, 330.
    See also Language, Linguistics
Treblinka 288
Valéry, Paul 140
Vivaldi, Antonio 69, 219
Wagner, Richard 202
Watteau, Jean-Antoine 91
Waugh, Evelyn 4
Whitman, Walt 203
Wilde, Oscar 11, 183
Will, Frederic
    Autobiography as theme in the
        poetry of 21–7, 50, 65–96,
        134–214, 230, 234, 314–
        26, 329–30
    Death as a theme in the poetry
        of 5, 11, 26, 65, 136, 205–

9, 217, 235, 277–309, 329
Miroirs d'éternité 60
Poems:
  "A Little Brandy" **60–1**
  "Anonymous Assault" 5,
    243–274
  "Argg: Time for Breakfast"
    242
  "Begonia Rises Waxy, The"
    63–4
  "Being Here Site of the
    Poetic, The" (excerpts)
    17, **29–36**, 39, 44, 49,
    97, 104
    Tupus poems, the 17,
      37–39, 40
  "Bus" **60**
  "Circe" **140–44**, 313
  "Emphasis for Easter, An"
    12–7, 21, 25, 56, 58, 65,
    277–8
  Epics of America 49–54, 97,
    135, 206, 230
    II: "The Foreigner" 51–
      2
    IV: "Horses" 51, **52–3**
    XII: "Starlight in the
      American Stable"
      50–1,
    XXIX: "Zen" **53–4**
    XXXIII: "Shaman
      Days" **66**
    XXXIV: "Milktoast"
      49–50,
    XXXIX: "His Pale
      Color" **58–9**, 66
  "Figuratively Speaking" **229**
  Five Poems 61–3
    "German Fellow, The"
      62–3
    "In the Hollow
      Provided" **63**
    "Tom's Military Career"
      62
    "Tom and the Rebellion
      of the Carrots" **62**

  "Tom Washes the
    Minerals" **61–2**
  Flying to Byzantium 313,
    314–26
  "1951 December
    American School
    of Classical Studies
    Athens" **315**
  "1951 December 26"
    315
  "1951 December 27. *Ein
    ten polin*, Stamboul
    Rose,
    Constantinople"
    316
  "A New Continent" **317**
  "Africa!" **322–3**
  "And Now He's Flying
    to Byzantium!" **318**
  "And What You May
    Become I too May
    Become" **325–6**
  "Back to Being
    Historical" **323–5**
  "February 2017" **318**
  "February 28, 2017"
    319
  "December 27, 1951,
    7:30 p.m." **316–7**
  "July 2016" **317**
  "Historical is the
    Ground" **321**
  "Long Wail, The" **320–
    1**
  "Organisms" **319**
  "Sons, Suns" **320**
  "To Do" **321–2**
  "For Mike Quill" **76–8**
  Fragments **5–10**, 11–12, 17,
    25, 29, 58, 65, 136–7,
    205, 207, 277–8, 329
  "Death and
    Transfiguration" **8–
    9**
  "First Sin" **6**
  "Lament" **9**

"Nobility" **9–10**
"Plaint" **10**
Preface **5–6**
"Trends Recollected" **7**
"Trial and Error" **10**
"Tumor" **7**
"In Victory" **7–8**
Guatemala 21–7, 25. 29, 44, 50, 97–8, 135, 140, 205, 230
"Guatemala II" **22–3**
"I Am Dog-Tired This Morning" **241–2**
"I Have a Silent Childhood" **229–30**
"I Have Long Been Absent" **115–6**
"In the Furze" **228**
"It Wasn't Easy" **116–7**
"It's the Figueroa Principle" **237–8**
"King's Flute, The" **130**
"Let Your Voice Ring Out Loud and Clear" **227**
"Letter Back" **133**, 135–7, 205, 313
"Like a Geometry" **236**
"Long Poem in the Age of Twitter, The" (excerpts) 29, **40–3**, 97
"Love Me Love My Dog" 226–7, 242
"Lunch, Paint, Modern Ways" **57**, 60, 205
"Medical Transcriptionist at the End of Time, The" **278–9**
"Medical Transcriptionist at *Aigues Mortes*, The" **278**
"Medical Transcriptionist Books Passage, The" **279**
"Might Be Sattiday" 42, **43**, 205
"Minus" **204**

"My Room" 205, **206**, 209, 237, 313
"Myosotis: Ninety Canzonettas" 90, 97–8n., 140, **144–203**
Nine Poems of Striving
"Ambition" **110**
"He Sweltered" **108**
"He/she Strove" **106**
"Immobility" **111–2**
"Jubilance" **112**
"Magic in Poetry, The" **113–4**
"Odd Season" **108–9**
"There Was a Dranster" **106–7**
"Wrapping it up" **111–2**
"Odysseus" **209–11**
"Paths" **280**
"Patio Metaphysics" **67–8**
"Please Take My Truck and Drive It" **240**, 242
"Poetry and Philosophy" (1988) **218–26**
"Poetry and Philosophy" (2008–9) **68–76**
"Return Ticket" **231–2**
"Side, The" **232**
"Side 2" **233–4**
"Side 3" **234**
Six Poems (1965) **78–83**
"After Keats" **80**
"For a Childhood" **82–3**
"In Memoriam" **80–1**
"In Time of Tapping" **79**
"Né en Illinois" **81–2**
"Subaquatic" **78–9**
Six Poems (1982) **90–6**
"Flower Power at Last, You Said It" **94**
"L'histoire d'un soldat" **92–4**
"Lully and the Wrecked Ornaments" **92**
"Lully's Foot" **91**

"Two for You, Eyes of
    Blue" **90–1**
"Winter Nocturne" **95**
Some Dranster Poems **97–
    105**
"Aside" **105**
"Sentence, The" **98–100**
"Dog Days" **100–2**
"There Must Be No
    Limit" **102–3**
"Too Much to Watch"
    103–4
"Somebody Was in the
    Way" **114**
"Song from the Dark Ones"
    279
"Snail Said, The" **117**
"Space" **64**
"Teiresias" **208**
Three from China **83–7**
"Inter-Cult Talk" **85–7**
"Lo-Fu" **84–5**
"Scholar, The" **83–4**
Three Poems **88–9**
"Catechism" **88–9**
"Dawn" **88**
"Hands" **89**
"There Must Be No Limit"
    (2006) **102–3**
"There Must Be No Limit"
    (2015) **281–2**
"This Autumn's Progress"
    133–4, 135, 137, 232,
    282, 313

"Three Snowmoods" **138**,
    140
"Too Much to Watch" **103–
    4**
"Word for Love in Danish is
    Hard, The" 53, **212–3**,
    214, 283
World of John Holmes, The
    5, **283–309**, 314, 330
"A Wall in the
    Imagination" **289–
    91**
"California Girls" **304–9**
"India" **295–301**
"Lyric We Are in, The"
    293–5
"Mercy and the
    Countryside" **291–
    3**
"Names of Things Eat
    the Things" **286–8**
"Saying" **301–4**
"Zikist, The" **283–6**
"Wound and the Grace,
    The" **136–7**, 206, 212
"You Said" **236**
"You Will See My Point"
    240
Williams, Oscar 12
Wittgenstein, Ludwig 11
Woolf, Virginia 315
Wordsworth, William 66, 137, 288
Xenophon 74
Yeats, W. B. 36, 77–8, 316, 320